Justice

Justice

Classical Foundations and Contemporary Debates

Young Kim

LEXINGTON BOOKS
Lanham • Boulder • New York • London

Published by Lexington Books
An imprint of The Rowman & Littlefield Publishing Group, Inc.
4501 Forbes Boulevard, Suite 200, Lanham, Maryland 20706
www.rowman.com

Unit A, Whitacre Mews, 26-34 Stannary Street, London SE11 4AB

British Library Cataloguing in Publication Information Available

Library of Congress Cataloging-in-Publication Data

Names: Kim, Young- author.
Title: Justice : classical foundations and contemporary debates / by Young Kim.
Description: Lanham : Lexington Books, 2018. | Includes bibliographical references.
Identifiers: LCCN 2018000936 (print) | LCCN 2017060882 (ebook) | ISBN 9781498559003 (electronic) | ISBN 9781498558990 (cloth : alk. paper)
Subjects: LCSH: Justice (Philosophy)
Classification: LCC B105.J87 (print) | LCC B105.J87 K56 2018 (ebook) | DDC 172/.2—dc23
LC record available at https://lccn.loc.gov/2018000936

∞™ The paper used in this publication meets the minimum requirements of American National Standard for Information Sciences—Permanence of Paper for Printed Library Materials, ANSI/NISO Z39.48-1992.

Printed in the United States of America

This book is dedicated to my parents,
Chang Soon Kim and Bok Duk Ryu, and to their respect for
intellectual inquiry, and as always, to my wife Jane.

Contents

Acknowledgments

I am indebted to SunHee Kim Gertz, Professor Emerita of English, Senior Research Scholar, Department of English, Clark University, for her thoughtful review of the manuscript. Her support of my writing endeavors has been invaluable. My thanks as well to Janet Coleman, Professor Emerita of Ancient and Medieval Political Thought at The London School of Economics and Political Science, who was especially helpful in my gaining insight into Plato's ruminations in *The Republic* and *The Statesman*. It was a pleasure to work once again with the editorial staff at Lexington Books and especially with Joseph Parry. I remain grateful for all their support.

Chapter 1

The Question of Justice

When Plato describes Socrates conversing with Phaedrus, the ostensible subject of the dialogue is the relationship between love and rhetoric, linked together since both a lover and an orator attempt to persuade others.[1] In their reliance upon persuasion, however, both love and rhetoric are treated as mere arts, the mechanics of which Plato uses to introduce the dialogue's actual subject. In the *elenctic* manner typically characterizing his dialogues, Plato has Socrates attempt to lead Phaedrus to understand that the ability to persuade, and love itself, should be subject to the pursuit of knowledge; a pursuit that in and of itself is a moral one, a pursuit that can enlighten the correct path an individual should take.[2]

In some ways, many contemporary discussions of justice seem analogous to the initial discussion in *Phaedrus*, insofar as they focus on the mechanics of justice, as seen primarily in their political considerations of institutions and public or civic affairs. That is, they do not go deeply into foundational moral concerns such as principles of right or wrong behavior and goodness or badness of human character, thus prompting the question: What is the point of justice if not to establish a moral framework for political interactions?

To explore the importance of a moral framework, I accept an essentially liberal political context, but one that makes the individual's will to act and take responsibility for her or his actions central. In a sense, then, I prefer the liberal political framework comprising the foundation of contemporary discussions of justice over the hierarchical political framework supporting the conceptualizing of justice by classical thinkers. I nonetheless return the discussion to the classical concern with moral responsibility. Adjusting to our times, and in accord with Immanuel Kant's focus on individual responsibility, I argue that justice must focus on right actions.

In this study, I elaborate on the principles of justice articulated by classical thinkers, and especially by Plato and Aristotle, to demonstrate the importance of their thought in contemporary debates of justice. In reminding of the importance of their views, I bring moral considerations more fully into contemporary discussions as well. It is clear in many ways how such a discussion is appropriate not only because of inexplicable crimes (e.g., the seemingly authorized murders of unarmed black men), but also because of violently competing moral systems (e.g., ISIS). Without recognizing the importance of moral constraints and responsibilities, however defined, contemporary discussions of justice can only treat the mechanics, the rhetorical competitions, in the face of our most pressing social issues, offering little normative guidance as to right actions.[3]

I divide this study into three parts. In the first, I discuss classical foundational approaches by exploring how Plato and Aristotle conceive of justice. From there, I construct Part II to analyze the components of justice and their relationships within societies. Finally, in Part III, I explore specific problems that justice must contend with today and demonstrate the need to address individual moral responsibility in establishing justice, in underscoring right actions.

To avoid misunderstanding, I do not subscribe to either the metaphysical framework of Plato or the insistence on character development found in Aristotle as articulated in their writings. Rather, it is the linkage of morality to justice I promote, a linkage that needs to be revisited often since, contrary to Plato and much of Aristotle, I believe that both morality and justice are dependent in large part on social norms. That is, social norms comprise common standards within various social groupings, with respect to acceptable or appropriate behavior in differing social circumstances. Such social norms vary by community, as do the strength or weakness of such norms within communities, and moreover, they change over time. In other words, social norms represent contingent circumstances, and as such require continual assessment, at least with respect to how morality informs justice.

Thus, the societies in which Plato and Aristotle lived had their own complexities. That is, both Plato and Aristotle wrote for an elite, male audience—their investigations were conducted by and for free, property-owning men, citizens of city-states.[4] Today's reading public and citizenry, at least in the Western world, evince more complexity and diversity, thereby requiring sustained consideration beyond the political.

Focusing on the political and ignoring the moral, many contemporary theories of justice not only fail to take into account the importance of shifting social contexts, ironically, they present arguments in an unacknowledged moral framework. That is, such discussions often set their analyses in a politically liberal context, and by taking for granted certain principles (e.g., regardless of race, ethnicity or gender, each individual has a right to justice), they are actually engaging in a moral discussion leaving the framework unexamined, the framework within which their investigations are made. It is in recovering the importance of moral arguments typically found in classical approaches and reasserting moral considerations adjusted to contemporary mores that I hope to offer a useful perspective to view the question of justice in today's dynamic, diverse, and complex societies.

PART I: CLASSICAL FOUNDATIONS OF JUSTICE

Though quite different, the accounts of Plato and Aristotle—which I examine in Part I of this study—both treat moral aspects of the question of justice. In doing so, they provide foundational resources for contemporary inquiries into the nature of justice including those focused on individuals, groups, and the ideal society.

Individual and Social Morality

In *The Republic*, Plato transforms the apparently simple question, "What is justice?" by means of the Greek term *dikaiosune*—a term for "justice" that captures both individual justice and the justice that informs societies, by mirroring the individual in the cosmic universe. His use of *dikaiosune* thus allows Plato to wed ethics to politics and therewith moor the central question epistemologically to inquire "What is the basis of moral and social obligation?"[5]

Plato's well-known answer rests upon the fundamental responsibility to seek wisdom, wisdom which leads to an understanding of the Good. For Plato, a moral universe is grounded upon the notion of foundational forms, forms that exist in the intelligible realm regardless of whether mortals apprehend them or not. Importantly here, good politics and justice depend on the knowledge of such forms. Plato further argues that such metaphysical understanding of forms produces and ensures the good communal life when ideally structured under a philosopher king in a society with three classes (philosophers, auxiliaries, and producers) that neatly mirror his triadic view of the individual soul (reason, spirit, and appetite). In this manner, justice is obtained when knowledge of how to fulfill one's moral and political function in society is put into practice.[6]

I explore Plato's views on justice in chapter 2, articulating later in this study how his metaphysical approach has proven critical in approaches to justice since at least the nineteenth century, as carried forward in the continental philosophical tradition of Jean-Jacques Rousseau and Johann Gottfried

Herder, Georg Wilhelm Friedrich Hegel and Søren Kierkegaard, Friedrich Nietzsche and Martin Heidegger, who focus on individual responsibility and hence on moral responsibility within the social network.[7] In addition to nineteenth-century philosophical discussions, Plato's insistence on individual moral responsibility plays a role in contemporary discussions as well. Thus, Jürgen Habermas—whose critical theory of communicative reason I use to interrogate a number of issues of justice considered here—belongs to those influenced by Plato's approach.[8] By articulating the importance of individual responsibility, these thinkers echo Plato's approach to justice, which considers how the individual and society mirror universal forms as argued through his use of the term *dikaiosune*.

Virtue and Well-being

While Plato yokes the individual to the metaphysical in his approach to *dikaiosune*, Aristotle locates justice within the individual as a learned disposition and virtue. Rather than representing an ideal of absolute truth unable to be verified by any method other than reasoned discourse, Aristotle defines virtues by an individual's actions. Thus, he argues that virtues (*arête*) are learned dispositions that result in well-being (*eudaimonia*) for those leading virtuous lives. He further explains that virtues occupy the mean between extremes; courage, for example, is the mean positioned between cowardice and recklessness.

It is in Book V of the *Nicomachean Ethics* where Aristotle presents justice as a virtue. In so doing, however, he abandons the simple location of this particular mean as between two extremes by asserting that justice is *a kind* of mean, in that "it relates to an intermediate amount, while injustice relates to the extremes," and that "injustice is both excess and deficiency."[9] This is not the only equivocation in his discussion of justice. For example, implicit in any definition of *dikaiosune* is society's role, since justice necessarily involves societal aspects. But Aristotle's analysis of justice seems forced here as well: while his overall analysis of virtue centers on the individual, the individual does not remain the focus in his discussion of the virtue of justice. Rather, in discussing justice, Aristotle marginalizes the individual and individual traits in order to analyze the individual's relation to others in political community.[10] In shifting focus from individual virtue to relations within a political community, Aristotle's primary concern with regard to what he terms particular justice, based on the underlying concept of equality, seems to be what some may term "social justice" nowadays.[11]

I explore Aristotle's views on justice in chapter 3. In today's discussions, his approach has been central to two fields exploring justice—virtue ethics and distributive theories of justice. It is his view of justice as a moral virtue and learned disposition, for example, that has been advanced in the virtue ethics of Phillipa Foot and Alasdair MacIntyre.[12] Likewise, various contemporary distributive theories of justice (whether focused on the distribution of social goods, wealth, or natural resources) have their foundation in Aristotle's distributive account of particular justice based on merit. Notably, such distributive theories have formed the predominant contemporary approach to the question of justice thereby responding to some of the complexities in today's societies. Although akin to Aristotle's approach they largely fail to take into account the individual's moral responsibility to act.[13]

PART II: THE INDIVIDUAL AND POLITICAL SOCIETY

As mentioned, Plato and Aristotle treat justice as *dikaiosune*, which is concerned with both individual justice and the justice that informs societies. Plato attempts to show how one mirrors the other, while in adjusting his definition of justice as a virtue, Aristotle moves his treatment of justice to somewhere in between, focusing on the relationship between the individual and society.

Echoing aspects of both classical thinkers, many if not most contemporary accounts of justice are embedded by and large in the analytical tradition pursued in the manner of David Hume and Immanuel Kant, Jeremy Bentham and Gottlob Frege, John Stuart Mill and Bertrand Russell.[14] One analytic approach to the question is teleological or consequentialist (Elizabeth Anscombe's term) in design, as framed in the utilitarianism of Jeremy Bentham, Henry Sidgwick, and James Mills.[15] Other contemporary approaches to the question of justice are deontological and articulated in a liberal framework resulting in views as vastly different as the libertarian views expounded by Robert Nozick with regard to his minimal state on the one hand, and by Ronald Dworkin with respect to his emphasis on the equality of resources on the other.[16]

Moral Inquiry

Plato's approach may be described as approaching justice in an extremely rational manner. In contrast, Aristotle relies on practical reason to examine the good life, thereby firmly situating concerns in the mortal and the variable. One of the most influential later thinkers regarding justice, Immanuel Kant, uses the phrase "pure practical reason" to describe morality as including the concepts of moral agency and moral responsibility based on pure reason. Thus, despite the similarity in terms to Aristotle, with his reliance on pure reason Kant's approach falls more in the platonic category (rationality) than the Aristotelian one (practicality).[17]

Based on a strong, but not extreme, view of rationality and especially on practical reason, Kant identifies good will as the one thing that is inherently good in humans. Immaterial, good will gives humans intrinsic dignity and represents our power of rational moral choice, of decision-making that through rational choice is clear-minded and not overcome by emotion. Importantly here, good will invariably leads to practical reason, the use of reason to decide upon actions.

Critically for Kant, good will stems from duty and thus informs human autonomy, which he defines as the ability to make deliberate, rational choices.[18] Indeed, it is self-governing reason that Kant offers as decisive grounds for viewing each person as possessed of equal worth and deserving of equal respect, as self-governing reason allows each individual to act as a moral agent. In other words, we must treat others with respect as rational persons formulating their own maxims. Similar to Kant's approach, I also argue for a concept of moral agency that includes elements of rationality and autonomy, but I diverge from his explanation of their relationship. That is, while I view rationality and autonomy as constituent elements of moral agency, I do not subscribe to Kant's view that rationality entails autonomy.[19]

From my perspective, it is important to articulate action-guiding principles to moral questions since I locate justice at the secular level of intentional actions by rational moral agents. Thus, what Bernard Williams identifies as morally thick concepts become quite useful. Williams, for example, identifies cowardice, truthfulness, brutality, and gratitude, as values that are embedded in societies—able to bear significant cross-cultural weight—and are likely to continue to frame and define Western cultures.[20] As Tim Scanlon expresses the matter, increasingly we must rely upon "parametric" universalism, which may be viewed as a benign treatment of relativism, grounded upon deeply embedded, culturally universal concepts sufficient to exclude genocide, murder, and totalitarian rule.[21] I explore further the moral dimensions of the question of justice in chapter 4.

Values

In chapter 5, I explore questions of value, which tend to cut across traditional categories of moral theory as normative or metaethical inquiries and also across ethical and political boundaries. Thus, I examine issues of value monism and value pluralism, as well as the shape of morality. For Plato, clearly, the pursuit of the knowledge of foundational forms and especially the form of the Good anchors the question of values. For Aristotle, values are seen as part of the moral character of the individual in the pursuit of living well.

While neither Plato nor Aristotle may be seen as value pluralists in any strong sense, or can be said to influence value pluralism, value pluralism nonetheless considers the kinds of deontological, moral questions posed by both Plato and Aristotle as well as by Kant. With regard to value pluralism, I examine the knotty issue of incommensurability and engage the contemporary deontological debate of the priority of the right over the good exemplified briefly below through the basic arguments of John Rawls and Joseph Raz.

Essentially, Rawls constructs and frames the debate of the right over the Good in a deontological manner, morally binding his theory of justice to fairness.[22] Nonetheless, the outcome-orientation of his second principle of justice, the difference principle, moves his theory outside a comfortably deontological framework as he seeks to solve the problem of how a society properly distributes goods, such as opportunities, income, and wealth. In doing so, Rawls recalls Aristotle's attempt to theorize the distribution of a society's goods according to merit; an attempt that jars against the moral framework Aristotle constructs, in order to theorize the individual's relationships in society. In other words, like Aristotle, Rawls too leaves the deontological for the political, in Rawls' case by means of the Kantian practical reasoning of moral agents, who are motivated by the principles of right and justice. As such, the priority of right is seen by Rawls as placing limits, in the interest of fairness, on the conceptions of the good that may appropriately be pursued for political purposes.[23]

In contrast, in promoting the good over the right, Joseph Raz develops a comprehensive form of liberalism that encompasses both political and moral theories, thereby evoking the approach to *dikaiosune* informing Plato's approach.[24] Thus, Raz constructs a platonically coherent perfectionist regime in which plural values, together with his concepts of personal autonomy and social forms, attempt to work mutually to support a liberal order. Not surprisingly, however, he struggles as a strong value pluralist to solve the problem of incommensurability.

Concerned with human well-being and self-creation, Raz believes that liberal neutrality is a "chimerical" ideal which cannot even be approximated. In like vein, he argues that the state not only should not be neutral, it cannot be so. In this framework, Raz continues to defend accounts of well-being and of the good life as good in and of itself, and not as goods desired or enjoyed by human beings. Ironically, and recalling the critiques aimed at Plato's hierarchical and potentially totalitarian scheme, Raz thereby develops a liberal perfectionist political structure that seems curiously lacking in many of the characteristics that one would expect in a liberal political order, namely, tolerance, diversity, and respect for other ways of life.

Political Liberalism

In many contemporary accounts, theorists set the framework for justice in a liberal political structure, whereby the term *liberal* is often thought to build upon freedom or liberty and equality as core notions.[25] While neither Plato nor Aristotle may be seen as supporting a liberal political order, nonetheless, contemporary work on justice, even in its complex variety of liberalisms, does owe some of its insights to these classical thinkers. Thus, while perhaps not accepting the evaluations of the six categories of political order as divided into correct or deviant constitutions, for many contemporary thinkers, Aristotle's description of democracy as a deviant constitution in which the many rule has proven useful.[26] Plato's observations prove similarly useful even if parts of his metaphysical ideas may not be accepted. Plato's approach, for example, argues for positive liberty (using Isaiah Berlin's term), while democracy represents only the third-best (lawful) and third-worst (unlawful) form of state.[27]

Berlin exemplifies the kinds of important but limited influence exerted by both Plato and Aristotle on contemporary thought. Thus, Berlin is aligned with many contemporary thinkers in that he situates his political views in a traditional liberal framework in opposition to both Plato and Aristotle. In his well-known essay, "Two Concepts of Liberty," Berlin nonetheless addresses Plato's ideal society as based on the concept of positive liberty, the freedom to do what one is supposed to do, a disposition that leads to a well-ordered and stable society.

But Berlin also maintains that in the process, Plato's system would create a stratified and hierarchal order which, although intended to provide the framework for a just society, can lead to the rise of totalitarian regimes.[28] Berlin argues as well that negative liberty is also promoted by Plato's approach, negative liberty such as is at the heart of John Stuart Mill's political views and articulated in Mill's harm principle, which provides that "the sole end for which mankind are warranted, individually or collectively, in interfering with the liberty of action of any of their number is self-protection."[29]

As I discuss in chapter 6, Berlin opts for value pluralism, which accommodates an "inescapable characteristic" of the human condition, that of making choices "between absolute claims,"[30] thereby reflecting the "immense value [individuals place] on the freedom to choose."[31] In other words, for Berlin, a liberal political order that protects the freedom to choose is the most legitimate kind of state. Value pluralism must consequently entail liberalism.[32]

While there are many criticisms of Berlin's approach, which makes an individual human trait—the freedom to choose—central to his political theory,[33] some contemporary thinkers have attempted to revive Berlin's project. For instance, William Galston argues that liberal value pluralism has the potential to "connect what one believes to be the best account of public life with comparably persuasive accounts of morality, human psychology, and the natural world."[34] It is because of the freedom to choose that Berlin demotes Plato's concept of the Good as value monist.

Indeed, the inference from value pluralism to liberalism seems simple and natural. That is, value pluralism may be seen as a theory of the moral universe that provides for many kinds of goods and a plurality of valuable ways of life. In this particular respect, then, value pluralism accords well with liberalism which, according to Mill, is a political order that attempts to provide the greatest possible freedom for individuals to "pursue [their] own good in [their] own way."[35] Moreover, as Galston argues, not all values are commensurable—they may neither be reduced to a single overarching value nor completely rank-ordered. Beyond these points, however, Galston's basic view of value pluralism proves problematic to those many forms of liberalism in which justice is viewed as the "first virtue of social institutions."[36] Likewise, his views can prove difficult for those liberals who—demonstrating some Aristotelian influence—favor a lexical ordering among goods. For Robert Nozick, for example, liberty represents such an overarching value,[37] while in Ronald Dworkin's liberal theory, equality serves a primary role.[38]

Further problematic to liberal political approaches, Plato supports his vision of the ideal society by means of the Noble Lie, an amalgam of myths of origin narrated to encourage devotion to a state.[39] Contemporary commentators typically reject the Noble Lie and similar uses of platonic myths as devious and fundamentally antidemocratic.[40] In John Rawls' view, for instance, Plato's structuring of society is tantamount to imposing a comprehensive conception of the good on a society. As such, Plato's approach proves antithetical to Rawls' own advocacy of the priority of the right over the good, promoted in his influential theory of justice as fairness and his maximin principle, which argues that the "basic structure [of society] is perfectly just when the prospects of the least fortunate are as great as they can be."[41] In contrast to Rawls, but still addressing platonic ideas, Joseph Raz engages the contemporary debate of the priority of the good over the right by constructing a liberal perfectionist regime where justice consists of the pursuit of the good by individuals who may choose among goods presented and as defined by their societal contexts.[42]

In various ways, Aristotle proves more amenable than Plato to contemporary approaches to justice, in large part because he articulates a societal framework in his thinking on justice, making him in several aspects closer than Plato to the views proffered by Rawls, Raz, and other contemporary thinkers. Essentially, in addition to universal considerations, Aristotle addresses the particular. Thus, for him, justice has both universal attributes grounded in a broad concept of lawfulness, as well as particular attributes grounded in the concept of equality.

With respect to the formalism of his universal approach to justice as lawfulness, Aristotle further nuances the universal perspective through concepts of natural justice and equity, which he introduces to provide flexibility to rules in particular situations—at the cost, however, of some analytical rigor.[43] As to particular justice, grounded on the concept of equality, Aristotle posits a theory of distributive justice in which an individual should not take more than his or her fair share of goods in society. He further postulates that an individual's fair share should be determined by merit. Particularly, this refinement in conceptualizing justice is picked up and debated in contemporary relational approaches to justice.[44] Aristotle's merit-based theory of distributive justice also points to differences in approaches that are culture- and time-bound. Thus, not surprisingly, Aristotle does not address key issues in today's discussions, such as the distribution of scarce necessary resources.

Happiness and Duty

Contemporary discussions also take up the questions of happiness and duty as core defining elements of justice. For Plato, justice is good not only for its consequences, but also good in and of itself; justice is an intrinsic good. He argues that justice is part of the happy life, continuing to reason that if virtues were only an instrumental means to happiness, individuals might be able to achieve happiness by appearing to be virtuous. If virtue is a paramount constituent of happiness, he concludes, then individuals cannot be genuinely happy without being virtuous and vice versa. Simply put, to describe justice, Plato constructs an account of happiness arguing that a just person is always happier than an unjust person.

In *The Republic*, for example, Plato answers Thrasymachus' claim that justice belongs to those with power by countering that individual justice is achieved when the three parts of the soul are in balance and that the just person has a better, happier life than one whose soul is out of balance. Aligned with the three parts of the soul, for his ideal society, Plato conceives three classes. When each person accomplishes the proper work of his class, a just society is generated, one which is orderly, stable, and hierarchal. The greatest happiness in such a society, critically, would only be achieved when philosopher kings rule since philosophers acquire knowledge of foundational forms more fully than any other individuals.

For Aristotle, on the other hand, justice is a virtue, the supreme virtue, and happiness consists of virtuous activity. That is, his concept of *eudaimonia*, of living well, describes an activity rather than a state of being or condition. In his *Nicomachean Ethics*, he develops a functional argument for the pursuit of well-being based in reason; that is, happiness is the result of using reason well over the course of a full life. Moreover, Aristotle argues that doing anything well requires virtue or excellence, and consequently, living well consists of activities arrived at by the rational soul in accordance with virtue or excellence.

This focus on living well is adapted in the eighteenth century, when classic utilitarianism such as that defined by Jeremy Bentham promoted a consequentialist approach to the question of justice, arguing that the moral worth of an action is judged solely by its utility in providing happiness or pleasure to human beings. The focus of Benthamite utilitarianism is maximizing and aggregating pleasure as a moral end. Pleasure is conceived of as a sensation, whereby pleasures that persist through time comprise quantitative *utiles*, useful and hence scientifically measurable entities. John Stuart Mill's account, which John Gray describes as indirectly utilitarian, complicates the Benthamite approach by means of his concepts of higher and lesser pleasures as well as by the seeming contradictory fallibilist and progressive views that he advocates, views that demote the provability of belief.[45] Moving yet further from Aristotle in contemporary times (as I examine in chapter 10), the utilitarian account of Derek Parfit explores the transgenerational aspects of the question of justice, an approach most well-known, perhaps, through the concept of reparations.[46]

Deontological approaches to justice contrast with such utilitarian accounts, in that in a deontological view, duty precedes any calculation of happiness. For example, as with many other deontologically inclined thinkers, Kant views justice as the most important of duties. This is particularly critical when considering Kant's further version of the Supreme Principle, the Formula of the End: "Act in such a way that you always treat humanity, whether in your own person or in the person of any other, never simply as a means but always at the same time as an end."[47] Thus, in Kant's universal and individual perspectives, especially as they are tied deontologically to duty, an echo of the classical concept of *dikaiosune* may be detected.

For many Kantians, though, the demands of justice are met when reduced to the formulaic demand that no proposal reduces others to mere means. With this approach, however, the individual is kept in the background thereby not focusing on the operation of practical reason or, for Kant, on the autonomy which is fundamental to his ruminations on what is just. Thus, when ascribing to a deontological, nonutilitarian approach to resolve moral questions, it is just as important to separate intention out and address the sense of psychological motivation, rather than simply testing maxims for their general value. While, conceivably, intentions and general maxims overlap at times, the act of identifying intentions underscores the entire reason-based process by which an individual gains respect when coming to a decision on her or his own. The emphasis is on the individual, not on a possible, universally accepted metric. Importantly, intention carries with it the possibility of (the *intent* to effect) action, while a maxim more or less represents a static state. Thus, Kant views human beings as rational, free, and responsible agents, each of whom should be treated as an end unto her- or himself rather than as a means.

PART III: DEBATES OF JUSTICE

Part III of this study treats certain disputes of justice, particularly those that pit individual rights and responsibilities against various group theories. In mapping the classical influence of Plato and Aristotle on such debates, I argue for integrating the concepts of tolerance and diversity into a liberal political platform including international and temporal frameworks.

The Nature of Justice

Although metaphysically grounded, there are relational aspects to Plato's account of justice as well, as seen in how the proper balance of the three components of the individual soul must accord with the proper ordering of persons in classes in society in order to establish justice effectively. Relational elements also structure Aristotle's account of justice, as seen in his development of justice as a virtue and character trait leading to the pursuit of excellence in a life well lived. Indeed, in his exegesis on particular justice—as contrasted with universal justice as lawfulness tempered by natural law and equity—distributive justice as based on the concept of equality serves as a forbearer to a dominant approach in contemporary theories of justice.

In chapter 7, the contemporary debate of whether justice is distributive or relational by nature is addressed along with the question of the proper task of justice. In taking up this debate, I examine the account of John Rawls and his distributive theory of justice as fairness, as well as Ronald Dworkin's distributive account, based on a complex view of equality.[48] What I underscore in this chapter is that many contemporary accounts of justice with distributive formulations fail to address important political issues, as focused on the individual who assumes responsibility for her or his actions, the Kantian criterion I deem crucial for a just society.

Moreover, contemporary distributive schemes do not directly consider societally defined power relations between and among individuals, or between groups and institutional structures in society. Nor do they address such important political considerations as various structures of decision-making, such as divisions of labor, culture, or the construction of social meanings. Rather, such distributive formulations stake out the task of justice as the development of political institutions, "just institutions," to distribute or redistribute liberties and goods of society—whether such distributions are based on merit as in Aristotle's account; on need as in Rawls' account; on resources as in Dworkin's account; or on some other formulation.

A relational view of justice, on the other hand, seeks to examine the connections between individuals and their relations in society with particular emphasis on how such relationships are established and configured. In a normative view, this focus includes an understanding of what these relations should be. In a political view, this focus includes the method of organizing persons in society. As discussed later, I foreground the importance of communication, thereby giving both normative and political views the ability to address the diverse complexities of today's societies.

Individual Rights and Responsibilities

Plato's and Aristotle's views on the individual and political society are typically thought not to contribute to the concept of individual rights in modern political society, a concept whose origins are often attributed to Thomas Hobbes and John Locke. Plato's functional argument of individuals doing their own work in society, however, may foreground the question. In Aristotle's case, scholars have linked his thought to the natural rights tradition claiming that his teleological view of human nature and his ethical theory of *eudaimonia* may serve as a foundation for a theory of individual rights akin to Locke's.[49]

Accordingly, in chapter 8, I trace Platonic and Aristotelian thought in interrogating the issue of individual versus group rights while addressing the political issue of liberalism as the common framework for many contemporary theories of justice. Consequently, the main question developed in this chapter is whether rights and responsibilities should be accorded to groups rather than to individuals. In doing so, I examine the question of moral agency and the group rights theory of Iris Marion Young,[50] in which she defines a group as "a collective of persons differentiated from at least one other group by cultural forms, practices, or way of life."[51] Importantly, Young asserts that the rights held by a group obtain over those of individuals—a position prompted by her views of a pluralistic human condition in which ways of life and commitments significantly differentiate one group from another. Her position is sometimes used, somewhat controversially, to further multicultural causes.

While diversity and pluralism reside easily within a liberal societal construct, the claim of equal recognition for groups, however, proves more problematic since the two linchpins of the liberal account, liberty and equality, focus on the autonomous individual rather than on groups as the relevant moral agent.[52] For example, some liberal thinkers, in supporting diversity and pluralism, antithetically maintain that rights should be awarded to certain groups, not unlike Plato's consigning of function to a hierarchy of societal groupings (albeit in a more uniformly conceived society). While cultural or religious groups may be allowed special exemption from a duty to obey, the reasons for such exemptions, as such liberal theorists claim, are based on political prudence or on an estimate of the balance of advantages.[53]

The problems emerging from assigning groups as the proper bearer of rights emerge from solipsistically presenting groups as individuals. That is, from a Kantian perspective, to attribute rights to groups supposes that groups have a being and integrity on par with those of individuals. This cannot be the case. Groups aggregate individuals and do not themselves simply form a human-like being to whom it would be appropriate to ascribe moral agency, values, reasoning, and moral decision-making.[54] Besides such issues of definition, moral standing should also not be accorded to groups; when it is, individuals tend to disappear from view.

The core problem becomes clear when considering membership in a minority group, groups distinguished by race, ethnicity, culture, or language. Thus, in the multicultural debate, Will Kymlicka makes the case that such membership is involuntary and not a true case of free association.[55] In other words, members may not exit such groups easily as they may with a club or association. Importantly as well, if the group's authority is oppressive or its way of life intolerable, group members may not have the type of options available to them that other citizens in a liberal society may have.

Fundamentally, social groups are not static since the individuals comprising groups all but guarantee constantly changing and unclear boundaries. Indeed, any social group that may be demarcated may be further subdivided into smaller entities. Thus, referencing Mill's harm principle and Rawls' first principle of justice as fairness, an indeterminacy challenge can also be directed at Young's core political concept of groups and group rights.

A challenge of a different order is presented by communitarianism and the concept of groups embraced by Michael Walzer, as witnessed in his *Spheres of Justice* argument.[56] One communitarian challenge to liberalism, for example, is the view that societies may not exist in a vacuum and must, and should, be framed by a larger vision of the Good, thereby echoing platonic thought. That is, it seems appropriate to rest rights on substantive, moral judgments of the ends that rights advance. Walzer thereby raises questions of cultural relativism and political pluralism along with the interesting issue of whether it is possible to have political pluralism without value pluralism.

International Relations

As indicated earlier, the moral frameworks presented in Plato's and Aristotle's accounts of justice are mapped onto closed and static models of political society. Geopolitical concerns and relations between and among nations, however, test the question of whether morality, or indeed justice, is a relevant consideration in international affairs. In chapter 9, I explore the reach of mandates of justice geopolitically and include the clash between human rights and theocracies, as well as the conflict between realist and cosmopolitan views of international relations. Charles Beitz's work on international relations functions as a touchstone here.[57]

In developing a contemporary theory of global justice, Beitz first posits and then rejects a realist view of international relations based on a Hobbesian state of nature, whereby anarchic war is widespread and might makes right, with the ruler obliged to act in Machiavellian manner and only in the self-interest of his people. In contrast, Beitz' normative view of international relations—initially based on interdependence and cooperation and later modified by a more Kantian moral view—grounds due respect and concern for others in his theory of cosmopolitan global justice. His view also mirrors the classical concept of *dikaiosune*, echoing Plato's approach to justice insofar as he incorporates both the moral and the globally political, while further seeming to count upon Aristotle's relationship of the individual to society as well in his distributive theory of natural resources among nations.

Future Justice

In today's societal contexts, I would be remiss not to treat justice in the future. Thus, in chapter 10, I examine issues of personal identity, the transmission of values over time, and population ethics in relation to the question of justice for future lives, issues made even more complex by the diverse constitution of increasingly heavily populated societies as well as by the global reach of the concerns of diverse groups.

Classical thinkers did articulate positions on future justice, albeit not taking into consideration such complexities as found in societies today. Thus, Plato views the incorporeal soul as immortal, thereby positing a metaphysical answer to the question of personal identity. However, he fears that his vision of the ideal society, even if instantiated, would eventually decay. Aristotle, on the other hand, focuses his attention on virtues, character traits that may be inculcated in mortals. Like Plato, he also accepts the notion of imperfect societies and imperfect constitutions, thereby recognizing the contingency of political orders.

In contemporary times, Derek Parfit develops a psychological account of personal identity, which he views as a bundle of experiences, thoughts, and feelings bound together by causal relations of memory and character. In *Reasons and Persons*, his utilitarian vision of future lives is put under stress by the issue of an expanding global population, which leads him to his Repugnant Conclusion.[58] The question of population expansion is not insignificant. Indeed, Rawls' formulation of justice as fairness may well be troubled by the possibility of overpopulation since his liberty and difference principles as applied to his distribution model prove more and more difficult to realize.

Parfit tackles the problem numerically, whereby for any possible population of minimally ten billion people, all with high qualities of life, there must be some much larger population whose existence, *ceteris paribus*, would be better off through the sheer gains in the aggregate quantity of good even though its members have lives barely worth living.[59] By bringing numbers into sharp focus, Parfit forces a calculus that, perhaps unintentionally but certainly necessarily, pushes issues of quality of life and personal identity into a less prominent space. He thereby loses sight of the Kantian ideal of respect for individuals as the macro, globally articulated, pole of *dikaiosune* dominates his model.

In contrast, I argue that the key to examining the reach of justice over time depends, in part, on what values are to be transmitted into the future, what the mechanism is for their transmission, and what provisions are made for future justice. In doing so, it proves necessary to remember both poles of *dikaiosune*, the individual and the societal, to keep the Kantian respect for individuals in focus while attempting to chart and provide for justice for future lives.

NOTES

1. Edition used: Plato, *Phaedrus*, trans. R. Hackforth, ed. Harvey Yuris (Cambridge: Cambridge University Press, 2011).

2. It is thought that *Phaedrus* is a middle-period platonic dialogue, as is *The Republic*, by which period Plato had linked a moral philosophy to metaphysical theory, a theory of cosmic order with first principles of nature and thought. See Janet Coleman, *A History of Political Thought* (Malden: Blackwell Publishing, 2000), vol. I, pp. 71–73.

3. The ancient Greeks had no term for what we refer to as "social." Thus, my use of the term is in the modern sense of referring to an aggregate of people living together in a more or less ordered community with shared laws, traditions, and values.

4. Hence, when referring to individuals in general in either thinker's works, I will be using male pronouns.

5. Edition used: Plato, *The Republic*, trans. Desmond Lee, 2nd ed. (London: Penguin Books, 2003).

6. See Plato (2003), Book IV.

7. See David West, "The Contribution of Continental Philosophy," in Robert Goodin and Philip Pettit, eds., *A Companion to Contemporary Political Philosophy* (Malden: Blackwell Publishing, 1995), pp. 39–71.

8. See Jürgen Habermas, *Between Facts and Norms*, trans. William Rehg (Cambridge: MIT Press, 1996).

9. Aristotle, *The Nicomachean Ethics of Aristotle*, trans. D. Ross, rev. Lesley Brown (Oxford: Oxford University Press, 2009), V.1133b–1134a and 1134a8–9, following the customary Bekker format.

10. For Aristotle, "man is by nature a political animal." *Politics*, trans. T. A. Sinclair, rev. Trevor Saunders (London: Penguin Books, 1992), I.1253a.

11. "Social justice" is a controversial term, variously defined in modern usage. In a narrow sense, it refers to distribution of wealth, opportunities, and privileges within a society, and thus an egalitarian distributive approach. In this sense, it has similarities to Aristotle's view that particular justice is based on the concept of equality. But see Friedrich von Hayek's famous charge of category error, in which he states that it is confusion to apply notions of justice (which refer to actions of individuals) to relative holdings of people across a free society. F. A. Hayek, *Law, Legislation and Liberty* (Chicago: University of Chicago Press, 1978), vol. II, ch. 9.

12. See Phillipa Foot, *Virtues and Vices* (Oxford: Oxford University Press, 2002), and Alasdair MacIntyre, *After Virtue*, 3rd ed. (Notre Dame: University of Notre Dame Press, 2007).

13. E.g., see John Rawls, *A Theory of Justice* (Cambridge: Harvard University Press, 1971); Ronald Dworkin, *Sovereign Virtue* (Cambridge: Harvard University Press, 2000); Charles Beitz, *Political Theory and International Relations*, 2nd ed. (Princeton: Princeton University Press, 1999); see also chapters 7 and 8 *infra*.

14. See Philip Pettit, "The Contribution of Analytical Philosophy," in Goodin and Pettit, 1995, p. 7: "1. There is a reality independent of human knowledge of which we human beings are part. 2. Reason and method, particularly as exemplified in science, offer us the proper way to explore that reality and our relationship to it. 3. In this exploration traditional—in particular, traditional evaluative preconceptions—should be suspended and the facts allowed to speak for themselves."

15. E.g., see Jeremy Bentham, *The Works of Jeremy Bentham* (Edinburgh: William Tait, 1843), vol. 1.

16. See Robert Nozick, *Anarchy, State, and Utopia* (New York: Basic Books, 1974); Dworkin (2000); chapters 6 and 7 *infra*.

17. Edition used: Immanuel Kant, *Groundwork for the Metaphysic of Morals,* trans. H. J. Paton (New York: HarperCollins, 2009).

18. These elements undergird Kant's fundamental principle of morality as expressed in his discussion on the Supreme Principle of Morality, which he also termed the Categorical Imperative. Id., p. 108.

19. Subject to much debate, some, including John Rawls, interpret Kant's stance as a constructivist account, in which autonomy and independence of reason are seen to produce objective moral ends. Notably, the particular constructivist account that Rawls attributes to Kant argues for a conception of objectivity that is

not metaphysical, but political. That is, he develops a foundation hosting objective standards in reasoning, aimed at solving practical problems of what to do in society, including principles of justice that govern the basic structure of society, as defined by major social institutions. There are nonetheless metaphysical realist strands present in Kant, as when he refers to our consciousness of moral law as the "fact of reason." Immanuel Kant, *Critique of Pure Reason*, trans. and eds. Paul Guyer and Allen Wood (Cambridge: Cambridge University Press, 1997); 5:31; cf. 5:6, 42f, 55, 91, 104. The citations use the standard A and B pagination of the first (1781) and second (1787) editions, respectively.

20. Bernard Williams, *Ethics and the Limits of Philosophy* (Cambridge: Harvard University Press, 1985), p. 140.

21. Based upon a loose definition of rationality and a contractualist framework, Scanlon develops "[a] view that allows for such variations in what is right, by applying a fixed set of substantive moral principles to varying circumstances, [which] is not relativism but rather what [he calls] 'parametric universalism.'" T. M. Scanlon, *What We Owe to Each Other* (Cambridge: Harvard University Press, 2000), p. 328.

22. See Rawls (1971).

23. See John Rawls, "The Priority of the Right and Ideas of the Good," *Philosophy and Public Affairs* 17; 4: 251–276 (1998), reprinted in John Rawls, *Political Liberalism* (New York: Columbia University Press, 1993), pp. 173–211; see also chapter 5 *infra*.

24. See Joseph Raz, *The Morality of Freedom* (Oxford: Oxford University Press, 1986).

25. While many of the contemporary writers discussed in this study engage with distributive schemes of justice and debate issues of equality, in regard to the individual, most embrace the Kantian notion of an equality of concern and respect for the person.

26. Aristotle (2009), I.7.

27. See Plato, *The Statesman*, trans. J. B. Skemp (London: Bristol Classical Press, 2002), 291d–e and 301b–c, following the customary 1578 Stepanus edition format.

28. Isaiah Berlin, "Two Concepts of Liberty," in *Four Essays on Liberty* (Oxford: Oxford University Press, 1969), pp. 118–172.

29. John Stuart Mill, "On Liberty," in John Gray, ed. *John Stuart Mill on Liberty and Other Essays* (Oxford: Oxford University Press, 1998), p. 14.

30. Berlin (1969), p. 48.

31. Id., p. 52.

32. But see Robert Talisse, "Does Value Pluralism Entail Liberalism?" 2007; http://ssrn.com/abstract=1005651.

33. John Gray, for example, asserts that Berlin's argument suffers from a classic Humean "is-ought" error. That is, even granting that individuals strongly value the freedom to choose, it does not follow that the state *ought* to provide or protect such freedom. Paradoxically, to do so would lead the state to recognizing an overriding value (free choice), thereby violating value pluralism. Gray, who makes this point, further argues that value pluralism is consistent with a range of non-liberal political orders. See John Gray, *Two Faces of Liberalism* (Cambridge: Polity Press, 2000).

34. William Galston, "Must Value Pluralism and Religious Belief Collide?" in George Crowder and Henry Hardy, eds., *The One and the Many* (Amherst: Prometheus Books, 2007), p. 252.
35. Mill (1998), p. 17.
36. E.g., see Rawls (1971), p. 2.
37. See Nozick (1974), and chapter 8 *infra.*
38. See Dworkin (2000), and chapter 6 *infra.*
39. Plato (2003), 414–415, following the customary 1578 Stephanus edition format.
40. For Example, Karl Popper, *The Open Society and Its Enemies* (Princeton: Princeton University Press, 1971); but see Leo Strauss, *The City and Man* (Chicago: University of Chicago Press, 2002).
41. Rawls (1971), p. 328.
42. See Raz (1986), and chapter 5 *infra.*
43. See Aristotle (2009), Book V.
44. See chapter 7 *infra.*
45. See Mill (1998).
46. See Derek Parfit, *Reasons and Persons* (Oxford: Clarendon Press, 1984).
47. Kant (2009), p. 96.
48. See Rawls (1971) and Dworkin (2000).
49. See Fred Miller, *Nature, Justice, and Rights in Aristotle's Politics* (Oxford: Oxford University Press, 1995); John Gray, *Liberalism* (Minneapolis: University of Minnesota Press, 1985).
50. Iris Marion Young, *Justice and the Politics of Difference* (Oxford: Oxford University Press, 1990).
51. Id., at 43.
52. E.g., see Brian Barry, *Culture and Equality* (Cambridge: Polity Press, 2000).
53. See Barry (2000); see also chapter 8 *infra.*
54. For instance, for the view that only individual human beings may be of ultimate value, see Chandran Kukathas, "Are There Any Cultural Rights?" *Political Theory* 20; 1: 105–139 (1992). Compare Will Kymlicka, *Multicultural Citizenship* (Oxford: Oxford University Press, 1995) and Barry (2000).
55. See Kymlicka (1995).
56. See Michael Walzer, *Spheres of Justice* (New York: Basic Books, 1983).
57. See Beitz (1999).
58. See Parfit (1984), 387.
59. Id., Part IV.

Part I

FOUNDATIONAL MATTERS

Chapter 2

Plato

A Moral Universe

Plato believes in a moral universe, one which is metaphysically grounded upon foundational forms including the form of the Good. Forms are perfect, eternal, and paradigmatic archetypes, and knowledge of the forms leads to genuine knowledge and wisdom. While such a view may seem far removed from current thought on justice, Plato's fundamental and metaphysical linkage of justice with ethical concerns nonetheless continues to animate contemporary debates on what justice means, even as communities become more and more particularized and their relationships concomitantly more complex. Resulting discussions may focus on distributive justice within a liberal political framework, but even the most numerically based, secular positions are still framed in Plato's ethical concerns.[1]

Essentially, for Plato good politics and justice depend on knowledge of the forms, which he metaphysically understands to exist in the intelligible realm regardless of whether mortals apprehend them or not. As articulated in *The Republic*, this metaphysical understanding of forms produces and ensures the good communal life, ideally structured under a philosopher king in a society with three classes that are analogous to the triadic soul of an individual. He thereby defines justice as knowledge of how to fulfill one's political and moral function in society, a viewpoint that has occupied philosophers for centuries.[2]

FOUNDATIONAL FORMS

The Republic begins with what on the surface appears to be a simple question: What is justice (*dikaiosune*)? Since the Greek term covers both individual and social morality, however, the inquiry actually extends into both ethics and politics while firmly linking both fields. Consequently, the question scrutinized in *The Republic* continually moves between individual and societal levels so that the question could be rephrased as: What is the basis of moral and social obligation?

In this framework, Thrasymachus is portrayed as the greatest danger to Plato's account of justice. While Thrasymachus does not present an amoral position such as that articulated by Thomas Hobbes' *Leviathan* in the seventeenth century, he does prove to be an immoralist, believing not only in self-interest but also in the dictum that might make right. At the political level, Thrasymachus articulates a dangerous position insofar as he refuses to recognize that laws apply to him, thereby posing a threat to the political stability of a well-ordered society. Just as dangerously, on the individual level Thrasymachus appears to be a hot-headed individual, an unnatural man, whose tripartite soul (reason, spirit, and appetite) is out of balance.[3] It is for these reasons that Plato presents Socrates as obliged to launch an attack on Thrasymachus' arguments, and on the sophist's own terms, in order to affirm that by nature men are mutual benefactors, cooperators rather than natural perpetrators of harm, that in other words justice does pay and that the just man is a happy man.[4]

Epistemologically, Plato tries to show that Thrasymachus' view of interest rests on ignorance, a lack of understanding of the form of the Good. From a secular point of view, that is, Plato appears to be arguing that virtue is its own reward, a stance that may obtain epistemologically and metaphysically but one that falls short when measured in knowledge of the visible world and its worldly goods. Indeed, for centuries it is along this moral-political continuum that tensions concerning justice have emerged for justice per se mandates a view greater than the individual and the concrete with ideas nonetheless situated, as I argue, in societal norms. In this case, by analyzing the elements of the human mind, Plato argues that a mortal's well-being, full development, and happiness are secured by doing right and not doing wrong, as metaphysically conceived in terms of universals, the eternal forms. Within this metaphysical framework, the proper balance among the three elements of the soul with each doing its job emerges as his individual answer to the question, "What is justice?" When an individual is in balance, the argument continues on the societal level, he will further the good of the state.

Lodged on the individual level in the pursuit of mutable goods, Thrasymachus with his out-of-balance soul may not be able to be convinced by any epistemological argument. As for justice writ large, he would deny that justice boils down to minding one's own business; that is, in fulfilling one's individual function in society. In other words, Thrasymachus' position represents the best case against a moral and political approach to justice.

While adhering to ethical principles lodged in a metaphysical understanding of political organization, Plato does not ignore the attraction of the visible and its claims. His inclusion of Thrasymachus points to his understanding of how justice may be defined in secular terms, leading him nonetheless to shift from the visible as the measurement of all things to the invisible. Thus, as led by the guardian of an ideal society, Plato's justice is manifest in the proper ordering of society and political stability. This recognition, resting as it does on metaphysical claims, predictably proves to be a constant concern for Plato, as seen for example in Books VIII and IX, and in his belief that even if a *polis* were able to be organized according to the lines he advocates, it would eventually devolve into more defective constitutions and eventually decay.

For Plato, we live in a moral universe of which we acquire knowledge through the intellectual apprehension of forms by means of our reasoning. Although *The Republic's* discussion and development of a theory of forms is far from comprehensive, it is clear that in Plato's account forms exist unchanging in an intelligible realm—whether mortals in their corporeal existence ever apprehend them or not—and that these forms represent what is ultimately real.[5] Humans, who are born into, live, and die in the sensible world, nonetheless have immortal souls and by means of reason may come to recognize, contemplate, and remember forms from prior times when earlier their incorporeal souls came into contact with the eternal forms. In other words, by exercising their rational faculties, humans may intellectually apprehend forms, see the eternal and hence true reality, and thereby come to understand how to live a good life. This metaphysically driven epistemology proves critical here because Plato's account of justice, of *dikaiosune*—of individual and social morality—is defined by his theory of forms.[6]

The Republic's main treatment of forms appears in two passages, first, when Socrates engages Glaucon in a discussion of the philosopher king and his education, and next, when the theory is presented by way of analogy through the myths of the Sun, the Divided Line, and the Cave. Forms represent the proper objects of reasoning and knowledge for philosophers since they exist as a realm of eternals and absolutes. As such, they are ontologically superior to the mundane realm of mortals or that which is governed by mutability. Dangerously though, the mutable's very tangibility leads humans astray since tangibility per se makes all objects in this world seem to be real. Nonetheless, according to Plato such objects comprise only intimations of the true forms. Consequently, how the everyday participates in the eternal forms is what Plato attempts to demonstrate.

Epistemologically then, good politics and ethics, or justice along with the roles justice plays in a moral universe, depend on knowledge of these forms. Since, as Plato sees it, humans are natural theorizers they can develop comprehensive explanations of a near infinite number of experiences in order to apprehend mortality and to situate life in an intelligible context that furthers understanding. Aiding them in such efforts, mortals may occasionally glimpse intimations of forms in the sensible world as they categorize and develop common names for things that share essential characteristics, and in so doing, they participate in what is ultimately real.

Theory of Forms

Plato's first discussion of forms in *The Republic* occurs in the context of developing a definition of the philosopher (474b–487a).[7] Here we learn that forms are eternal and unchanging ideals or patterns which have a real existence independent of our apprehension of them in a realm ontologically superior to that of the visible world (477–479; 597). Moreover, there is a form for "each set of particular things, to which we apply the same name" (596a). The relation of forms to particulars reflects the forms' superior status in that they are present in particulars; concomitantly, particulars are said to partake of forms. Put another way, particulars exist in the temporal, sensible world and merely partake of forms, while imperfectly reflecting them, as is most evident in the fact that sensible particulars are subject to change.[8]

While it can be argued that the imperfection of sensible particulars renders them only approximate forms, a better view may be that this imperfection of sensible particulars derives from their possessing the properties of forms in an incomplete manner; that is, they are not *completely* perfect.[9] Hence, sensible objects may be both partly beautiful and partly ugly, partly just and partly unjust, partly good and partly evil, to the extent that they participate in the beauty or justice or goodness of the forms. It is only the forms that are really and wholly beautiful, just, and good, without qualification and in every context.[10] Plato's theory of transcendental and separated forms is thus seen as relational in character, with separation responsible for the relational character of his account of universals.[11]

While Plato does not delineate the extent of the realm of forms in *The Republic,*[12] he does adumbrate how forms may be intellectually apprehended through reasoning and explains how reasoning is developed in the philosopher's education through the study of mathematics and dialectic (525e–534e). Such training allows individuals to grasp the coherent wholeness of the universe. This process of learning right reasoning is intended to lead to moral knowledge, as evident in and conveyed by the harmonious and coherent whole. Explicitly, forms may be mentally "seen" and intellectually apprehended through correct reasoning which includes the conceptual tool of definition that, in turn, aids mortals to grasp the essential nature of a form.

Basically reversing secular reasoning as represented in Thrasymachus' viewpoint, forms alone can be truly known, whereas sensible things comprise objects of belief. In order to display this theory of forms more fully, Plato further paraphrases the argument by analogy and simile as articulated in certain myths that will be discussed after first briefly sketching his epistemologically framed explication of the form of the Good, his metaphysically defined orders of reality, and how he relates illusion to reality.

The Form of the Good

Among other things, for Plato, knowledge affirms the Good in its apprehension of forms. As one commentator has noted, "matters of fact in the world, in some sense independent of our ideas and judgments, about which these ideas and judgments may be correct or incorrect."[13] Plato argues that forms exist before sense data, and ideas are confirmed by the instantiations of forms in the sensible world. On one level, individuals are born with conceptual and intellectual capabilities before experiencing anything in the sensible world. This is possible, Plato argues, because while mortal bodies may undergo metempsychoses, the human soul is immortal and it is immortal because its own specific fault, evil, cannot destroy it (608c–611a). Thus, the soul remembers truths or forms, having experienced them before being born into bodies. It follows that education should further the process of training individuals to stimulate these recognitions into consciousness.

It is clear in *The Republic* that all efforts of education are directed to acquiring knowledge so that the Good, the ultimate object of knowledge, may be apprehended. Indeed, Plato presents the form of the Good as *the* firm foundation. In order to arrive at knowledge of the Good, he proffers the above-mentioned dialectical method by means of which individuals might set out from starting points provided by hypotheses and reach absolutely firm, unconditional conclusions. In such exercises of pure reasoning, dialectic provides the guidelines, the map, for the process of rational argument since, for example, the philosopher attempting to educate a future philosopher king must have a conceptual basis for describing errors made along the way to acquiring knowledge. In this context perhaps a false judgment may be seen as a misfit perception of thought.

Mortals may initially apprehend by opposites (as, for example, in good versus evil), with each oppositional pair representing starkly articulated dichotomies. In part, relying on oppositions represents a categorization or taxonomic exercise in which the essential character of items that should be grouped together and that share the essence of the category is perceived.[14] According to Plato, for example, all mortals apprehend in terms of sensory perceptions, that which possesses beauty, the good or the just. Since these qualities are culturally and historically specific and thus relativistic, the philosopher who pursues knowledge of the forms is better equipped to recognize intrinsic first principles (see 476a), which instantiate the originary form of Beauty, the Good, and the Just, as intrinsic conceptual categories. As a result of a philosopher's efforts, individuals can learn about forms through these conceptual categories, as partially embodied in learned opinions that have become authoritative.

Complicating the path toward knowledge of the Good is a mortal's living in two realms. The body resides in the mutable world, which is perceived through the senses as the real world, while the immortal soul can grasp the nature of forms and do so more easily when unencumbered by its corporeal shell. As mentioned earlier, forms do not depend on humans' apprehension in order to exist; for Plato, forms eternally exist in the intelligible realm and individuals may occasionally glimpse intimations of forms in the sensible world as they, through the pursuit of knowledge by means of reason, categorize and develop common names for things that share essential characteristics. In so doing, they participate in what is truly real.

Any other intellectual pursuit is an illusion, as exemplified in Thrasymachus' immoral pursuits. Thus, whether a philosopher using reasoned argument and dialectic pursues the form of the Good, a craftsman uses *technai* to engage in the representation of forms, or, at yet another remove, illusionists derivatively imitate things in the visible world, it is impossible for humans—whose immortal souls have come into contact with forms while in their incorporeal state—to live without forms.

The Sun, the Divided Line, and the Cave

In the context of discussing the education of the philosopher who ideally governs a just society, Plato describes the qualities of character which the philosopher must have, emphasizing that these qualities must be based, ultimately, in the knowledge of the Good. Rather than attempting to define the form of the Good, however, Plato offers analogies to convey the unintelligible realm beyond the range of mortal sense perception. Thus, *The Republic*'s use of the Sun, the Divided Line, and the Cave briefly summarized here not only provide guidelines for the aspiring philosopher king but they also demonstrate how Plato pursues a comprehensive understanding of *dikaiosune*, as he balances the metaphysical and the analytical, the political, and the moral.

Mapping the progress of proper intellectual education, the analogies of the Sun, the Divided Line, and the Cave illustrate how a student depends less and less on individual instantiations of abstract, metaphysical, universals, and learns to think in increasingly abstract, analytical ways. To begin with, in the visible world, the Sun allows sensible objects to be seen and grants the faculty of sight to the eye. Analogously, individuals may apprehend objects of thought in the intelligible world of eternal forms and thereby achieve the power of knowing, the faculty of knowledge, for the mind's eye (507a–509c). Having apprehended the forms, however, does not suffice; the mind must be trained to abstract the eternal from the mortal. Here, Plato presents the analogy of the Divided Line to illustrate an individual's ideal relationship to the forms while delving further epistemologically into the relation between the two orders of reality.

Although presented *seriatim,* in a continuum, the Divided Line may nonetheless be viewed as a hierarchy consisting of forms, physical things, and shadows and images (509d–511e).[15] The forms exist in the intelligible realm and can be apprehended by means of training in mathematical reasoning and dialectic resulting in knowledge. While physical things, as well as shadows and images, all exist in the visible world, importantly, for the development of discerning acuity, there is a difference between physical things and their shadows and images, that difference primarily comprising degrees of truth or genuineness in what is apprehended.

As suggested by these metaphysically based, analytically framed analogies, Plato specifies certain states of mind (see 511d) in which individuals can apprehend knowledge and perceive opinion in, respectively, the eternal and visible realms. With respect to knowledge, two states of mind—intelligence and reasoning—allow for understanding eternal forms, although each state of mind apprehends them in a different way. For intelligence, which considers only forms (511c), the intellect moves upward to a first principle, before turning back to a conclusion (511a–b). For reasoning, which reflects upon both forms and mathematical postulates (510c–511b), the intellect moves downward from assumptions to conclusions, as is the case with geometry and similar *technai* (511a–b, d).[16]

In contrast, in the visible world when individuals pursue opinion rather than knowledge, as does Thrasymachus, two other states of mind are activated, belief and illusion, which Plato relates to two objects of the physical world represented in the Divided Line analogy. Thus, belief, as in "commonsense assurance," and illusion (511d–e) are what engage sophists, poets, and artists, who do not pursue true knowledge. More specifically, on the one hand, beliefs relate to animals, plants, manufactured objects (510a), and models or drawings of geometrical figures (510d–e). Illusions, on the other hand, relate to images, shadows, and the reflections of the original objects of beliefs.[17]

Finally, Plato further adumbrates the difficult ascent to true knowledge in the analogy provided by the Myth of the Cave. Perhaps the best known of Plato's analogies, this myth describes people in a dark cave watching shadows cast on a wall, believing that these shadows constitute reality. One individual—like the others, facing forward and chained to a wall so that he can only see the shadows of objects cast by a fire blazing behind him—is freed from his chains. He sees that these shadows are actually mere illusions, and he now believes the objects to be real. Upon leaving the Cave, however, after initially being dazzled by the Sun, the form of the Good, he apprehends that the Cave's objects and shadows only encourage beliefs and illusions, not true knowledge. This philosopher, upon having achieved this supreme vision, is required to return to the Cave to serve his companions, to free them from their chains. Thus, the cave dwellers are depicted as the ignorant masses, and the philosopher as one who escapes the ignorance imprisoning them, ultimately leading to his achieving a vision of the Good, the source of all truth. Importantly, his lack of desire to return to the Cave identifies the chief qualification for the philosopher and, consequently, characterizes the reluctant philosopher king as well (514a–521b).

The analogies of the Sun, the Divided Line, and the Cave most effectively cohere when read against each other (see 521c and 534). Thus, the Cave's chained prisoner corresponds to those trapped by illusion, as located on one end of the Divided Line as shadows and images (517d). The freed prisoner takes cognizance of objects and thus believes he can distinguish between the shadows as illusions and the objects as real, thereby moving to belief and to physical things on the Divided Line. The freed prisoner's ascent to the world outside the Cave allows him to move along the Divided Line to the forms (517b); moreover, his apprehension of real things in the world outside the Cave depends upon his ability to reason as he is confronted by this truly beautiful world where the true forms of those objects in the Cave reside (516a–b).

Finally, when the freed prisoner looks at the Sun he understands that the Sun is the form of the Good instantiated in the Cave's fire (516b, 517b–c). More than simply allowing objects of sense to be seen, the Sun, the form of the Good, comprises the source of reality and truth, allowing for objects of thought to be apprehended as real and granting the power of knowing, the faculty of knowledge, to the mind. Consequently, the philosopher thinks in increasingly abstract ways and becomes less and less dependent on concrete articulations of abstract universals.

Education of the Philosopher

As mentioned earlier, the main treatment of the theory of forms in *The Republic* is presented in the context of defining the characteristics of the philosopher king and describing his special education. Beyond the basic training described in Part III of *The Republic* (376d–412a), the further education of the philosopher is intended to provoke thought and to train the mind, with the vision of the Good as its ultimate objective. The training of the philosopher is one of rigorous intellectual discipline, effected by means of the technique of exact and increasingly abstract thinking. The teacher turns the student's eye to the light. Thus, the student is not a passive recipient of knowledge; he must grasp the truth himself. The long and difficult education of the philosopher is necessary (521c–592a) since, for Plato, an understanding of theory precedes practice for a ruler or anyone else pursuing wisdom. As noted earlier, this training includes the disciplines of mathematics and dialectic. More specifically, five mathematical disciplines are pursued: arithmetic, plane geometry, solid geometry, astronomy, and harmonics (524e–531c), and each is used to further abstract thought. These disciplines correspond to the escape from the Cave allowed by the reasoning that categorized what was seen in the Cave as transitory objects and shadows, mere reflections of the forms (532b–c).

Mathematical studies serve as a prelude to the study of dialectic, which is viewed as an exercise in pure thought and the last stage in the ascent from the Cave, when the eye can look upon the Sun itself as the Good (526d). Dialectic is critical of assumptions, even those of mathematics and is, in fact "the only procedure which proceeds by the destruction of assumptions to the very first principle, so as to give itself a firm base" (533a). It tries to grasp what "each thing is in itself" (533b) and culminates in coherent knowledge (537c) in the apprehension of the form of the Good (532a–b; 534b–c). Consequently, it is dialectic that will allow the lover of knowledge, finally, to grasp truth by himself. Dialectic, as exemplified in Plato's dialogues by means of Socrates' destroying the arguments of his interlocutors, is seen as a thorough testing of arguments to arrive at true beliefs.

THE INDIVIDUAL AND ACTIONS

The individual as depicted in Plato's vision of *The Republic* has an "immortal soul, corrupted by vice and purified by virtue, of whom the body is only an instrument" (129a–130c). The soul consists of three parts which mirror the classes of Plato's ideal state; achieving balance among the elements of the triadic soul is a mark of a just individual, just as peace and stability is a mark of a just political order, "the best is neither war nor faction—they are things we should pray to be spared from—but peace and mutual good will" (628c). It is in this context that Plato views Thrasymachus as having an unbalanced soul and argues against the view that "justice is nothing else than the interest of the stronger." By contrast, Plato sees justice as a moral, universal value.

The Good and the Soul

Plato argues that the essential and unitary Good is linked to the gods and the divine and, concomitantly, that the immortal soul loves wisdom, or knowledge of the form of the Good (611e–612a). Thus, even though a good individual may also be rewarded by society in this mortal life, philosophers who pursue knowledge of the Good find the pursuit its own reward (612b–613e). Indeed, it seems that Plato cannot imagine greater happiness than occurs when the immortal soul in its disembodied state joins a great procession and sees "what is outside the heavens" (247b), the whole realm of the forms. As relayed in Plato's recounting of the Myth of Er and the Spindle of Necessity (614a–621a), not only does the soul always retain the ability to recollect what it once grasped of the forms but also the soul, which undergoes metempsychosis, is dependent upon the lives led while on Earth, resulting in greater or lesser contact with these forms, relationships that constitute, to some extent, rewards or punishments for our choices.[18]

The Just Person

Given Thrasymachus' position on justice, the obvious question that emerges is "why should a person be just?" Plato answers this individually situated question: for one's psychological health and pleasure. In taking up Thrasymachus' conventional immoralist challenge to justice, whose purpose he asserts is to have the weak serve the interests of the strong, Plato argues that justice as a virtue allows the soul to perform its function well. That is, justice allows the tripartite soul to be balanced, so that a person who performs his function well is "blessed and happy." His metaphysically lodged argument is at once both deontological as well as teleological in its claim that justice belongs "in the highest category, which anyone who is happy welcomes for its own sake and for the sake of its consequences" (358a1–2). In this manner, Plato constructs an account of happiness insofar as he argues that a just person is always happier than an unjust person.[19]

As indicated earlier, mirroring the three classes of society—philosophers, auxiliaries, and producers—every human soul consists of three parts: reason, spirit, and appetite. *The Republic* understands these separate parts of the soul in psychological terms, as becomes clear when Plato addresses complications such as psychological conflict (defined as parts of the soul warring against each other) and psychological constitutions. In developing the role of virtues in mental conflict, Plato also presents an account of *akrasia* that speaks to agency and motivation—*akrasia* comprises expressions of an agent's character that allows judgments without the use of reason.[20]

Thus, a person is wise when his rational faculty is functioning well "knowing as it does what is best for each of the three elements and for the whole made up of them" (442c5–7),[21] and an unwise person has a faulty conception of what is good for himself. In similar vein, a person is courageous when his spirited attitude does not alter in the face of pains or pleasures, but remains constant to what has been rationally discovered to be fearsome or not

(442b–c), while a coward facing the prospect of pain will fail to bear up to what has been rationally determined not to be genuinely fearsome. Likewise, a rash person anticipating pleasure will rush headlong into what according to the dictates of rationality should be avoided.

A person is viewed, then, as temperate, balanced or moderate, when the three parts of his soul are in agreement, and an intemperate or immoderate person is seen as having spirited or appetitive attitudes because the three parts of his soul are out of balance. In this tripartite view of the balanced soul (441d12–e2), justice on the individual level is the virtue that brings all other virtues into balance, and importantly, anyone who is just is seen as entirely virtuous.

Just Actions

Plato's psychological account of the just person as defined through his just actions is thus fundamental to the philosopher's view of the universe. Linking the just person to just actions, Plato further underscores both an essential attribute of knowledge—the motivational power of knowledge—as well as the need to develop that attribute by means of training the young early on in a wide range of attitudes. As to the motivational power of knowledge, Plato actually makes the case that an individual is virtuous if and only if he is a philosopher and can intellectually apprehend the form of the Good (cf. 474b–480a). It follows that with such knowledge, philosophers are motivated to take just actions.[22] From a developmental perspective, Plato also suggests that the motivation to do what is right may be inculcated early in the moral education of guardians (the military elite), thereby allowing the soul to become, eventually, perfectly just.

The balance that Plato examines in response to Thrasymachus' challenge supplements the idea that it is better to be just than unjust with the corollary that a just person is a happy person. In making the case for the just life being superior to the unjust life, Plato argues in terms of psychological health and pleasure insofar as he contrasts the tyrannical soul with the aristocratic soul, the most unjust with the most just. Consequently, the individual ruled by lawless attitudes is enslaved, least able to do what he wants, full of disorder and regret, poor, and fearful (577c–578a). In contrast, the philosopher is most able to do what he wants to do, and what he wants to do is what is best. Significantly, the comparison necessitates that there is a close correlation between the capacity to do what an individual wants to do and human success or happiness.

To bolster this axiom, Plato offers additional illustrations concerning pleasures, which he does not have Socrates define (580c–d, 583b). These pleasure proofs, however, remain problematic and unconvincing. The first pleasure proof proceeds as follows: each part of the soul has its characteristic desires and pleasures. Depending on which part of the soul rules a person, a particular pleasure will dominate. The characteristic pleasure of philosophers, for example, is learning; the characteristic pleasure of those striving for honor is being honored; the characteristic pleasure of money-lovers is making money. Each of these different kinds of persons would say that his own pleasure is best. To decide which pleasure is really best, Plato insists it must be determined which person's judgment is best. The answer is obvious in his framework. It is, of course, the philosopher.

The second pleasure proof complements the first since it relates pleasure to pain but also points to what might be mistaken for pleasure. Thus, pleasure and pain are opposites, separated by a neutral middle ground that affords neither pleasure nor pain. The removal of pain may seem pleasant, and the removal of pleasure may seem painful, but these perceptions are deceptive; pleasures that fill a lack by replacing pain are not genuine pleasures. Not surprisingly, the philosopher's pleasures do not fill a painful lack and therefore represent genuine pleasures. In contrast, those activities that are founded on the mutable, such as bodily pleasures, do fill a painful lack and therefore cannot be genuine pleasures.

Essentially bracketing out any trait or activity that does not fulfill one's character or that is lodged in the transitory, Plato argues that balance produces pleasure as it allows for harmony and the furthering of justice on both the individual and societal levels.[23]

POLITICAL SOCIETY

Fundamentally, for Plato, an understanding of forms produces and ensures the good communal life by means of a philosopher king who presides over three balanced classes in society to ensure that the polity is well ordered and organized. In this manner, a practical constitution emerges from theoretical reflection. For Plato, without theory, there is no politics, just chaos. Moreover, not only does his form-dependent theory of the state articulate an ideal system of governance, but by means of it philosophers can also properly understand what justice is and why it matters. The task then becomes one of implementing the theory so that men who seek justice may actually enjoy it.

Not surprisingly, Plato's views on justice in *The Republic*, including the connection between a just society and a just individual, are founded on his theory of forms, his metaphysical and epistemological approach to the universe, to comprehend what is ultimately real (cf. 485b). As discussed above, Plato views reality as comprising two orders, the realm of the unchanging, eternal forms and the mutable, sensible world of appearances.[24] Nonetheless, he has a unitary understanding of the world, not a binary one, although he often uses a binary approach to explicate a concept, even his most fundamental belief. Thus, reality is presented as a bifurcation between the sensible, observable world in which objects may appear good, beautiful, just, and true, on the one hand, and on the other hand, the eternal world, in which the incorporeal object that is goodness, beauty, justice, and truth—the form of the Good—exists, the form of the Good from which the many sensible things receive their names and defining characteristics. Yet, the forms and the sensible world are not intended to be dichotomous; rather, one is an intimation of the other.

Moreover, Plato's ideal state as depicted in *The Republic* abandons dualities when depicting a closed society with the three classes of persons, in which the best political order values peace and stability in a government led by philosopher rulers, who are attuned to virtue and illuminated by goodness, who rule for the common benefit of all citizens and who regard justice as the most important and essential virtue (540e). Plato expresses what just relations between persons and classes are in the phrase: "doing one's own work and not meddling with what isn't one's own" (433a–b). In contrast, democracy is depicted as an unstable form of rule dependent upon chance and must be held together with competent leadership (501b). In fact, Plato criticizes unchecked democracy because of its dominant features, freedom and equality (557a–564a).

Constitutions

These various arguments underpin Plato's demonstration that a just society is one that is well ordered, with the three classes each providing a necessary function to society as a whole. In order for a society to be stable, and thereby provide one of the conditions still considered necessary for a just society, the society should not only be stratified, it should also be hierarchical.

Complying with this vision, Plato delineates six imitative constitutions in his later treatise *The Statesman*, which he arranges in a hierarchy proceeding from most to least tolerable forms of governance.[25] First, he notes the three most tolerable law-abiding societies: kingship, aristocracy, and democracy. If, in contrast, a society is not law-abiding, again proceeding from most to least tolerable, governance finds articulation in democracy, oligarchy, and tyranny.[26] The seventh constitution he names is the true constitution under the rule of the philosopher king.

Likewise, the dividing line between law-abiding and not law-abiding constitutions is generated in terms of the principle of balance. Critically, law-abiding constitutions are involved in the pursuit of knowledge whereby the motive of rulers is to seek the common good. In contrast, constitutions that are not law-abiding are characterized by ignorant self-interest. In this framework, democracy has some limited purchase on the Good since it at least has the common good as its stated object.

The Statesman and Political Rule

In Plato's *polis*, rulers would be chosen from a military elite, the guardians, because they are good at shepherding and caring for the interests of the community. For his purposes, the middle class of auxiliaries may be seen as guardians in training. As Plato further explains in *The Statesman,* there is an art or technique (*techne*) of ruling and its best practice is engaged in by the statesman, the familiar philosopher king with knowledge of forms as well as insights into the use of due measure, which are unchanging standards of what is right, insights that he applies to particular circumstances.[27]

The *techne* of the statesman, then, comprises political theorizing and furthers the skills of both thinking and ruling. The rational statesman has the collective well-being and common good of each citizen as his disinterested main interest—he is the released prisoner who returns to the Cave in order to help his fellows. The success of his project (and its proper object) is the harmonious fellowship of different individual types and *technai* in society; he artfully weaves the warp and weft, the courageous and the moderate types found in society, into a harmonious whole.[28] Hierarchically, he also orchestrates the different *technai* of individuals, the functional specialists, to serve a balanced society.

In other words, the statesman is a generalist, who coordinates and integrates the various activities and character types that on their own would not coalesce into a well-ordered *polis*. His work, which is one of maintenance, involves control and oversight and he achieves success when he is able to link all citizens, to convince them to share the same ideals and ultimate values, using persuasion and as appropriate coercion to effect the truth. Acting as an absolute shepherd, one who remains very close to his flock, the statesman rules with the consent of those governed. Under such leadership, Plato suggests, the state—having devolved from the cosmological Age of Kronos to the Age of Zeus, the age in which mortals are left to their own resources—can work against the tendency to degeneration.

Again hierarchical, but also in a limited sense distributive, the attempt to define such a statesman and his education leads Plato to distinguish a taxonomy of *technai*. By means of these divisions, and others that he rejects, he tries to demonstrate that all other arts are subordinate to the art of politics. Distinguishing the statesman from others in the political community, Plato relegates various groups to subordinate functions such as the sophists along with orators per se, military men, and judges. Interestingly, Plato describes judges more as collaborators in the social enterprise because of their skills while they remain nonetheless under the control and direction of the statesman. In other words, in the practice of his art the statesman is entitled to unchallenged knowledge-based authority—similar to the scientific authority granted physicians in the practice of their *techne*—for the statesman is the one who interweaves individuals' skills for the communal whole and takes charge of the entire process.

Since he is unchallenged in his superiority, the true statesman may rule with or without laws, for his authority is absolute over all laws. Indeed, having achieved sufficient knowledge of the forms by means of reasoning and intelligence, the true statesman may skillfully use his *techne* to meet the contingencies of every situation appropriately. This is critical since laws are more or less mathematical—insofar as they are rigid, inflexible, and general—and at their best they attempt to imitate the rules or prescriptions that a true statesman might issue. Nonetheless, in the absence of any true statesmen—of which at any period of time there may be one or two—laws are entitled to the fullest authority, provided they become secondary when true statesmanship is present. Consequently, it is only the statesman in the practice of his art of ruling who may develop a true constitution.

The Polis and the Soul

In creating a harmonious whole, Plato would have rulers convince the people of the Noble Lie—that the categories of rulers, auxiliaries, and producers obtain not due to circumstances within the people's control, upbringing, or education, but rather, because of God's intervention. God, as the myth goes, had put certain metals in each person's blood and these metals determined their stations in life: rulers have gold, auxiliaries have silver, and producers have bronze. Most children of philosophers also have gold in their blood, but some may have silver or bronze and would then be demoted to a lower class, whereas auxiliaries and producers born with gold in their blood may be promoted (414–415).

Plato viewed the Noble Lie as necessary to keep a stable social structure and his claim is that this fictional account, though false, if believed by the people would result in an orderly and harmonious society.[29] The so-called Noble Lie is "noble" then, by reason of its purpose of keeping the masses under control and happy with their lots in life. Of course, in developing the Noble Lie, Plato reveals his belief that most people either are not intellectually capable of looking after their own and society's best interests or, perhaps, in contrast to the true guardians, belong to Thrasymachus' camp and thus would be too unbalanced to apprehend the need for a stable social structure. Of course, another response to the Noble Lie's faith in the true guardians is, as made popular by Juvenal's cynical question regarding the deficient faithfulness of wives, "Who will guard the guardians?"[30]

The question of whether good and effective politicians can be completely truthful and still achieve the necessary ends of society has been raised by, among others, Leo Strauss, who asks his readers whether noble lies have a positive role in uniting and guiding the *polis*. That is, are myths needed to give people meaning and purpose and to ensure a stable society or can men relentlessly examine, in Friedrich Nietzsche's words, those "deadly truths" and still flourish freely? In effect, the question becomes one of whether there are limits to the political, and concomitantly, what can be known absolutely.

In *The City and Man,* Strauss discusses the myths in *The Republic* that he believes are essential to all governments. These include the myth that the state's land belongs to it, even if it had been illegitimately acquired, and that citizenship is rooted in something more that accidents of birth. In this sense, Strauss himself may be seen as endorsing noble lies, suggesting that dissembling and deception comprise "the peculiar justice of the wise."[31] The difference in their approaches is found in their foundations. That is, Plato bases his belief in the Noble Lie on a moral good, while Strauss presents the superiority of ruling philosophers as an intellectual superiority and not a moral one, thereby interpreting Plato in a rather cynical manner.

More typically, contemporary commentators have also rejected the Noble Lie, mainly as devious and fundamentally antidemocratic. Thus, Karl Popper accuses Plato of trying to establish religion on a noble lie as well. In *The Open Society and Its Enemies,* Popper writes, "It is hard to understand why those of Plato's commentators who praise him for fighting against subversive conventionalism of the sophists, and for establishing a spiritual naturalism ultimately based on religion, fail to censure him for making a convention, or rather an invention, the ultimate basis of religion."[32]

As is clear from the above, Plato's political ruminations on civic justice and civic happiness, including his advocacy of the Noble Lie, are guided by his reliance on *dikaiosune*. Thus, he constructs an analogy between a just state and a just person, one which represents a deep belief in the connection between the macrocosmic *polis* and an individual's microcosmic soul. Governed by a philosopher king who successfully mediates among the three classes of society to achieve harmony, the state operates much as the triadic soul of an individual, and both are at their best when the three components operate in balance. In such conditions, the practical constitution and the polity emerge well ordered and organized by means of theory, the only path Plato argues, to politics. It is here that the formal theory of the real, of forms and the formal theory of the state, contributes to a true understanding of what justice is and why it matters. The philosopher king's task becomes one of implementing the theory, so that those who seek justice may actually achieve and receive it.

In responding to Thrasymachus' predilection for power and raw strength, Plato attempts to show that the immoralist's limited perception of "interest" actually constitutes ignorance, a lack of understanding of the form of the Good. Thrasymachus' self-interested approach may indeed articulate a danger to the state as well as to the individual, in part because it hinders the pursuit of knowledge of the forms. But his approach also proves dangerous in part because a state subsists in the mortal world and his observations carry weight in this realm. Nonetheless, on the political level, Plato attempts to demonstrate—by creating an analogy between the elements of the human soul and the state—that its well-being, full development, and happiness are secured by each individual fulfilling his purpose, by doing right and not doing wrong, and thereby underscoring that virtue belongs to the general order of the eternal.

NOTES

1. See generally, Terence Irwin, *Plato's Ethics* (Oxford: Oxford University Press, 1995). Further distinguished here are religion-based views in which justice is seen as an expression or objective of God's will, as discussed further in chapter 9 *infra*.

2. See Janet Coleman, *A History of Political Thought* (Malden: Blackwell Publishing, 2000), Vol. I, ch. 3.

3. See Richard Kraut, "The Defense of Justice in Plato's *Republic*," in ed. Richard Kraut, *The Cambridge Companion to Plato* (Cambridge: Cambridge University Press, 1992), ch. 10; Julia Annas, *An Introduction to Plato's Republic* (Oxford: Oxford University Press, 1981), ch. 6.

4. The generalized referencing of individuals as male in Part I's chapters reflects the conventions of various writers, and not my position. As to his views concerning women, interestingly, in Book V of *The Republic*, Plato states that the function of guardianship is to be performed by men and women alike (451c–457b); since the major distinctions between male and female guardians is that women give birth to children and are physically weaker than men, there is no justification for barring women from the guardian class. Further, for guardians, the private household and therefore the institution of marriage is to be abolished (457b–466d), since the guardians do not own property and the care of children is to be a communal responsibility. See discussion regarding guardians later in this chapter; see also Julia Annas, "Plato's 'Republic' and Feminism," *Philosophy* 51; 197 (July, 1976): 307–321; Gregory Vlastos, "Was Plato a Feminist," in ed. Richard Kraut, *Plato's Republic: Critical Essays* (Lanham: Rowman & Littlefield Publishers, Inc., 1997). Contrast Aristotle's views on women in chapter 3 *infra*.

5. Plato uses the word *eidos* or "idea," and *paradeigma* or "standard" or "pattern," for what we have come to term *form*. For these translations, as well as for a translation of *The Republic,* generally, I rely upon Desmond Lee's text in Plato (2003).

6. See Nicholas White, "Plato's Metaphysical Epistemology," in Kraut (1992), ch. 9.

7. The reference annotations here follow the customary 1578 Stephanus edition format.

8. See Irwin (1995), ch. 10.

9. In his essay, "Plato on the Imperfection of the Sensible World," *American Philosophical Quarterly* 12; 2 (1975): 105–117; Alexander Nehamas develops the view, *contra* the approximation view, that Plato envisaged sensibles as incomplete predicates, whether they are attributive or relational predicates. See *Republic* 523–525.

10. Implicitly, I have subscribed to the view that there are no separate forms for beauty and ugliness, just and unjust, and good and evil. Although Plato often approaches concepts in a binary manner, in the case of forms, it seems that the absence of a relevant character (goodness, justice, or beauty) coheres better to the incompleteness view of sensibles referred to in note 9. See *Republic* 476. Gail Fine in her essay, "Aristotle's Criticisms of Plato," in ed. James C. Klagge, *Oxford Studies in Ancient Philosophy* (Oxford: Oxford University Press, 1992), pp. 13–41, presents related issues argued in Aristotle's objections, at least in the case of the forms of equal and unequal. I discuss these issues later in this chapter.

11. Some make the argument that Aristotle's theory of universals is non-relational in character because of his rejection of separation. But see Gail Fine, *Plato on Knowledge and Forms: Selected Essays* (Oxford: Oxford University Press, 2003), ch. 13 and references therein.

12. As Francis M. Cornford notes in his *Plato's Theory of Knowledge* (London: Routledge and Kegan Paul, 1960), p. 9, Plato does not provide the answer to this question in the *Theaetetus* or in the *Sophist* either, the subject matter of which is his treatment of the theory of knowledge. However, Plato does have Socrates acknowledge that there are forms for two classes, those in Zeno's dilemmas (likeness, unlikeness; unity, plurality; motion, rest; etc.), and the moral forms (the just, beautiful, good, etc.). Moreover, he has Socrates cast doubts about the class of products of divine workmanship (living organisms and the four elements) and certainly about the class of undignified things (hair, clay, dirt, etc.). Id., pp. 8–9.

13. Nicholas White, *Plato on Knowledge and Reality* (Indianapolis: Hackett, 1976), p. xiii.

14. Since a form represents an essential character, it follows that each form is unique. Gail Fine responds to Aristotle's objections that, as to the form of equal, Plato's uniqueness assumption of forms violates the self-predication operation of forms in his theory (White 1976, pp. 25–31). Further, this same self-predication principle is violated with regard to the form of unequal when taking into account Plato's uniqueness assumption of forms. As to the second objection, it is not clear that Plato is committed to forms of opposites. See note 9 above.

15. A diagram of the Divided Line could look like this.

Forms Physical things Shadows and images

16. See Fine (2003), ch. 3 and 4.

17. For Plato, sophists, poets, and artists are all illusionists, in the sense that they represent or imitate what craftsmen do in the exercise of their *technai*. Craftsmen, on the other hand, represent or imitate truth and forms. Plato reserves especial antipathy for sophists, whom he regards as intellectual harlots, since they use reasoned argument instrumentally to persuade, rather than properly in the search for truth and the forms. It is in this vein that Plato would also exclude poets from the state, in fear of their persuasive powers. See *The Republic* 595a–608b.

18. See Plato (2003), Appendix II, n. 11 for discussion of the Spindle of Necessity.

19. See Irwin (1995), ch. 15.

20. See Plato (2003), Book VI. But see the competing argument of *akrasia* and ethical hedonism set forth in *Protagoras* (352c; 358b, c, d); see also A. W. Price, *Virtue and Reason in Plato and Aristotle* (Oxford: Oxford University Press, 2015), pp. 253–268.

21. Price (2015), ch. 13.

22. See Eric Brown, "Plato's Ethics and Politics in *The Republic,*" http//plato.stanford.edu/entries/plato-ethics-politics.

23. See note 3 and related text.

24. Cornford makes a number of criticisms, of which I list three here, to conclude that Plato's theory of forms may best be viewed as metaphor, since upon serious scrutiny, he finds no intelligible account with regard to forms and their relation to things: (1) In recognizing a common name for each form, there must be an unlimited number of forms. The unlimited, however, cannot be known, and if forms are then unknowable, their *raison d'être* in a theory of knowledge is abrogated. (2) Since forms are not mental existents, they must be objects of thought, of which any number of minds may, or may not, contemplate. (3) While forms may have a separate reality, in having sensible objects partake of them, there may be copies or images of them as well. Hence, an original may have many copies, which leads to an infinite regress. Cornford (1960), pp. 10–11.

25. Plato, *The Statesman*, trans. J. B. Skemp (London: Bristol Classical Press, 2002).

26. The following chart is derived from *The Statesman,* 291d–e and 301b–c.

RULE OF	LAW-ABIDING	NOT LAW-ABIDING
One	Kingship	Tyranny
Few	Aristocracy	Oligarchy
Many	Democracy	Democracy

Source: Created by the author.

27. For Plato, humans must theorize politics before realizing them. See discussion earlier regarding Plato's theory of forms and its relation to politics. Further, as to the art of measurement, one part is concerned with relative dimensions, although the more important part treats due measure and includes the concept of the mean between two extremes.

28. The young are to be educated before being interwoven into the fabric of society. If they are uneducable—not evincing virtuous tendencies—they are to be exiled. The statesman also acts as a breeder who matches up men and women, pairing the courageous types with moderate types.

29. Desmond Lee takes issue with the translation of "noble lie" (414b) and states that the proper translation should be "magnificent myth." This mistranslation, in his view, has led to the criticism that Plato countenances manipulation by propaganda. In Lee's more benign view, the magnificent myth is meant "to replace the national traditions which any community has, which are intended to express the kind of community it is, or wishes to be, its ideals, rather than to state matters of fact." Plato (2003), p. 112.

30. "Sed quis custodiet ipsos custodies"; see Juvenal, *Satire* 6, ed. Lindsay Watson and Patricia Watson (Cambridge: Cambridge University Press, 2014), II. 347–348.

31. Leo Strauss, *The City and Man* (Chicago: University of Chicago Press, 2002), p. 108.

32. Karl Popper, *The Open Society and Its Enemies* (Princeton: Princeton University Press, 1971), vol. 1, p. 142.

Chapter 3

Aristotle

The Virtuous Life

Aristotle frees justice from the metaphysical constraints of Plato's utopian views and instead locates the concept as a virtue in individuals positioned in society. His concept of virtue includes both intellectual virtues and moral virtues.[1] More specifically, he argues that virtues (*arête*) are learned dispositions of individuals that formulate a mean between extremes; courage, for example, is the mean positioned between cowardice and recklessness. Importantly here, in Book V of the *Nicomachean Ethics*, Aristotle presents justice as a moral virtue, and in so doing, he applies the doctrine of the mean to various aspects and types of justice. In trying to present justice as a moral virtue, however, Aristotle's analysis lacks rigor and accomplishes less for his theory of justice than might be expected because, in part, he is not as concerned with the individual and individual traits (the touchstone for his definition of virtue) as he is with the individual's relation to others in political society.

In this framework, justice has both a universal side, grounded in a broad concept of lawfulness, as well as a particular side, grounded in the concept of equality.[2] The formalism of Aristotle's concept of universal justice is further ameliorated by concepts of natural justice and equity, which he introduces to provide flexibility to a rigid concept of lawfulness. In doing so, however, his definition of justice as a moral virtue loses analytical rigor. Distributive justice and fairness (corrective justice and reciprocal justice)—aspects of particular justice—come into play in the claim that an individual should not take more than his fair share of goods in society and an individual's fair share is determined by merit, a proposal that does not adequately address such key issues as distributions of scarce necessary resources, among others.

In this chapter, I examine Aristotle's account of justice as a virtue, and his concepts of universal justice and particular justice.

JUSTICE AS VIRTUE

For Aristotle, justice is a moral virtue, a learned disposition. While using similar definitions as Plato does and also examining justice in the framework of *dikaiosune*, on individual and societal levels, he does so with different emphases. Unlike Plato, Aristotle examines justice as individual virtue in ideal relations in political society, insisting that the activities of a citizen, ruling and being ruled, comprise the best life for the fulfilled man, who by nature is a political animal living in a *polis*.[3] In significant contrast to Plato then, Aristotle's definitions are lodged in the mutable world rather than in the eternal realm of forms. More specifically, he assigns individual virtues, especially justice, to the world of just actions.

In describing various kinds of justice in Book V of the *Nicomachean Ethics*, Aristotle treats justice as a complete or perfect virtue. He further claims that justice is not complete or perfect in an unqualified way, but rather, in relation to other elements (1129b25–27). Thus, when moral virtues are exercised in accordance with the law for the greater good, justice is perfect in relational terms, just as when an individual acts courageously for the good of the political community (1129b17–19). To treat justice as a moral virtue distinguished by its relational character, Aristotle also applies his doctrine of the mean, thereby theoretically situating the virtue of justice between undesirable extremes. The application of the doctrine of the mean, however, yields an atypical and asymmetric result.

Virtue and Well-Being

Aristotle wrote the *Nichomachean Ethics* as a preliminary discussion to his *Politics*,[4] and in both works he examines virtue (*arête*) and human well-being (*eudaimonia*) as the foundation of questions raised in the treatises. As did his mentor, Plato treated the question of justice in *The Republic* and explicated the well ordering of society, justice writ large, along with the best constitution (the manner in which a community is organized) in another treatise, *The Statesman*.[5] For Aristotle, well-being (*eudaimonia*) or the good life—a life worth living—is the proper goal of human beings, a definition bespeaking a teleological orientation.[6] In contrast to Plato, however, Aristotle does not fundamentally posit the human being's true self as residing in an immaterial soul, for he views mortals as essentially embodied, as living a political life. As stated above, Aristotle bases his ethical views not on an appeal to forms or universals; but rather, it is practical wisdom that proves foundational to Aristotle's ethical views as well as to his views of human nature and virtue.

Similar to Plato in his focus on excellence of character, but differing in its anchoring in the here and now, for Aristotle well-being belongs to those living virtuous lives, to individuals partaking in the superior activity of intellectual contemplation and the practice of virtue. In practicing virtue, Aristotle argues that individuals can cultivate a virtuous character and a learned disposition. Given these conditions, it is not surprising that virtuous action is what a person with practical wisdom would freely choose to do. Simply put, Aristotle views virtue as living according to our natures as rational animals.

Ethics and Politics

Aristotle's conception of morality differs from those accounts that merely attempt to define what is good and bad, right and wrong. Instead, he attempts to present a blueprint for living well, even though he offers what appears to be an asymmetric equation to do so. That is, we know the right thing to do because that is what a person of good character would do, but this assertion is not so clear-cut when reversing the terms: can we know whether a person has a good character in light of his just actions? With this question, it is evident that Aristotle shifts his focus from individuals (a virtuous man acts virtuously) to political relationships (right actions, not inherent virtue, define justice).

In consonance with his focus on the societal, Aristotle posits that an individual's powers of reason bifurcate into theoretical reason, the intellectual faculty deployed in philosophy and the sciences, and practical reason, the intellectual faculty central to ethical life. Identifying the intellectual faculty governing *ethos* as practical, Aristotle further links an individual's practical reason to certain excellences of character or virtues, which he treats as internalized dispositions of action, desire, and feeling.[7] Essentially, the freedom to choose to act in a virtuous manner and hence experience well-being defines a life worth living.

Aristotle thus interweaves and defines the concepts of well-being, virtue, and practical wisdom with and against each other, and in developing a theory of virtue (*arête*), he attempts to clarify why what is good seems so to the virtuous.[8] Unlike Plato, who views justice for an individual as a matter of balance among the three parts of the soul and political justice as a matter of the well ordering of class divisions of society according to function, Aristotle views justice as an exercise in treating others in accordance with the rules of society, even though that society may very well be less than perfect. Thus, ethical life for Aristotle is ultimately a social matter concerning an individual's coming to terms with the laws, rules, norms, and customs of political society.

Aristotle's approach has generated much discussion over the centuries. Indeed, as time has demonstrated, his approach has proven paradigmatic. Particularly in current debates, for example, the topic of treating others in accordance with the rules of even a less than perfect society dominate ever more approaches to justice. This is especially the case with respect to his notion of particular justice and its concerns with equality as articulated in distribution and fairness. Especially provoking controversy, however, is his belief that the distribution of benefits and burdens of society should be tied to the notion of merit, as I explore in more detail in chapter 7.

The Doctrine of the Mean

The main project that Aristotle undertakes in Book V of the *Nicomachean Ethics* is to wrest justice from the metaphysical framework informing platonic thought in order to position it into a general framework of virtues, since he views justice as not only a moral virtue, but also, in fact, as the primary virtue.[9] In accordance with this position, Aristotle situates justice in his doctrine of the mean since he argues that all virtues of character are located in the mean between two undesirable extremes, the extremes of excess and deficiency.[10] Thus, Aristotle states that "with regard to justice and injustice we must consider what kinds of actions they are concerned with, what sort of mean justice is, and between what extremes the just act is intermediate" (1129a3–5). Critically, being located between extremes, virtue requires that an individual makes a choice. In this manner, virtue is enacted via a rational principle by a man of practical wisdom.

While Aristotle's focus on choice and action follows from the location of justice as a mean between extremes in the practical realm, his insistence on the virtue's foundation proves resistant to clean, binary analyses. With generosity, for example, an individual curbs his miserly or spendthrift disposition to act in a given situation that will effect a greater good. For Aristotle, however, justice is a *kind* of mean "but not in the same way as the other virtues, but because it relates to an intermediate amount, while injustice relates to the extremes" (1133b32–1134a1), and "injustice is both excess and deficiency" (1134a8–9). In other words, for justice to occupy the medial position, its extremes are not articulated as opposites, but instead have a more complicated and asymmetrical formulation.

This focus on, essentially, the context to which the virtue relates (rather than on dispositions) reflects Aristotle's location of virtues in the physical as opposed to the metaphysical world. In practice, he attempts to apply the doctrine of the mean to the concept of justice, but the various types of justice that he posits seem contorted, and indeed, the application is less effective than might be expected from a theory focusing on the pragmatic. Nonetheless, the doctrine also has proven influential, as it fuels the need to consider matters of distribution, the Aristotelian perspective of most interest to contemporary commentaries on justice.

UNIVERSAL JUSTICE

In examining justice in society, Aristotle is occupied with various kinds of justice. In Book V of the *Nicomachean Ethics*, for example, he explores a broad or general sense of justice—universal justice—which has lawfulness as its essential aspect. Here, a just man is a lawful man, and conversely, an unjust man is an unlawful man. Characteristic of his examination of justice as *dikaiosune*, alongside the universal sense of justice, Aristotle also posits a particular or narrow sense which focuses on equality, in terms of distribution and fairness.[11] Moreover, for society at large, political justice comprises both natural justice and legal or conventional justice, while for the narrow sense of political justice, Aristotle develops the notion of equity to translate the spirit of the law into particular situations, thus correcting the inherent rigidity found in the nature of law itself (1137a31–1138a3).

But in adumbrating universal justice, Aristotle expands the term "lawfulness" (*nomos*) to include not only the enactments of a lawgiver or legislature, but also the norms, customs, and traditions of a polity.[12] In other words, the societal virtue of lawfulness is far greater than being law-abiding—it possesses every other ethical virtue. In the same vein, a just person who is just in the broad sense is more than a just individual in that he possesses every other ethical virtue as well (1129b25–1130a10). This view appears to commit Aristotle to the proposition that whoever is just in the broad sense of lawfulness also possesses the virtue of justice in the narrow sense. That is, a just man in the narrow sense is one who aligns with the virtue of equality, or of being fair. Put another way, justice in the universal sense of lawfulness is the whole of justice, while justice in the particular sense of equality is only one portion of the whole (1130b10–14).

Essentially, Aristotle broadens the sense of universal justice to take into account its various possible contexts. For instance, what if the laws of a particular government are judged by some accepted measure to be barbaric, foolish, or wrong-thinking? In other words, can unjust laws exist? Propelled by this question, Aristotle articulates three complex responses or scenarios to demonstrate that for universal justice to prevail as lawfulness, relations and contexts must be considered:

1. Under universal law, specifically in natural law, justice is not based on human legislation or convention, so that a particular government's corruption of universal law docs not affect the concept of lawfulness.
2. Should there be gaps in the application of laws to particular cases, these can be filled by means of equity, also a kind of universal law which, as seen below, Aristotle describes as a sort of justice.
3. In an individual's own relationship to justice as applied to one's self, lawfulness must obtain.[13]

Regarding the third scenario, as to the question of whether an individual may treat himself unjustly, Aristotle investigates the matter in Book VII of the *Nicomachean Ethics* in terms of *akrasia* (incontinence).[14] In doing so, he adopts Plato's tripartite model of the soul to develop the idea that an akratic person goes against reason as a result of some *pathos* (emotion, feeling), a *pathos* for either pleasure or anger and which can lead to two possible types of *akrasia:* impetuosity and weakness. Consequently, there are four forms of *akrasia*: (1) impetuosity caused by pleasure, (2) impetuosity caused by anger, (3) weakness caused by pleasure, and (4) weakness caused by anger. Interestingly, his analysis of *akrasia* is rather more complicated than a conflict between reason and feeling.[15]

In order to make sense of the equation of Aristotle's various applications to universal justice as lawfulness, it may be best to view lawfulness as a goal, an aspiration, so that a just man is seen as a person who not only abides by the laws, but who also serves his community by means of its legal system and its established pattern of norms. This may be the more effective way to approach Aristotle's definition of justice in the broad sense of lawfulness since he does not, in fact, provide any criteria for how to act in particular cases. Indeed, none of his definitions of the virtues provides action-guiding principles. Rather, they are intended as prescriptive formulations of the kind of person an individual ought to become.

Political Justice

As a form of universal or broad justice, political justice is justice in a state under the rule of law and not under the rule of a tyrant (1134a35–b1). A state ruled by law is one in which citizens who "share the life with a view to self-sufficiency" are free and have equal shares, or have shares which are proportionate and fair, in "ruling and being ruled" (1134a26–28, b15). Political justice, in other words, governs the relationships among members of a political community. Deeply anti-platonic in this regard, Aristotle's conception of political justice rests upon the thesis that justice requires active participation in the political affairs of one's society, even if only limited opportunities for reform exist. Rather than idealistically remaining aloof to the mundane business of politics, Aristotle argues that, actually, the approximate forms of justice negotiated by hostile factions are important: one way to lead a worthwhile life is to promote some measure of legality and justice in defective regimes.[16]

As noted above, Aristotle bifurcates political justice into natural justice and legal or conventional justice. Natural justice "has the same force and does not depend on what is thought to be so or not so" (1134b19–20); that is, natural justice seems to consist of the laws, norms, and rules that would ideally govern relationships in a political community. This allows Aristotle to appeal to the concept of natural laws as an authority and thereby to override the view that universal justice consists of lawfulness in the sense of merely abiding by society's laws and conventions, which could prove less than perfect. The second aspect of universal political justice, legal or conventional justice, comprises the principles or rules observed in a community that fall short of an ideal community, rules that may accord with human nature and conditions of human happiness as expressed *in vivo,* in the mutable world.

Equitable Concerns

Treating justice in a patently more pragmatic manner than does Plato, Aristotle formulates the concept of equity (*epiekeia*), categorized in the narrow side of political justice, as "a sort of justice and not a different state of character" (1138a2–3). Although the generality inherent to laws, particularly in Plato's analyses, evince analytical strength, their generality also harbors weaknesses insofar as laws are inevitably too general, and potentially too rigid, for all particular cases. Aristotle recognizes the difficulty and formulates equity as a gap-filler to wield in the spirit of the law and legislator. Equity thereby provides, in a sense, a pragmatic margin of error or escape valve conceived in order to support legal or conventional justice. The equitable is "what the legislator himself would have said had he been present, and would have put into his law if he had known" (1137b22–24).

In this regard, equity seems to safeguard the law from adhering too rigidly to its own rules and principles, especially when these rules and principles produce injustice. In other words, judges are allowed to depart from legal principles in order to promote justice. Problematically, this conclusion is somewhat inconsistent with some of Aristotle's other claims about justice, raising rival conceptions of what is just as well as creating ambiguity about who or what is just in a particular instance, let alone who determines "what the legislator himself would have said had he been present."

Thus, taken together, Aristotle's view of justice—as adherence to generally accepted rules, on the one hand, and how nonetheless to allow a genuine virtue to respond more flexibly to particular situations, on the other—creates tensions in his pragmatically oriented system. As further discussed in chapter 6, by including flexibility, Aristotle leaves the realm of the eternals to bring customs and traditions into consideration, a broadening of the field of analysis that also occupies contemporary thinkers exploring how multiple voices affect the concept of justice. His complex approach allows for some flexibility. For instance, Aristotle calls for the just person to take a lesser amount than deserved as "equitable," so that even in narrower aspects, the argument may be made that a just person is one who knows when to set aside the law, rigid guidelines, even to accept less than deserved in particular situations (1137b34–1138a3).[17]

Constitutions

Missing from his *Nichomachean Ethics* is a discussion of the ideal state, one in which the common good of all citizens is achieved, as well as the question of what constitution—the manner in which a city-state is organized—is best, a question that Aristotle does take up in his *Politics*.[18] In *Politics*, the model political community is a city-state composed of citizens who have the right to participate in deliberative or judicial office, with a more direct involvement of citizens in governance than in the representative democracy model (I.1252a1–7). Still restricted from citizenship, however, are women, slaves, foreigners, those of the working class, and others.

In addition to more direct involvement in governance, Aristotle's model constitution provides a method to organize the offices of the city-state. Addressing the question of a sovereign office, he adapts six possible constitutional forms from Plato's *Statesman*. Thus, the three correct forms of constitution are kingship, aristocracy, and polity, and the three incorrect forms are tyranny, oligarchy, and democracy (*Politics,* VII). In distinguishing between correct and incorrect constitutions, Aristotle claims that "constitutions which aim at the common advantage are correct without qualification, whereas those which aim only at the advantage of rulers are deviant and unjust, because they involve despotic rule which is inappropriate for a community of free persons" (I.1279a17–21).

Having accepted Plato's guide to types of constitutions, Aristotle further claims that oligarchs mistakenly think that those superior in wealth should have superior political rights, while democrats mistakenly believe that those who are equal in birth should have equal political rights. Both these perspectives of political justice are mistaken since they both assume a false conception of the ends of the city-state. That is, the city-state is neither a business association to maximize wealth (oligarchy) nor is it an agency to promote liberty and equality (democracy). Rather, Aristotle contends that "the good life is the end of the city-state." For Aristotle, the correct conception of justice is aristocratic, assigning full political rights to those who make a full contribution to the political community, that is, to those with virtue as well as property and freedom. The rule of the *aristoi,* the best persons, fulfills the aristocratic, the ideal, constitution, one in which the citizens are fully virtuous. Rejected are the rival claims of the rule of law, as well as the rule of a supremely virtuous person, since absolute kingships are actually a limiting case of aristocracy (*Politics*, III).

PARTICULAR JUSTICE

While Aristotle claims in Book V of the *Nicomachean Ethics* that in its broad sense, or on the societal level, universal justice effects the characteristic of lawfulness, on the individual or particular level, in the narrow sense, particular justice defines through the principle of equality (1130a,ff.). Thus, on the individual level, a just man is equal or balanced in his claims, and conversely, an unjust man is unequal or unbalanced in his claims. Further, as mentioned above, because the societal virtue of lawfulness possesses every ethical virtue, Aristotle is committed to the view that lawfulness also possesses the virtue of justice in its narrow sense, in equality. Consequently, while there may be just acts that cannot make a claim to equality or inequality, they are nonetheless just due to their lawfulness. There are, conversely, no acts of equality that are not at the same time lawful.

This view leads Aristotle to conceive of justice as emanating from the excellences of character—generally from moral virtue, and particularly justice in society. This foundation of character defines injustice as well. In the particular or narrow sense, for example, injustice is motivated by greed, by an individual's particular desire to have more than his share (1129a26–b11). Indeed, when addressing injustice in the narrow sense, Aristotle uses the term "greedy" (*pleoneketes*) to underpin his analysis of that which is "unequal" (1129a32–33). Importantly, the greed that Aristotle refers to is not greed in an individual per se, but rather, a pernicious desire to have more at the expense of others, thereby looking at the ramifications an individual trait has on societal relationships.

In applying the doctrine of the mean to justice on the individual level, whenever an unjust act occurs, one person has more than his share and another individual has less, thus having unequal shares on the two sides of a societal equation. The unjust person, because of his greed, aims for such an imbalance, while the just person seeks to avoid the extremes. Grounded in such pragmatic considerations, Aristotle further distinguishes among various kinds of particular justice: justice that "plays a rectifying part in transactions between man and man," also known as rectificatory or corrective justice (1130b30–1131a9), reciprocal justice, and justice in the distribution of goods or distributive justice.

Corrective Justice

Aristotle's category of justice as grounded on equality, on the individual level or in the particular sense, includes rectifying or correcting wrongs committed in either voluntary or involuntary transactions. Voluntary transactions include such matters as promises, sales, or loans. Involuntary transactions include such matters as theft, assault, and adultery. For this aspect of justice, Aristotle makes the point that distributions of justice should be matters of arithmetic and not matters of proportionate or geometric equality. That is, no scale of merit should be applied to contestants in determining appropriate rectifying or corrective measures. When one person steals from another, for instance, the parties involved in the act should not be weighed on some scale of merit. Rather, the law should treat these parties as equals and should only ask whether the defendant has indeed committed the wrong of which he is accused (1132a5).

Consistently, Aristotle believes that the aim of corrective justice is to restore the parties involved to a position of equality, a position that has been disrupted by an unjust act (1132a24–27). In this framework, that is what punishment of a guilty party attempts to achieve. That is, those who willfully perform acts that upset the equality among citizens—by seeking gain for themselves and creating loss for others—must be made to suffer a loss in order to undo the inequality they have caused. Thus, corrective justice may be seen as the ethical appropriateness that allows for a loss to be compensated by some good that appropriates some good because of selfish gain or that corrects an injury inflicted upon a person by another. The application of the mean to corrective justice thereby reinforces the operational aspects of Aristotle's theory. Perhaps it also provides a psychological account of matters, affirming why, for example, a just judge or juror cannot be bribed, or how an unjust judge or juror who has accepted a bribe is perceived to engage in both excess and deficiency.

Reciprocal Justice

A second kind of individual justice in the particular sense of equality is reciprocal justice. In his treatment of this topic, Aristotle focuses on commercial activities such as buying, selling, lending, and the like. In doing so, not surprisingly, Aristotle's basic notion is that goods should be exchanged for goods on an equal basis. His treatment of this notion, however, becomes complicated as he attempts to demonstrate what type of equality this application promotes and how it is effectuated. At least the application of the doctrine of the mean to reciprocal justice is relatively straightforward. The question arises here, however, of whether there is any added value in the exegesis; that is, whether the principle of equality actually obtains here.

In developing his explanation of commercial exchange as a form of reciprocal justice, for example, Aristotle first criticizes the concept of justice as reciprocity attributed to certain Pythagoreans, who hold to the maxim "should one suffer the things one did, right justice would be done" (1132b27). This has been taken to mean something akin to the Old Testament principle of an eye for an eye. Aristotle then posits a corrective to the simple restitution model.

First, Aristotle says that the Pythagoreans engage in category error by equating justice, the whole virtue, with reciprocity. Certainly, he continues, corrective justice cannot be subsumed under the reciprocity principle; miscreants, for example, are punished not because they did evil as such, but in order to correct what has gone wrong and to restore equality among citizens. Importantly, that is, Aristotle treats laws as instruments intended to promote the common good.

It is this very privileging of the common good, however, that causes his approach to become murky. As indicated above, for example, Aristotle divides corrective justice into voluntary and involuntary transactions. With respect to this category of reciprocal justice, Aristotle places the justice of commercial exchanges under the heading of voluntary transactions. As such, restoring balance in these instances is geometrical rather than mathematical. For example, Aristotle poses the case of an ordinary citizen striking an official. Aristotle says, "If he struck the official, it is necessary not only that he be struck, but that he be punished as well" (1132b29–30). Rather than merely responding to harm with reciprocal harm, Aristotle views as necessary the element of punishment, again, in order to restore the status that serves the public good. Thus, those who are just in their commercial exchanges may be relied upon to give equal return for what they receive. Those driven by greed, however, not only cheat those who deal in commercial activity by not yielding an equal share, they also undermine the common good by creating distrust in all commercial exchanges. For equality to be restored, the act along with the greater injustice must be redressed. With such conceptual gymnastics, the question remains whether the emerging principle provides enough effective guidance.

In the last of the three categories comprising justice as equality—distributive justice—aspects of both corrective and reciprocal justice may be glimpsed, while relational contexts are foregrounded.

Distributive Justice

With regard to distributive justice, Aristotle understands that different kinds of equality and inequality prove fundamental to his concept. First, there is the question of equality in the distribution of benefits and burdens in society. In this instance, Aristotle's theory of the mean postulates, as with corrective and reciprocal justice, that it is not virtuous for an individual to take more than his fair share. The problem remains, however, in determining what is an individual's fair share. Also here, though pragmatic in perspective, Aristotle does not examine individual instances, subjecting any application of the pragmatic principle to a considerable amount of ambiguity. Be that as it may, to treat persons unequally with respect to the distribution of a society's benefits and burdens (absent a relevant difference) represents a likely definition of injustice, and in terms of distributive justice, an unjust person would be an individual who gives more of a good to one person and less to another without taking into consideration their merits or lack of his actions.

Although Aristotle begins with the proposition that such benefits and burdens should be allocated equally among members in society, this initial paradigm undergoes a significant alteration based upon the merit of the recipients, the problem occupying the contemporary theorists examined in chapters 6 and 7 of this study as well. If recipients are of equal merit, they should receive equal shares. If they are of unequal merit, they should receive unequal shares. Thus, similar to the escape valve of equity with regard to the universal view of justice, this measure tries to particularize as far as generalizing allows. As if trying to adjudicate for most if not all instances, Aristotle thus terms these unequal distributions of shares as a sort of justice that can be called equality (from the individual perspective) by means of the application of a formula in which the ratio on one side of the equation is made equal to the ratio on the other side of the equation. Rather than arithmetic equality (1132a1–2), which obtains in corrective justice and which would distribute equal shares to all alike, regardless of merit, Aristotle considers the distributive ratio as an instance of proportionate or geometrical equality (1131a29–32), as may be found in reciprocal justice.[19]

It is relatively clear, however, that going beyond the category of ethical merit would probably remove Aristotle far from even geometrical equality. Indeed, he does not articulate guiding principles for ethically just distributions such as may be required for contributions, need, desert, and such factors, the very defining of which would likely result in a high degree of rigidity. How should the distributive principle of merit be applied, for example, to a situation in which scarce food is to be shared? Should larger amounts be distributed to those who have greater need, that is, who are starving, or to those who carry out critical state functions? Aristotle is silent on such scenarios.

Instead, the principal question Aristotle addresses in his discussion of distributive justice is political: who should have power in society? His answer is that those better qualified to hold office should have greater power. In positing this solution, Aristotle recognizes that criteria for determining who is better qualified—for determining merit—are contestable. Again, he makes no further attempt to resolve the issue in the *Nicomachean Ethics,* although he does take up the discussion in his *Politics.*[20] There, his conclusion seems to be that in choosing among various criteria for determining merit, consideration should focus on what it takes for citizens to live well. That is to say, the kind of merit to hold as a standard is that which best serves the common good of the whole community. This explanation, of course, appeals to Aristotle's belief in the ultimate goal of political society which, for him, is to create and to sustain those conditions under which the pursuit of the good life can best be achieved by all citizens.

Distributive justice may thus be seen as concerned with the ethical appropriateness of who receives benefits and burdens in society and to what extent they receive them. In distributive matters, as contemporary discussions attest, there is a presumption of treating persons equally unless an appropriate and relevant difference obtains. In other words, while Aristotle's starting point in just distributions is the notion of equality, actually, his main criterion for distribution is merit. Critically, the criterion of merit raises additional questions, including who is to determine which distribution is more meritorious, and to what extent, as well as the more abstract problem of what criteria or guiding principles determine such distributions. The problem remains today; merit may be an inappropriate distributing criterion in some circumstances, such as in the case of distributing scarce necessary resources among members of a society.

In our own times, interest in Aristotle's theory of *arête* and virtue ethics has reemerged.[21] His treatment of justice as one of the moral virtues, however, is not as elegant as Plato's construct. Having determined in the *Nicomachean Ethics* that justice as a moral virtue needs to be treated like other moral virtues, Aristotle's argument suffers from forcing the doctrine of the mean upon the concept of justice. Added to these infelicities, both tensions and inconsistencies in his treatment of universal justice result from his desire for flexibility in particular situations. Likewise, Aristotle's attempt to base particular justice, especially in the distributive sense with regard to society's benefits and burdens, on the concept of merit is problematic.

For all this, many of his particular ideas about justice are much more influential in contemporary theories than are Plato's. Indeed, grounding a society's distribution of benefits and burdens in the concept of equality, Aristotle proposes that, absent an appropriate relevant difference, persons should be treated equally, a principle that informs and frames many contemporary discussions of justice. In fact, John Rawls' *A Theory of Justice,* which has been credited with reviving interest in and generating many contemporary discussions of justice, may be seen to owe its distributive approach to justice to Aristotle.[22]

NOTES

1. Aristotle, *The Nicomachean Ethics of Aristotle*, trans. D. Ross, rev. Lesley Brown (Oxford: Oxford University Press, 2009), II V, following the customary Bekker format.

2. As Richard Kraut notes, many scholars use the terms "universal" or "general" justice when it has the quality of lawfulness, and the terms "particular" or "special"

justice when it exhibits the aspect of equality. Kraut prefers to use the terms "broad" and "narrow" justice instead. I use both sets of terms interchangeably. Kraut makes the further translation point that Aristotle is frequently made to say that justice in the narrow sense consists of equality and that the person who has this quality is "fair." However, Kraut notes that the text does not use two different terms, one for "equality" and one for "fair." Aristotle uses the word *isos* and its cognates to designate both the virtue as well as the person who has the virtue. I take his point and accept that the particular sense of justice refers to equality as well as fairness. See Richard Kraut, *Aristotle: Political Philosophy* (Oxford: Oxford University Press, 2002), Section 4.1, note 6.

3. See Janet Coleman, *A History of Political Thought* (Malden: Blackell Publishing, 2000), Vol. I, ch. 4.

4. Edition used: Aristotle, *Politics,* trans. T. A. Sinclair, rev. Trevor Saunders (London: Penguin Books, 1992).

5. Editions used: Plato, *The Republic*, trans. Desmond Lee, 2nd ed. (London: Penguin Books, 2003); Plato, *The Statesman*, trans. J. B. Skemp (London: Bristol Classical Press, 2002).

6. See Christopher Shields, *Aristotle*, 2nd ed. (New York: Routledge, 2014), ch. 8; see also, Terence Irwin, "Conceptions of Happiness in the *Nicomachean Ethics*," in *The Oxford Handbook of Aristotle,* ed. Christopher Shields (Oxford: Oxford University Press, 2012), ch. 19.

7. Contrast Aristotle's concept of practical reason with that of Immanuel Kant, discussed in chapter 4 *infra.*

8. Aristotle's full development of his theory of virtue lies beyond the scope of this chapter. Certainly, his theory and a concern for virtue ethics and moral character have recently seen a revival of interest in normative ethics. For example, see Phillipa Foot, *Virtues and Vices* (Oxford: Oxford University Press, 2002), and Alasdair MacIntyre, *After Virtue*, 3rd ed. (Notre Dame: University of Notre Dame Press, 2007).

9. Indeed, John Rawls views justice as "the first virtue of social institutions." John Rawls, *A Theory of Justice* (Cambridge: Harvard University Press, 1971), p. 3.

10. For a balanced discussion along with criticism of Aristotle's doctrine of the mean, see Sarah Broadie, *Ethics with Aristotle* (Oxford: Oxford University Press, 1991), pp. 95–103; see also W. F. R. Hardie, *Aristotle's Ethical Theory*, 2nd ed. (Oxford: Clarendon Press, 1980), pp. 129–151. As put by one commentator, "The theory [of the mean] oscillates between an unhelpful analytical model (which Aristotle himself does not consistently follow) and a substantively depressing doctrine in favor of moderation." See Bernard Williams, *Ethics and the Limits of Philosophy* (Cambridge: Harvard University Press, 1985), p. 36.

11. See note 2.

12. See Kraut (2002), regarding the superiority of Terence Irwin's translation in *Nicomachean Ethics*, 2nd ed. (Indianapolis: Hackett Publishing Company, Inc., 1999) over David Ross' with regard to this point.

13. Aristotle's treatment of *akrasia* (incontinence) leads him to conclude that neither in the universal or particular senses of justice may one treat oneself unjustly. Aristotle (2009), V.1130a13–1131a10.

14. See *Aristotle's Ethics VII,* ed. Carlo Natali (Oxford: Oxford University Press, 2009).

15. See Richard Kraut, "Aristotle on Becoming Good: Habituation, Reflection and Perception," in *The Oxford Handbook of Aristotle,* ed. Christopher Shields (Oxford: Oxford University Press, 2013), pp. 529–557.

16. See Aristotle (1992), IV.

17. See John Lloyd Ackrill, *Aristotle's Ethics* (London: Faber & Faber, 1973), pp. 105–107.

18. See Aristotle (1992), VII and VIII.

19. Aristotle does not consider such situations where there may be only one good available for distribution. One commentator suggests that this oversight is due to Aristotle's principal concern with the political problem of how should the positions of honor and power be distributed among citizens. See Kraut (2002), 4.11.

20. See Aristotle (1992), III and discussion *infra.*

21. See note 8 above.

22. See Rawls (1971), and chapter 7 *infra.*

Part II

THE INQUIRY INTO JUSTICE

Chapter 4

The Moral Inquiry

The moral framework structuring their inquiries into justice allows Plato to expound upon the metaphysically ethical quest for wisdom and Aristotle to explore justice as a moral virtue in the everyday world. In stark contrast, moral aspects are underserved in contemporary accounts of justice. While disparate and influential contemporary accounts of justice express concern for the individual as a moral agent, often in the Kantian sense of due respect and concern, these theories nonetheless tend to be dominated by their framing of the question in political concerns. That is, often the engagement with political institutions and attendant elements are more or less driven variously by the distribution of social goods to those least advantaged in society, by the equality of economic distributions in society, and by the belief in individual freedom and a minimal state.

In this chapter, I examine moral aspects of the justice inquiry, focusing on the importance of concepts of rationality, agency, and responsibility. Further, since I argue that the question of justice involves a search for the right thing to do in given circumstances, I look forward to develop a normative framework for the justice inquiry in the form of action-guiding principles.

REASON AND AGENCY

Practical Reason

Plato's metaphysical linkage of individual and social morality to his theory of foundational forms undergirds his pursuit of the question of justice, while Aristotle distinguishes between pure reasoning and practical reasoning. Ethical virtue is fully developed, Aristotle argues in Book V of his *Nicomachean*

Ethics, only when it is combined with practical wisdom (1144b14–17).[1] Somewhat similarly, I distinguish between theoretical and practical modes of analysis in the conceptual framework for the moral inquiry into justice.

Grounded in a moderate view of rationality as a precedential method for acquiring knowledge, I address two different systems of norms: those for the regulation of belief (theoretical reason) and those for the regulation of action (practical reason). In other words, I view theoretical reason as concerned with questions of explanation and prediction. I view practical reason, on the other hand, as a foundational resource in the moral inquiry into justice. More specifically, I see practical reason as the general capacity of human beings to resolve, through reflection, the question of what action should be taken after taking into consideration questions of value which should lead to a thorough review of intentional actions.

Generally, practical rationality entails instrumental rationality, which requires that considered examination of the means to effect an end are taken into account. In thereby making an often complex judgment of what is desirable (which end is preferred), instrumental rationality generates a relationship between action and value. As is often the case in today's debates, proponents of instrumental rationality tend to take into account psychological motivations. In my view, when considering intentional actions psychological motivation may well seem as an important part of the inquiry. For my purposes here, however, even proponents of instrumental rationality agree that such an instrumental principle does not in and of itself generate reasons for action.[2]

In other words, I look to the reasons for action, on the reflection required to resolve the question of what should be done. Thus, I see issues to be explored from the perspective of practical reason to include: whether and how deliberative reflection can give rise to action, what norms for the assessment of action are binding upon us as agents, and whether such norms are purely instrumental. When practical reason weighs such issues, moral responsibility is evoked. That is, moral responsibility, treated in more detail below, depends upon the rational and autonomous individual to judge, act, and deliberate norms in such a manner that a particular type of reaction—generally speaking, praise or blame—is elicited. It is important to underscore here that in deliberating a particular type of reaction, the conditions and objects of moral responsibility intrinsically require analyses that consider societal norms to some degree.

Not surprisingly, the rational authority of moral norms often proves to be a complex analysis.[3] One approach, inspired by Aristotle, centers on practical reflection, based in the question of what it means to act well.[4] Another strategy to address this problem has been to maximize rationality in various manners (e.g., decision theory).[5] Yet another approach has been to look to values and theories of values as an important focus for practical reflection.[6]

I argue that respect for others is a pivotal criterion in the justice inquiry and thus norms, including a plurality of values, need to be taken into consideration whether, as various approaches have done, foregrounding reason, values or actions. Critically, since the conditions and objects of moral responsibility entail an analysis of relevant norms, practical reason comprises an important tool for the inquiry into justice. Yet, even though Kantians make respect for others central—and thereby participate in considering societal norms—they often argue from constructs that maximize rationality, thereby not only *not* taking norms into full account, but also eliminating morality as a source of limiting conditions in the rational pursuit of ends. In so doing, they thereby suggest, in contrast to Hume, that values may not be a source of the demands of practical reason. Instead, I see norms acting as constraints, or as a source of limiting conditions, on one's moral responsibility for intentional actions. Further, through their reference to the external world and experience, norms function as a repository of moral resources since they empirically reach into the particular communities in which individuals are situated.

Rational and Autonomous Agency

For many contemporary justice theorists, the Kantian concept of due respect and concern for others represents a central moral concept even while such theories focus on the political aspects of the question and develop distributive accounts of justice. Tracking the moral concept throughout the analytical process, I start with the view that justice involves a moral inquiry, based on a rational and autonomous view of moral agency, and pertains to beings who are capable of acting with reference to some notion of right and wrong. In this approach, then, human beings are viewed as rational, moral, free, and responsible moral agents.

This view accords with the Kantian notion of treating persons with respect, as derived from his Formula of the End in Itself: "Act in such a way that you always treat humanity, whether in your own person or in the person of any other, never simply as a means but always at the same time as an end."[7] The Formula of the End in Itself represents one of Kant's versions of the Supreme Principle of Morality and his Categorical Imperative, which places a focus on a person's intentions, rather than on the results of intentional actions, thereby differing sharply from the end-valuation of consequentialist views. In this manner, Kant's account is not only deontological in approach, but also attempts to be value-neutral.

In exploring moral agency, Kant includes the components of rationality and autonomy, beginning his exegesis in the *Groundwork of the Metaphysic of Morals* with the proposition that the one propensity that is inherently good in humans is good will. Immaterial, good will bestows intrinsic dignity upon humans. It brings together rationality and autonomy, which he defines as the ability to make deliberate, rational choices. Thus, good will represents our power of rational moral choice of decision-making that is clear-minded and not overcome by emotion. Importantly here, good will invariably leads to practical reason, to the use of reason to decide upon actions. Underscoring choice rather than desire, good will stems from duty.

As such, rather than proposing an instrumental view of rationality, Kant develops the striking doctrine that a rational will must be regarded as autonomous, as free, so that the agent is the author of the law who is bound by it. It is the presence of this self-governing reason that Kant offers as decisive grounds for viewing each person as possessed of equal worth and deserving of equal respect, the grounds, that is, for acting as a moral agent. In contrast to the Humean "slave to passions," the reach of Kant's concept of reason necessarily extends into practical affairs and directly addresses the normative question. Kant thereby bases his account on the individual, although he nonetheless shares with Aristotle a concern for justice in society.

Underlying Kant's Formula of the End in Itself is the belief that each of our acts reflects one or more of our maxims, the principles that propel our actions.[8] In this context, to use someone *as a means* is to involve the person in actions to which she or he could not, in principle, consent. Kant does not say that it is wrong to use someone as a means. Certainly, we do so in any cooperative scheme of action, for instance, in playing any team sport. The issue for Kant is that we should not use others as mere means, since to do so denies their freedom to formulate maxims of their own. In other words, acts that are done in deception or coercion of others (precluding their consent) are wrong. In this manner, Kant argues that we must treat others with respect, as rational persons formulating their own maxims.

While I agree that the concept of moral agency includes the constituent elements of rationality and autonomy, I diverge from Kant's view that rationality entails autonomy. Rather, as I see it, rationality *requires* autonomy, since the rational deliberation defining justice requires freedom to enact it. Thus, essentially, I loosen the linkage between autonomy and reason from a directly dependent relationship. Further, I acknowledge that I have in part an instrumental view of rationality, insofar as in my view, rationality guides agents to take those actions necessary in relation to given ends. I recognize, though, that instrumental rationality thereby provides an incomplete explanation as to further independent standards for evaluation of those ends, and it does not, in itself, generate reasons for action. Thus, I arrive at the conclusion that instrumental rationality functions as a structural component of one's attitudes. Necessarily, in order to map out the nature and scope of practical reason, instrumental rationality must be seen as one of various structural requirements of rationality.

On metaethical grounds, an ongoing debate questions whether Kant's account is realist or constructivist, which itself raises the question of whether morality is grounded on rationality. Consequently, one of the battles waged has to do with the correctness of moral judgments based on non-ontological grounds.[9] Rather than enter the metaethical fray directly, I suggest that questions raised by Kant's conception of rational agency, for purposes here, are best met on the grounds of normative ethics.[10]

RESPONSIBILITY

For Kant, then, the criteria for a moral agent depend upon agents who are both rational and autonomous. That is, while Kant champions the principle granting each individual respect, by also asserting that moral agents must be rational and autonomous, he articulates limits as well. In similar vein, Aristotle avers that only moral agents are properly subject to ascriptions of responsibility, and moral agents are those individuals who possess a capacity for decision-making. While both thinkers underscore the importance of rationality in the process, Aristotle contrasts with Kant in identifying the source for rational assessments of moral actions. That is, Kant identifies the source for the good will to deliberate the morality of an action as duty. For Aristotle, a moral decision represents a certain kind of desire resulting from deliberation, one that expresses the agent's conception of what is good (1111b–1113b3).

In addition, while agency is important to both Kant and Aristotle, Aristotle further bestows emphasis to the other end of moral actions. That is, rather than individual agents with good will assessing the moral nature of their own actions, for Aristotle, moral agents who can claim moral responsibility are assessed in part by others' judgments of their characters and their actions. In both schemes, the agent and the social context are important, but in Aristotle, social approbation plays a more pronounced critical role. Thus, in Book V of the *Nicomachean Ethics*, Aristotle states that it is sometimes appropriate to respond to an agent with praise or blame on the basis of the agent's actions and/or dispositional traits of character (1190b30–35) but, if and only if, his action or disposition is voluntary.

For such agents, providing guidance requires acknowledging the conditions and objects of moral responsibility, concepts about which tend to divide into two competing views: (1) the merit-based view, by which praise or blame is an appropriate reaction toward an agent if and only if the agent "deserves" such a reaction, and (2) the consequentialist view, by which praise or blame is an appropriate reaction toward an agent if and only if such a reaction would lead to a desired change in the agent and/or the agent's behavior.[11] The former foregrounds social norms, and the latter directs attention to the individual's actions.

Outside this dichotomy, and marginalizing autonomy, the concept of moral responsibility is challenged by what is known as causal determinism. Causal determinism proffers the view that everything that happens or exists is caused by antecedent conditions, making it impossible for anything to happen or exist other than as it does or is. Scientific determinism may thus be viewed as a variety of causal determinism, whereby the antecedent conditions identified are a combination of the prior states of the universe and laws of nature. With regard to the threat causal determinism poses for moral responsibility, there are two main kinds of proponents: (a) the incompatibilist, who believes that if causal determinism is true, then there is nothing for which a person may be morally responsible, and (b) the compatibilist, who believes that a person can be morally responsible for some things, even if both who the person is and what the person does are causally determined.

Those who accept a merit-based conception of moral responsibility have tended to be incompatibilists. Kant, with respect to his duty-for-duty's-sake morality, may be cited as an example of this view. On the other hand, those who accept a consequentialist conception of moral responsibility have traditionally inhabited a compatibilist framework, contending that determinism poses no threat to moral responsibility, since the Aristotelian measures of praise and blame may still be an effective means of influencing an agent's behavior, even in a deterministic world. Thomas Hobbes, David Hume, and John Stuart Mill may be seen as such compatibilists.

Accountability

In response to these two camps and kinds of thinkers, P. F. Strawson effected a change in the nature of the discussion of moral responsibility by challenging the commonly shared assumption that holds persons responsible based on a tautological, theoretical judgment of their being responsible. According to Strawson, the attitudes expressed in holding persons morally responsible encompass more than just the express theoretical assertion of responsibility, and include a wide range of attitudes that derive from their participation in personal relationships (e.g., resentment, indignation, hurt feelings, anger, gratitude, reciprocal love, and forgiveness).[12]

These attitudes represent reactions to the perception of another's good will, ill will, or indifference, and further, they are expressed from the stance of a person involved in interpersonal relationships who regards the agent held responsible as a participant in such relationships as well. In other words, the central criticism Strawson directs at both consequentialist and traditional merit-based views is that they have both over-intellectualized the issue of moral responsibility. The practice of holding persons responsible is embedded in our way of life, and "neither calls for nor permits, an external 'rational' justification."[13]

Strawson attempts to reformat the traditional debate by arguing that judgments about being responsible are understood in relation to the role *reactive attitudes* play in the practice of being held responsible, thereby echoing Aristotle's focus on the social context. Thus, Strawson's views may be seen, somewhat by default, as a compatibilist view of moral responsibility, but one that is merit based. That is, unlike prior consequentialist forms of compatibilism, Strawson's merit-based views foreground social norms, as they attempt to explain why some agents may merit our praise or deserve our blame, reactions that thus have value. While versions of Strawson's views continue to be promulgated and defended, incompatibilists, however, remain largely unconvinced and thus have continued to propound more or less traditional merit-based views of the concept of moral responsibility.

I too subscribe to a merit-based, incompatibilist view of the concept of moral responsibility. Nonetheless, Strawson's emphasis on the social aspects of responsibility does reflect my interest in metaphysical treatments of freedom and moral responsibility, or that which makes my views differ from Kant's. In other words, I agree with Strawson that the place and role of reactive attitudes in human lives may be accommodated in a theory of moral responsibility which draws a distinction between responsibility understood as attributability, and responsibility as accountability.[14] While my views on moral responsibility may be classified similarly to Kant's as those of a merit-based incompatibilist, I nonetheless accommodate Strawson's insights regarding reactive attitudes by viewing responsibility as accountability rather than as attributability, thereby further differing from Kant's views with regard to the problem of moral luck in the correlation of moral responsibility with voluntary action.[15]

Moral Luck

The question of merit in addressing moral reponsibility along with the evaluation process in assessing good will leads inexorably to the question of moral luck. Put simply, moral luck raises concerns about how to integrate a person's given circumstances (such as being born in a rich suburb or a poor ghetto) or other circumstances beyond their control into a judgment of whether an action is moral or not. At the center of the concept is a fundamental debate pitting an absolute concept of morality, regardless of circumstances, against a more granular view of how an individual acts in given circumstances, the latter of which often occurs in legal judgments, perhaps most obviously implemented in the various types of degrees of murder in various legal systems.

The question of moral luck was also addressed by both Plato and Aristotle. Thus, in the context of laws and punishment, Plato raises the question in the *Laws* of how moral luck should affect punishment, of how judgment can be made for circumstances not under an individual's control.[16] Plato positions his thoughts on the absolute side of the debate. In contrast, luck enters Aristotle's account of moral responsibility via *eudaimonia* in Book V of the *Nicomachean Ethics*, to consider at least two aspects: (1) whether an individual receives the upbringing and training, creating dispositions, to lead a virtuous life, and (2) whether the external world more or less allows an individual to be virtuous, and so truly happy, since "happiness needs the external goods as well; for it is impossible, or not easy, to do noble acts without proper equipment" (1099a 31–33).[17] In this manner, Aristotle argues for a more granular consideration of moral luck.

The span of possible positions persists into today's world. Closer to Plato, for example, Kant stimulated the view that matters of morality are immune from luck.[18] On the other hand, reviving Aristotelian questions, Bernard Williams and Thomas Nagel have once again raised the question of whether we should be morally responsible for only those matters that are within our control, and further, whether two persons should be morally assessed differently, if the only differences between the two are outside their control.[19] Although Williams had initially intended the term "moral luck" to be an oxymoron, he has nonetheless addressed the seemingly contradictory term in correlating moral responsibility with voluntary action as well as in exploring the phenomenon whereby a moral agent is assigned moral blame or moral praise for an action or its consequences, even when it is clear that the agent did not have full control over the act or its consequences.

To illustrate the problem of moral luck, the following conveys a rendition of the familiar traffic accident example: Two people drive cars down a road, Driver A and Driver B. They are alike in every way. Driver A, in a moment of inattention, runs a red light as a child is crossing the road and slams on the brakes in an attempt to avoid hitting the child, but unfortunately, she or he hits and kills the child. Driver B, in the meantime, also runs a red light in a moment of inattention, but since no one was crossing the road at the time, she or he merely gets a traffic ticket. The question, then, is: are both Drivers A and B equally worthy of moral blame? The only difference in the example is the occurrence of an external uncontrollable event, a child walking onto the road.

Kant would answer yes, both drivers are morally to blame, since in his rationalist view, moral luck does not play into the calculus of whether an agent has done her or his duty for duty's sake. That is, for Kant, equal fault equates with equal blame. In contrast, Nagel might classify the traffic accident as resultant (or consequential) moral luck: both drivers were affected by moral luck in that a particular set of circumstances turned out in two different ways.[20]

To address the problem of moral luck, I combine the rationalist with the consequentialist approach, by constructing an internal/external view of the problem. Thus, in the above example, if both drivers failed to check their brakes, from an external perspective, they should be equally at fault and equally blameworthy. If both drivers did everything correctly, including checking the brakes of their cars, then externally (and rationally), they should, again, be equally blameworthy. In the latter variation, however, if Driver A hits and kills the child, then internally, Driver A may view her or himself as deserving of more blame than Driver B, in whose case no child crossed the road. This view accords with Williams' observation that Driver A, who may have done nothing wrong with respect to her or his driving, nonetheless has "reasonable regret" for the consequences of her or his actions. This view also incorporates, echoing Strawson, reactive attitudes into the notion of accountability.

Moral Relativism

A fragment attributed to Protagoras has been interpreted to endorse a form of relativism: "Of all things the measure is man, of the things that are, that [or "how"] they are, and of things that are not, that [or "how"] they are not."[21] Nearly contemporary with Plato, Protagoras' *homomesura* variable and mortal-bound approach may have actually contributed to Plato's philosophical search for transcendental absolutes. Be that as it may, Plato addresses the *homomesura* concept in his epistemological work, *Theaetetus*,[22] and true to moral realism, Plato—and Aristotle as well—denies moral relativism on metaethical grounds. That is, for both Plato and Aristotle, moral realism proposes that in some sense an objective moral reality obtains.

In contrast, moral relativism argues that cultural influences and traditions inform morality, and since these differ from one culture to another, one culture's moral framework does not apply in another's. As with any theory, moral relativism should be amenable to testing per se against other moral theories, for validity, coherence, as well as for explanatory and predictive power. Yet, simply put, moral relativism tends to pay more attention to the micro- rather than the macro-level. Important to note in this regard, moral relativist accounts are coherentist, in that they especially look to the internal consistency of an account. In his defense of moral relativism, for example, Gilbert Harman develops the concept of moral frameworks in a coherentist manner, whereby through a process of continuing rational reflection, an individual refines an original set of values until she or he arrives at a coherent set of "corrected values" in a stable equilibrium, and hence, a moral framework.[23]

Of course, the question must be posed: what probative worth does an individual's corrected values have? The critique is not insignificant, for metaethical questions arise *a fortiori* since moral relativism posits that there can be no universal moral principles, since moral systems are incommensurable. Consequently, claims analyzed with one moral system, simply put, may emerge superior to another. Indeed, Alasdair MacIntyre has argued that through an exercise in imagination, one could conclude that a conflicting and incommensurable moral tradition is rationally superior to one's own.[24]

Nonetheless, in an empirical outlook, some moderate forms of moral or cultural relativism may be seen as providing constraints, albeit thin constraints, as well as resources for moral decision-making. Foregrounding social reactive attitudes, moral relativism may be taken to mean an ethical theory that denies the existence of universal moral truths and proposes that right and wrong must be defined variously, based on differences in cultural norms and mores. What is seen as morally right is relative, then, to an individual's society as well as to its time and place in history. Some versions of moral relativism, multiculturalism, for instance, not only justify individual actions based upon a particular group's cultural norms and mores, but also award rights to groups, thus denying, in effect, individual moral agency (see chapter 8). Thus, such a version of moral relativism falls short of the justice question and fails to further the development of normative, action-guiding principles.

Theoretically, we could exclude an extreme version of normative relativism, which would hold that no one should ever pass judgment on others with substantially different values or try to make them conform to another's values, since it would be inappropriate to apply an ethic of nonjudgmental toleration to condemn the intolerant. Simply articulating such an extreme view reveals its porosity, so that in leaving it, we could then arrive at a more moderate version of normative relativism that would allow us to pass judgment on others with substantially different values.[25] Doing so, however, begs the question of competing moral values and sidesteps a decision-making procedure for moral reasoning.

Even in moderate forms of moral relativism there appears to be thin provision for moral judgments and a moral decision-making apparatus. For instance, Harman's precondition to moral judgments of "shared motivational attitudes" does not appear to provide any guidance in moral decision-making to those outside the particular framework considered—it is for all intents and purposes a closed system. For example, it is rather easy to find situations in which this precondition is not met, and consequently, genuinely moral decisions may not be made.[26]

Bernard Williams extends the scope of Harman's coherentist analysis by means of his internal reasons thesis with regard to normative reasons for action, whereby he posits that an individual cannot have genuine reasons to act that have no connection with anything she or he cares about. The extension of his internal reasons thesis moves beyond the tradition of rationalism in ethics to arrive at, however, some other place at once intuitive and subjective. And this extension is only somewhat limited by his modifying phrase that such internal reasons should be reached by a "sound deliberative route."[27]

In his treatment of moral relativism, however, Williams also develops the concept of real and notional confrontations for ethical disagreements, whereby he understands that for relativism to be true, there must be a real confrontation between two moral systems such that at any given time there is a group for whom two moral systems meeting a "condition of exclusivity" comprise a real option. In contrast to Harman's stronger precondition to moral judgments of "shared motivational attitudes," Williams' formulation of a real confrontation precondition results in an approach that has a broader reach for the proper extent of moral judgments.

Williams' formulation thus extends the internal refining process offered by Harman. Along these lines, Tim Scanlon further argues that morality is a question of what we owe each other. In treating moral relativism from this perspective, he develops a theory of "parametric universalism." While Scanlon's theory may be viewed as relativistic, it is nonetheless grounded on certain universal, cross-cultural concepts, making external analyses possible while minimalizing intuition as a standard.[28] In identifying these concepts, Scanlon states that they should be deeply embedded culturally and sufficient to exclude genocide, murder, and totalitarianism. Thus, in Scanlon's account of moral relativism, as well as in Williams' benign treatment of relativism, there are empirical constraints formulated, as well as resources provided, that may be used in moral decision-making.

ACTION-GUIDING PRINCIPLES

Indeed, echoing Aristotle, it is hard not to imagine that human nature requires virtues such as courage, temperance, and justice for any plausible conception of a good life. In this respect, as argued here and elsewhere, I approach the question of justice deontologically to develop normative, action-guiding principles. In attempting to provide normative guidance to questions of justice, I look to constructing rules or principles.

As a moral theory, utilitarianism is consequentialist in approach, rather than relational, based in its principle of maximizing utility or pleasure. Thus, the classic utilitarianism of Jeremy Bentham, Henry Sidgwick, and James Mill propounds that the moral worth of an action is judged solely by its utility in providing happiness or pleasure.[29] Some contemporary accounts of justice are utilitarian as well, such as Derek Parfit's account, which I consider in chapter 10.

In stark contrast to such utilitarianism, Kant's will to universal law, a fundamental concept to many contemporary deontological moral theories, looks to rules or duties to determine what moral choices should be made. Thus, in the *Groundwork,* Kant presents one of his versions of the Supreme Principle of Morality, the Categorical Imperative, known as The Formula of Universal Law, in which he famously states that one should "act only on that maxim through which you can at the same time will that it should become a universal law."[30] Since John Rawls' theory of justice as fairness, many contemporary accounts have taken a deontological approach to the question.

Located in a deontological rather than a consequentialist approach, I maintain that the proper political context of justice may be seen as a form of liberalism, including the components of liberty and equality, while I also argue that a view of liberalism as concerned with notions of tolerance and social diversity extends the argument for justice into political considerations, both across societies and temporally (see chapter 6). Influenced not only by Plato's and Aristotle's emphasis on deontological necessity, my approach reflects as well Kant's focus on the individual as central to considerations of justice, thereby leading to an emphasis on the concept of negative liberty as Isaiah Berlin has articulated. Rather than removing obstacles or barriers, however, I see relations to be central. Thus, echoing classical reliance on *dikaiosune* in its macro- and micro- considerations, I see the task of justice as providing normative, societal guidance in an individual's relations to others, with the key to this relational view of justice being communication, both in a substantive sense as a rational, discursive method of resolving disparate conflicting views, but also in an instrumental sense of conveying ideas, especially the transmission of values through time.

In order to address moral questions of justice by means of relational rather than distributive analyses (see chapter 7), within the *dikaiosune* span of considerations, from societal to individual, I examine the question of justice in an analytical, rules-based approach. In so doing, I attempt to be value-neutral, acknowledging, however, an underlying thin theory of the good, while weaving in the Kantian concepts of rationality, autonomous moral agency, and equal concern and respect for others. While I view personal identity as shaped by norms, expectations, and conventions, and hence, as largely a social construct, such societal shaping does not obviate, in the political arena, the responsibility of the individual, rather than groups, as the proper bearer of rights and responsibilities.

NOTES

1. Practical irrationality for Aristotle is known as *akrasia,* meaning incontinence or weakness of will (VII.1–10). See also https://plato.stanford.edu/entries/aristotle-ethics/#VirDefConInc, Sections 4 and 7.

2. Instrumental rationality as inspired by David Hume's view that: "Reason is, and ought only to be the slave of the passions." See *A Treatise of Human Nature*, ed. David Fate Norton and Mary J. Norton (Oxford: Oxford University Press, 2001), Bk. II, Part 3, Section 1, p. 399. I discuss questions of value more fully in the next chapter.

3. See Christine Korsgaard, *The Sources of Normativity* (Cambridge: Cambridge University Press, 1996) for a strong Kantian approach to the question of norms, their source and authority.

4. For Aristotle, practical wisdom proves foundational to his ethical views as well as to his views of human nature and virtue, with well-being (*eudaemonia*) belonging to those living vituous lives. See Aristotle (2009); see also Philippa Foot, *Natural Goodness* (Oxford: Clarendon Press, 2001).

5. Compare Philip Pettit and Michael Smith, "Parfit's P," in *Reading Parfit*, ed. Jonathan Dancy (Oxford: Blackwell, 1997), ch. 5.

6. For example, Joseph Raz, *The Morality of Freedom* (Oxford: Oxford University Press, 1986).

7. Immanuel Kant, *Groundwork of the Metaphysic of Morals*, trans. H. J. Paton (New York: HarperCollins, 2009), p. 96.

8. A maxim may be seen as the principle underlying the particular intention or decision upon which one acts, a rule for action. Strict Kantians may even view maxims and intentions as synonymous; I do not, as I discuss later in this chapter.

9. For example, see R. M. Hare, *Moral Thinking* (Oxford: Oxford University Press, 1981), ch. 9.

10. See ch. 1, n. 19 and accompanying text *infra.*

11. It is unclear whether it would be appropriate to categorize Aristotle's concept of moral responsibility as merit based or consequentialist.

12. P. F. Strawson, "Freedom and Resentment," in *Freedom and Resentment and Other Essays* (New York: Routledge, 2008), pp. 1–28.

13. Id., p. 23.

14. See, generally, Eshleman, Andrew, "Moral Responsibility," *The Stanford Encyclopedia of Philosophy* (Summer, 2014 ed.), Edward N. Zalta (ed.), http//plato.stanford.edu/archives/sum.2014/entries/roal-responsibility/.

15. Some have made distinctions between responsibility as attributability, answerability, and accountability. See David Shoemaker, "Attributability, Answerability, and Accountability," *Ethics* (Chicago: University of Chicago Press, 2011), Vol. 121, pp. 603–632. Meanwhile, others have argued that all three concepts are just one: answerability. See Angela Smith, "Attributability, Answerability, and Accountability," *Ethics* (Chicago: University of Chicago Press, April 2012), Vol. 122, pp. 575–589.

16. Plato, *The Laws*, trans. Trevor Saunders (London: Penguin Books, 1970), Vol. IX, pp. 876–877.

17. A third way that luck may enter Aristotle's account of *eudaimonia* is through provision, or not, of minimum external goods such as health, security, access to resources. See Terence Irwin, *Classical Thought* (Oxford: Oxford University Press, 1988), p. 445.

18. See Kant (2009), p. 62.

19. See Thomas Nagel, *Mortal Questions* (New York: Cambridge University Press, 1979), ch. 3, and Bernard Williams, *Moral Luck* (Cambridge: Cambridge University Press, 1981).

20. Refining the concept of moral luck, Nagel develops three additional categories in his essay: circumstantial moral luck, focusing on the environment of the moral agent; constitutive moral luck, emphasizing the personal character of the moral agent; and, more controversially, causal moral luck, which some interpret as an alternative presentation of the problem of free will. Nagel (1979), ch. 3.

21. DK 80b1, in the Diels-Kranz numbering system.

22. Plato, *Theaetetus*, ed. Bernard Williams, trans. M. J. Levett, rev. Myles Burnyeat (Indiannapolis: Hacket Publishing Company, 1992), 151d7–e3, ff.

23. Gilbert Harman, "Moral Relativism and Moral Objectivity," in *Moral Relativism and Moral Objectivity*, ed. Gilbert Harman and J. J. Thompson (Cambridge: Blackwell Publishers, 1996), pp. 3–64.

24. See Alasdair MacIntyre, *Whose Justice? Whose Rationality?* (Notre Dame: University of Notre Dame Press, 1988), ch. 18. For an overview on moral relativism per se, see Chris Gowans, "Moral Relativism," in *The Stanford Encyclopedia of Philosophy*, ed. Edward N. Zalta (Winter 2016 Edition), https://plato.stanford.edu/archives/win2016/entries/moral-relativism/.

25. For example, see Philippa Foot, "Moral Relativism and Moral Objectivity," in *Moral Dilemmas and Other Topics in Moral Philosophy* (Oxford: Clarendon Press, 2002), pp. 20–36.

26. For instance, some moral judgments are not applicable to those whose actions are "beyond the pale"; it would seem strangely weak to say that Hitler's perpetration of the holocaust was merely "wrong." Harman (1996), pp. 28–30.

27. Bernard Williams, *Ethics and the Limits of Philosophy* (Cambridge: Harvard University Press, 1985), ch. 9.

28. T. M. Scanlon, *What We Owe Each Other* (Cambridge: Harvard University Press, 2000), pp. 328–361. See also Scanlon's discussion of Williams' "all external reasons are false" argument in the Appendix.

29. See Jeremy Bentham, *The Works of Jeremy Bentham* (Edinburgh: William Tait, 1843), Vol. 1.

30. Kant (2009), p. 88.

Chapter 5

Values

Underlying many discussions of justice are questions of value, since values undergird the framework for moral decision-making. These questions tend to crosscut classifications of moral theory as metaethical and normative inquiries. For instance, both Plato and Aristotle are moral realists who believe in the pursuit of the Good; however, their theories of foundational forms and virtue ethics lead to different normative approaches to questions of value, metaphysical and pragmatic, respectively.

Basic questions of value theory include the variety of goodness (including disputes such as the right vs. the good); concepts of good, better, and bad; and the shape of morality, as gathered in the theories of value monism versus value pluralism along with the issue of incommensurability. Arising from such questions are teleological or consequentialist approaches to moral decision-making, in contrast to deontological approaches.

VALUE MONISM

In value theory, one of the questions addressed is whether there is more than one fundamental intrinsic value. Value monists (Isaiah Berlin's term) say no, since the question concerns intrinsic values of which, clearly, more than one instrumental value exists. From this perspective, Plato may be seen as a pluralist in terms of the number of forms, but a monist about the number of basic forms, since he maintains that all foundational forms are sustained by the single form of the Good.[1] As discussed further below, Aristotle espouses contrasting views regarding value.

Happiness

Plato appears to accept that the Good is happiness, and he attempts to arrive at a theory of values dealing with what is good and bad, and with moral duty and obligation, through the concept of *eudaimonia,* by which he understands that the highest ethical goal is happiness and personal well-being. He identifies three parts to *eudaimonia*: (1) living in harmony with one's self (justice); (2) living in truth with one's self (integrity); and (3) combining the first two parts, a feeling of happiness arising from the activity of self-fulfillment, attainable only through the exercise of certain virtues (wisdom, courage, temperance, justice, and integrity).

Likewise, Aristotle defines happiness as the Good in the *Nicomachean Ethics*: "Human good turns out to be activity of soul in accordance with virtue."[2] He further observes that there are three types of life thought to be happy: (a) the life of enjoyment; (b) the political life; and (c) the life of contemplation. However, he approaches the concept of the soul differently than does Plato. Rather than Plato's tripartite soul consisting of reason, spirit, and appetite, Aristotle argues that there are only two parts to the soul: (1) the rational element and (2) the irrational element.[3] Further, the purest exercise of the rational capacity is contemplation, the highest human activity since it furthers understanding.[4] Consequently, Aristotle argues that only contemplation can serve as a source of value. Indeed, for Aristotle, both metaphysically and ethically, contemplation is the final purpose of human life and the world.

As such, both Plato and Aristotle are seen to express a teleological understanding of the ends or purpose of human life. Classic utilitarianism also presents a teleological or consequentialist approach to the question of justice as well, since utilitarianism propounds that the moral worth of an action is judged solely by its utility in providing happiness or pleasure to human beings. Thus, Jeremy Bentham links happiness and utility in the formula: "the greatest happiness of the greatest number."[5] In placing one value above all others, classic utilitarianism may thus be seen as value monist. But Isaiah Berlin errs in describing John Stuart Mill's embrace of utilitarianism as representing a value monist moral theory. Mill defends a rather complicated version of utilitarianism, made complex in part by his harm principle, which has proven highly influential. His harm principle, that is, may be seen as setting forth a foundational view of classic political liberalism (see chapter 6).

Resembling both Plato and Aristotle, Mill is a moral realist, in the sense that he believes that there is an objective moral reality. Typically, realist accounts provide reasons for actions. To articulate a reason for any action, an individual must have a desire, and desires are subjective in the sense that one person's desires may not resemble the desires of another, making it difficult to generate general criteria. Mill does not have this problem. On the contrary,

Mill believes that moral judgments can be determined as true or false and that they can be known. Starkly unlike both Plato and Aristotle, however, Mill argues as a naturalist, one who believes that goodness or rightness can be identified with, or reduced to, a property as identified in human nature. Like Plato and Aristotle, Mill's concept of goodness or rightness is identified as happiness, but in Mill's approach, happiness is not identified with either Plato's universals or Aristotle's contemplation.

Thus opposed to a moral realist theory of intuitionism, Mill furthers utilitarianism as an empirical matter. G. E. Moore critiques this naturalist approach as making an illegitimate inference from "is" to "ought," and calling Mill's propensity to derive values from facts, a "naturalist fallacy."[6] Be that as it may, for Mill utilitarianism was not only a moral theory, but also a political calling, as part of a reform movement in Victorian England. Clearly located in the natural realm—and as propagated by Jeremy Bentham and Mill's own father, James Mill—classic utilitarianism theorizes the maximizing of pleasure. From their standpoint, pleasure is a sensation, whereby pleasures that persist comprise quantitative *utiles*, useful entities, and hence, they are scientifically measurable. Notably, from this time-dependent basis, Mill broadens the scope, so that utility embraces the concept of human beings as progressive individuals.

The goal of happiness proves central to Mill's view of himself as an utilitarian; indeed, he never directly repudiates Benthamite utilitarianism, with its focus on the maximizing and aggregating of pleasure or happiness as a moral end.[7] Despite his claim to utilitarianism, Mill's thought has proven difficult to categorize. Thus, classic utilitarians view the prominent position that Mill gives liberty in the utilitarian scheme as heretical. Likewise, by additionally incorporating the concept of higher and lesser pleasures into his account, and thereby appearing to adhere to value pluralism—which holds that values are plural and that some values may be equally fundamental and correct—Mill does not readily fit into the category of a value monist who, in contrast to value pluralists, believe that all goods are somehow commensurable.

Mill's insistence on different levels of pleasures indeed marks a significant departure from utilitarian orthodoxy. In doing so, Mill concomitantly articulates certainty as to the appropriate hierarchy of societal values. That is, the higher pleasures of Mill comprise those of the intellect and are superior to those gratifying the body; indeed, higher pleasures outweigh lower pleasures, regardless of the quantity of the latter.[8] In this assertion, Mill seems close to Plato and Aristotle. While the theoretical ramifications of Mill's incorporating the higher and lower pleasures into the utilitarian account have been much criticized, the underlying notion that some pleasures are to be preferred over others does have theoretical appeal.[9]

Critically, Mill allows a competent judge to determine what these higher pleasures are. In contrast to the Benthamite felicific calculus, that is, Mill's method of measuring value employs the judgment of competent agents. Thus, the preferential ranking of pleasures by knowledgeable judges is foundational to Mill's measurement of value. Additionally, relying upon competent judges allows Mill to use utility as a principle to understand and interpret marginal cases and to make decisions in cases where incommensurable moral values are at play. In installing other judges, Mill does remove himself yet further from classic utilitarianism. One view, espoused by John Gray, is that Mill embraced a qualitative hedonism, which ultimately places unbearable pressure upon his theory of value and thereby transforms his political liberalism into a form of perfectionist ethics, further providing the concept of higher pleasures an "infinite weight, or lexical priority" in comparative judgments.[10]

In addition to installing competent judges, Mill provides controls on higher and lower pleasures through the principle of self-discipline. That is, Mill views self-discipline in terms of Aristotelian virtue and as concomitant with external individual liberty.[11] As such, the pursuit of higher pleasures maps onto the internal self-discipline that Mill sees as necessarily operative in the realization of liberty. Given Mill's views on higher and lower pleasures and the fundamental role of liberty in his political thought, it is indeed no easy matter to apply the utility principle, since Mill does define happiness as pluralistic and hierarchical. Thus, in its application, Mill's utility principle proves aggregative and maximizing. As such, it thus sanctions unequal distributions of liberty and creates an indeterminate sphere within which liberty is to be protected. Consequently, except in limiting cases, Mill's calculus may actually undermine the ability to make judgments about greater, or greatest, happiness.

In his version of utilitarianism, Mill thus fails to provide any rational decision-making procedure for resolving conflicts among vital human interests. Mill's failure to do so, his failure to fulfill the value monist promise of happiness as a concept to arbitrate among various goods, leads Gray to conclude that Mill's ethical theory "collapse[s] into an unwitting and incomplete form of value-pluralism."[12] Further eroding his claim to utilitarianism, at least in the classic sense, is Mill's basic belief—similar to Aristotle's—in the value of individuality and in the development of an individual's capacities. Drawing criticism as well is the political value of liberty he espouses and the role of perfectionist self-discipline in the exercise of liberty. Indeed, his advocacy of freedom from governmental interference as well as from societal constraints articulated in the harm principle, and which extends his views on liberty, has been criticized for indeterminacy in what constitutes harm, in its underlying concept of human interests, and in its application of the subsumed utility principle.

Regardless of these aberrations, Mill does refer to utility as a definitive ethical touchstone. He argues that "utility [is] the ultimate appeal on all ethical grounds; but it must be utility in the largest sense, grounded on the permanent interests of man as a progressive being."[13] Propelled by a notion of the greatest good, similarly to Plato and Aristotle, Mill's thought nonetheless resides far from Plato's fundamental universals as well as from Aristotle's polity-based and -aimed concepts of equality. Instead, Mill posits the individual as the liberal measure by which an ideal society should govern and adapts utility as a tool to effect the greatest possible good for the individual and hence for society.

I examine further Mill's views of progress and fallibilism in the context of classic political liberalism in chapter 6. Ultimately, though, Mill's version of utilitarianism is made inconsistent by his introduction of the concept of higher and lower pleasures, as well as by his notions of progress and fallibilism, thus straining a value monist view of his account. Mill cares about diverse choices as the empirical expression of individuals engaged in self-realization and adopting different lifestyles. He is not, however, a value pluralist in any strong sense. That is, even though Mill holds plural values, he provides moral decision-making resources in his ethical theory such that he is able to overcome the classic, strong value pluralist problem of incommensurability. The central place of liberty in his views, as discussed in chapter 6, along with its extension through the harm principle, allows him to avail himself of that tool in deciding between conflicting moral values. Further, his ordering of higher and lower pleasures, his notion of progress and, at the margins, utility, provide additional tools that may be deployed to help make decisions involving incommensurable moral values.

Duty

Immanuel Kant reverses Aristotle's argument regarding contemplation as the final good and source of value—that is, the final purpose for human beings must be also regarded as the final purpose of the world. Since whatever is chosen with a good will is good, Kant argues that we can construct the ideal of a totality of all good things.[14] Thus, Kant does not agree with Aristotle's unconditional value of contemplation since, on metaphysical grounds, Kant sees the only value that exists is what human beings give to their own lives. Q.E.D., we must be the source of value.[15]

Further, in contrast to Plato and Aristotle, in the *Critique of Practical Reason*, Kant claims that the good is a rational concept. For Kant, this means that if the ends are to be good, they must be determined by reason, not by merely inclination or pleasantness.[16] Further, to be determined good in the judgment of every reasonable man, the reasons for calling a thing good must have universal value. Thus, as discussed in chapter 4, in terms of rational and autonomous agency, for Kant the rational nature of human beings specifically confers value on the objects of its choices and is itself the source of all value.

Kant may be understood as a value monist then in the sense that he embraces one overarching principle, arising from practical reason and to which all other principles are derived. While Kant does not deny happiness, in the *Groundwork of Metaphysic of Morals*, Kant presents a classic deontological moral theory, whereby the rightness or wrongness of actions depends not on their consequences, but rather, on whether they fulfill moral obligations. To determine what these moral duties are, Kant formulates the Categorical Imperative, which some view as expressing a constructivist (anti-realist) account of morality. One version of the Categorical Imperative is found in The Formula of Universal Law, articulating a version of the Supreme Principle of Morality, cited earlier: "Act only on that maxim through which you can at the same time will that it should become a universal law."[17]

For Kant, a maxim represents a subjective principle of action and should be distinguished from an objective principle—namely, practical law. Kant's subjective principle of action contains a practical rule determined by reason in accordance with the conditions of the subject (often the agent's ignorance or inclination), formulated as the principle upon which the subject acts. A law, on the other hand, is an objective principle valid for every rational being, and it is consequently a principle upon which an agent ought to act—that is, an imperative. Kant thus expresses his fundamental principle of morality as the Categorical Imperative, which may be seen as the law of an autonomous will. As mentioned previously, the basis of this principle is a concept of reason that goes well beyond that of a Humean "slave to the passions" or instincts, and it is this self-governing reason in each person that Kant thought offered decisive grounds for viewing every person as possessing equal worth and deserving equal respect.

The operation of the Categorical Imperative, which may also be viewed as a rule for testing rules, is complicated and requires a number of steps. First, before an individual acts, she or he must consider the maxim or principle upon which she or he is acting. Next, the individual must generalize that principle. Once generalized, if that principle no longer makes any sense, because it contradicts itself, it is wrong to use that maxim as a basis for action. However, if the generalized version makes sense, then the individual must ask whether it is good to live in a world where the maxim is followed by everyone else. Finally, she or he must act on the maxim only if the answer is "yes." Thus, to test a proposed maxim for its universal adoption, an individual asks whether the proposed action is consistent (i.e., possible) and acceptable to rational beings.[18]

Being rational means for Kant being able to act based on motives that are universally defensible; when human beings do this, they fulfill their obligation to duty, duty for duty's sake. Acting on the basis of good will, human beings are thus moral when they are the authors of their actions, autonomous, and morally responsible for the intentions, not the consequences of their actions. His views have been challenged in recent times by changes, for example, in medical ethics and approaches to ecological concerns, but nonetheless, Kant's respect for human life remains a foundational element in his deontological approach, as expressed in his view of humans as ends in themselves and in his respect for human dignity and autonomy. Critically, it is the possibility of rationality that makes humans morally significant, although rationality does not articulate specific justifiable ways to act.

Indeed, among the differences between Kant's views and consequentialist moral theories (as witnessed especially in utilitarian ethics) is the focus on intentions underlying actions for Kantians versus the focus on results of actions for utilitarians. Since, following the Categorical Imperative, an individual assesses actions by examining the maxims of agents, Kantian ethics assess only intentional acts, to the neglect of results. For utilitarians who value happiness or pleasure and the absence or reduction of misery, it is the results of actions that are paramount, to the exclusion of intentions, whether good or not.[19]

Ultimately, the debate of whether or not a universal moral law exists is at the heart of critiques of Kant's theory.[20] Questions range from whether or not we should give credence to an objective morality to whether an objective morality, necessarily general if it is to be universal, can handle ambiguous cases located at the margins of applications of the Categorical Imperative. Likewise, due to its universal nature, the application of the Categorical Imperative cannot easily provide for choosing between conflicting duties. Along with these challenges is the practical difficulty of formulating maxims according to Kant's theory, especially with respect to social interactions. For instance, an individual may adopt a maxim that can indeed be universalized in favor of pacifism and consequently act accordingly. However, if others do not adopt the same maxim, then Kantian pacifists could be challenged by non-Kantians, or even Kantians, who do not adopt pacifist maxims. Moreover, while the actions of both parties could be correctly deemed moral, nonetheless, unlike Jeremy Bentham who believed in rehabilitative justice, Kant also gives credence to retributive justice, an unforgiving view of the moral universe.

VALUE PLURALISM

By value pluralism, I specify here moral pluralism rather than political pluralism. Value pluralism questions whether values (such as freedom, happiness, and welfare) are plural or monist, engaging in discussions concerning the shape of morality, as when probing how many values can or should be included in a moral theory.

Both Plato and Aristotle are typically seen as value monist, in large part because of their accounts of *eudaimonia*, although they do differ in their views of values. Moreover, both evince a teleological orientation, characteristically associated with value monism. The virtues considered in Aristotle's theory of *arête,* however, are plural. This becomes apparent when he attempts to apply the doctrine of the mean to the primary virtue of justice. As discussed in chapter 3, while virtues are generally found between two undesirable extremes, the extremes of excess and deficiency, with regard to justice, however, Aristotle notes an asymmetric application of the doctrine of the mean, as described in his *Nicomachean Ethics*, in that justice is "a kind of mean because it relates to an intermediate amount, while injustice relates to extremes" (1133b32–1134a1); moreover, "injustice is both excess and deficiency" (1134a8–9). In other words, Aristotle does not approach the value of justice in a value monist manner.

It is perhaps Aristotle's incorporation of practical reason—together with virtue and well-being—in developing his full theory of *arête* that generates value pluralism in his account. Thus, Martha Nussbaum argues that Aristotle's account of practical reason in his account of ethics is conditioned by value pluralism, and further that only pluralism can explain his concept of *akrasia* as weakness of will.[21] Similarly focused on Aristotle's practical reason, George Crowder notes that his insistence on particularity and diversity of ethical experience is such that no general rules can be formulated in all cases.[22]

Not surprisingly, as suggested by Nussbaum and Crowder, the debate between pluralists and monists often focuses on the complexity of moral choice and whether such complexity implies that values are plural, or whether such complexity can be adequately explained by monists, such as utilitarians of the Benthamite persuasion. Further, since morality is often viewed as action-guiding, pluralists must navigate the additional tensions between explaining how comparisons among values are made and/or defending widely dispersed value incommensurability. One strategy of pluralists regarding the problem of incommensurable values has been to appeal to practical wisdom, the faculty described by Aristotle—a faculty of judgment that the wise and virtuous person has, which enables him to arrive at the right answer—not unlike Mill's dependency on competent judges.

Essentially, value pluralism holds not only that values are plural, but also that there may be many goods, as well as ways of life, that are equally fundamental and correct. In contrast, value monists believe that there is an overriding value that all goods are somehow commensurable and hence, value hierarchies may be generated. The problem for the monist is to determine which goods are superior to others. The controversies occupying value pluralists, on the other hand, stem from the belief that some values conflict and consequently are incommensurable. The moral life of a nun, in one of John Gray's examples, is incompatible with that of a mother, but there is no rational measure of determining which is preferable. To complicate matters, not all value pluralists are committed to the view that all ways of life are good, and some would indeed allow for hierarchal value rankings.[23]

Incommensurability

John Rawls' account of justice as fairness is charged with incommensurability due to his adopting of multiple permissible comprehensive conceptions of the good underlying his theory of justice.[24] Moreover, Rawls presents the problem of the ranking of values (his social goods) in his first principle of justice, the liberty principle. Thus, John Gray is correct when he points out that beyond the indeterminacy charge to Rawls' liberty principle, even as reformulated in *Political Liberalism*, what is disabling to Rawls' enterprise is that "incompatible applications of his principles can be justified by different conceptions of the good."[25] Further, conflicts among incommensurable values can be resolved, if at all, "only by reference to the understandings of the good that are found in particular ways of life."[26]

While value monists believe that all goods are somehow commensurable, what proves controversial in the argument of value pluralists is that they believe that some values may conflict and in fact be incommensurable. By acceding to a view that there may be various comprehensive conceptions of the good underlying his account of justice, Rawls indicates a strong value pluralist approach to the question. And for a strong value pluralist, the problem of incommensurability is especially keen, as may be exemplified by a brief comparison with the work of Joseph Raz, particularly with regard to his central notions of personal autonomy and social forms.[27] Raz situates his theory of value pluralism in a liberal perfectionist regime, one in which the good trumps the right.[28]

For a strong value pluralist, then, solving the problem of incommensurability proves essential, and for Raz it is also pivotal, particularly with regard to his fundamental notion of personal autonomy. At first blush, Raz appears to make a functional argument for the overriding principle of personal autonomy in modern life, based on fast-moving technology and the free movement of labor. Given this argument, the question emerges as to whether Raz views autonomy as an intrinsic good or not.[29] Oddly, for a perfectionist concerned with goods, Raz' approach poses no theory of values. Indeed he makes no ontological inquiry into the existence of values, let alone determines a hierarchy of values. The problem emerges more clearly when examining Raz' notion of social forms—the particular social practices and institutions in a given society—and whether they generate value.

In his 1994 essay collection, *Ethics and the Public Domain*,[30] Raz treats some of these issues in the first set of essays, emphasizing the importance to an individual's well-being of belonging to a cultural group and of the good life configured as an active rather than a passive life. Moreover, in his 2003 essay, "The Practice of Value," Raz further argues for the social dependence of values, but without relativism.[31] Caught in a conundrum, Raz' strong value pluralism precludes him from deploying his concept of autonomy (as well as the various social goods that constitute his perfectionist regime) for purposes of ranking or for lexical priorities when making moral decisions.[32]

Indeed, in moral decision-making situations that involve incommensurable moral values and where reason is incapable of guiding action, Raz ignores an examination of the nature of value. Instead, he analyzes the nature of agency and rationality in two kinds of relationships. Thus, he distinguishes human agency, in which reasons require action, from what he terms a classical conception of agency in which the will (which Raz views as separate from desire) chooses "among options that reason merely renders eligible."[33] In articulating his classical conception of agency, Raz employs rationality in a weak sense (and not in the Aristotelian sense of appealing to practical reason), which is the strategy that some pluralists adopt when attempting to solve the comparison problem between competing moral values.[34] Raz' value pluralism account is thereby left without any strong action-guiding principles for when incommensurable moral values are at stake.

Instead, Raz' solution to the problem of incommensurability balances on the claim that when there are no further reasons for favoring X over Y, it can be rational (in a weak sense) to choose X over Y. This may be a plausible approach when faced with a nonmoral choice, as exemplified in Raz' own example of choosing between a banana and a pear. In the context of making moral choices, however, the proposal does not suffice. For Raz, when reasons have run their course, individuals should take the object of desire as the preferred choice, opting for a mere appeal to basic preferences. In choosing without reasons, however, the slide into subjectivity vitiates any credible decision-making process. While less than satisfactory as an approach, more problematically, given Raz' concern for values derived from communal life and social forms, is the danger of relativism. That is, his account of communities and social forms provides individuals with valuable options and choices. As such, Raz shares a kinship with communitarians and their focus on the discourse and traditions of particular communities and societies.[35]

Incommensurability does indeed require conceptual attention. With respect to the problem of conflicting moral values, for example, Brian Barry suggests that fundamental values may be compared, even when they are incommensurable. His view is that deliberative argument can provide reasons for choices among qualitatively different claims, even when no common measure of value is available.[36] Yet another method of dealing with the problem of incommensurability is simply to accept that there may be situations in which a reasoned choice among plural values cannot be made. Isaiah Berlin takes this approach, when he claims that such goods as liberty and equality may conflict at a fundamental level. Albeit expressed in the context of political pluralism, Berlin's views in defending political liberalism have been influential in the discussion of moral pluralism as well.

Bernard Williams, for instance, believes that occasionally, there are indeed genuinely irresolvable conflicts among values and to expect a rational resolution in such situations is wrong-thinking. Williams does, however, suggest that there are methods of comparison, even when a common scale is not shared (e.g., ethical or aesthetic considerations against economic ones). Further, in *Moral Luck*, he makes the interesting point that even when a right choice has been made, the rejected option can be reasonably regretted, demonstrating that the choice involved a genuine value conflict.[37] Williams does not, however, suggest how weighting of irresoluble methods of comparison might occur.[38]

THE RIGHT AND THE GOOD

To close this chapter, I focus on a disjunction in theories of justice that has evolved from the work of Plato and Aristotle, the disjunction between the right and the good. Both Plato and Aristotle address the macro- and micro-sides of *dikaiosune* in their treatments of justice. However, Plato's metaphysically defined concept of justice, the Good, has been largely left behind in contemporary times for the societal side of Aristotle's theory of justice (especially particular justice), namely, what is fair and how are goods to be distributed. In the last section of this chapter, I compare the professed views of the priority of the right over the good presented in John Rawls' theory of justice as fairness, and the contrasting priority of the good over the right in Joseph Raz' account.

In his work, John Rawls set out to construct a conception of justice that he perceived as neutral and anti-perfectionist, one that "constitutes the most appropriate moral basis for a democratic society."[39] His moral inquiry results in an egalitarian distributive construct in which justice, generally, requires that primary social goods (liberty and opportunity, income and wealth, and the bases for self-respect) be distributed equally within a society, unless unequal distribution is to everyone's advantage.[40] In other words, liberty may only be restricted for the sake of liberty, and everyone is to have "an equal right to the most extensive basic liberty compatible with a similar liberty for others."[41]

Under favorable social conditions, a special concept of justice as fairness may obtain. Rawls' first principle of justice as fairness, however, provides for the priority of liberty as a supervening good to the second principle, the difference principle, which allows for social and economic inequity as long as society as a whole benefits. Besides bringing into question the importance of fairness, and in spite of his claims to a deontological approach, the outcome-orientation of Rawls' difference principle moves his theory outside a comfortably deontological framework.

H. L. A. Hart formulated the famous criticism of Rawls' equal basic liberty principle as being indeterminate in application, since Rawls includes no reference to external measures or values. In his essay, "Rawls on Liberty and its Priority," Hart closely analyzes Rawls' first principle, the principle of greatest equal liberty, and the associated priority rule that "liberty can only be restricted for the sake of liberty."[42] Hart finds this principle—which treats only the maximizing and extent of liberty—indeterminate, since in trying to apply it, the concept of greatest liberty cannot be distinguished from judgments about which liberties are more important than others, and, just as problematically, determining which liberties are more important than others depends on what ends they serve: "Conflicts between basic liberties will be such that different resolutions of the conflict will correspond to the interests of different people who will diverge over the relative value they set on the conflicting liberties."[43]

Questions remain, then, as to whether Rawls successfully affirms the priority of right over the good. If applied to a situation in which an agent is confronted with having to make a decision between incommensurable values, the basic liberties principle provides guidance when one of the values is a basic liberty, or when one of the values in conflict may refer to a basic liberty and the other does not. As such, the lexical priority of basic liberties proves a useful tool in moral decision-making. When all the conflicting moral values in question are basic liberties, however, Rawls' explanation of adjusting and regulating basic liberties so that they operate in a central range of application is unpersuasive and unhelpful in moral decision-making.

In Rawls' vigorous attempts to present a neutral liberal account, he does acknowledge various conceptions of the good in his theory of justice. Thus, while continuing to assert the priority of right, Rawls understands that five ideas of good are embedded in his account: "(1) the idea of goodness as rationality, (2) the idea of primary goods, (3) the idea of permissible comprehensive conceptions of the good, (4) the idea of the political virtues, and (5) the idea of the good of a well-ordered (political) society."[44]

While reason plays a critical role in the first idea of good in justice as fairness, Rawls' four other concepts require judgments or publicly accessible and reasoned decisions that are not likely to be in accord in a pluralistic society. Because the last four concepts require publicly reasoned discussion, Rawls attempts to accommodate all five ideas by taking the discussion into the political realm, and in the process, he appears to accede to a thin theory of the good as part of his full theory of the good: "I have supposed first that the rational plans satisfy the constraints of right and justice (as the full theory of the good stipulates)."[45]

More specifically, Rawls argues that a well-ordered society requires that people exercise their sense of justice for its own sake, and in doing so, they make justice supremely regulative of their plans for life. In this sense, he continues, right and goodness are congruent since doing what is right contributes to each person's good. To establish the validity of his viewpoint, he distinguishes deontological from teleological moral theories, arguing that deontological theories do not subscribe to the idea that right depends on what is good, while teleological theories, such as utilitarianism, do. His own theory of justice, Rawls insists, is deontological, because his two principles of justice privilege the right over the good.

Rawls seems to contradict himself, however, as he insists that the right is consistent or congruent with the good, diminishing thereby the privileging of the right over the good. He makes this argument in two steps. First, he posits that for a person to enjoy any good life, the person requires a supply of primary goods. He develops the point further through the Aristotelian Principle, by which persons, other things being equal, can exercise their developed faculties; the enjoyment they derive from such rights, he continues, increases the more developed the faculties and the more complex the activities. In adapting the Aristotelian Principle, Rawls gives primacy to choice, to psychological principles, by which persons in the original position may not only specify the content of primary goods, but in choosing the two principles of justice, they also promote their share of such primary goods. Rawls, then, makes end orientation critical in his account of a person's good, acceding to a thin theory of the good, one that allows parties in the original position to adopt a weak or noncontroversial conception of what is good for them.

Next, Rawls attempts to demonstrate that his vision of a just society would be stable and consistent with the good of its members. Since a stable conception of justice is fundamental to a stable society, he avers, fairness proves indispensable for fairness generates a strong sense of justice and, consequently, also promotes a person's good. Ultimately, Rawls appears to say that what is our good cannot go against our nature, and it is in our nature to be "free and equal rational being[s]," whose nature can only be fulfilled by acting on "principles of right and justice having the first priority."[46] This view concomitantly provides the basis for Rawls' rejection of utilitarian thought which, in his opinion, misunderstands our nature, viewing persons as concerned primarily with the mere satisfaction of desires and refusing to recognize the importance of freedom and equality.

Rawls' move from a moral viewpoint to a political one strains and confuses his argument for the priority of the right over the good. The individual as a moral agent thus tends to disappear from his account, and his underlying intuition of human beings having an innate sense of justice is certainly contestable. Further, his argument for the congruence of the good and the right, equating the good with the right, attempts by definitional fiat to explain how justice operates. On the contrary, for a theory of justice to function effectively, it must take into account *both* moral and political roots, *dikaiosune,* as termed by the ancient Greeks. Thus, Rawls' attempt to give priority to the right over the good fails, as does his attempt to make them congruent.

Further, the attendant theoretical problems that emerge from a right-over-the-good approach make the communitarian challenge to a liberal neutral view still relevant, since communitarianism holds that a society may not exist in a vacuum and must, as well as should, be framed by a larger vision of the good.[47] It thus seems appropriate to rest rights on substantive, moral judgments of the ends that rights advance. Necessarily, the composition of societies plays an important role in conceptualizing these ends, whereby their diversity takes on an empirical dimension in what various societies define as good. Thus, the question arises as to whether rights may be identified and justified in a manner that does not presuppose any particular conception of the good life, at the opposite end, so to speak, of Plato's metaphysical starting point. That is, may principles of justice that govern the basic structure of society be developed that are neutral with respect to competing moral commitments of a society's citizens?

In contrast to Rawls and Kant, Mills approaches the political debate of the good over the right with a vision of the good life defined as that which allows individual freedom from governmental interference, subject to the constraints of his harm principle, which provides that "the sole end for which mankind are warranted, individually or collectively, in interfering with the liberty of action of any of their number, is self-protection."[48] In considering political dimensions of justice, Raz likewise develops an account of human well-being which embraces values, but in contrast to Mill, Raz argues that government may even engage in coercive action to protect a vision of the good life and the underlying personal autonomy of individuals, thereby making values the ultimate determining factor in his vision of liberalism.[49] He thus creates a liberal perfectionist regime in which, as stated earlier, the good trumps the right.

Raz bases his notion of liberalism on autonomy-based freedom and embraces a triadic view of liberty, including negative and positive liberty as well as personal autonomy. For Raz, liberalism need not rest on individualistic grounds alone.[50] In fact, Raz develops an account of liberty in which his conception of personal autonomy coalesces with and feeds into his notion of social forms, and his theory of value pluralism is designed to support the liberal ordering of society, albeit in a perfectionist regime.

In other words, the development of a liberal perfectionist state committed to protecting and promoting personal autonomy proceeds from the value of individual well-being. An individual's well-being, for Raz, depends on success in the pursuit of valuable goals, and such valuable goals in turn are largely determined by the social forms of an individual's community. Fundamentally, the social forms characterizing modern liberal states reflect the pervasiveness of autonomy. The critical question, consequently, is to what extent liberal societies should promote autonomy as a way of life. If autonomy is as pervasive a fact of life of modern liberal societies as Raz asserts, then a case may be made for its further promotion. On the other hand, if autonomy has a more limited role, then perhaps a less interventionist state may be appropriate. In either event, in Raz' view, there is no sacrosanct "self-regarding" sphere that political authority need to protect; indeed, success in making goals available as social forms requires the effective exercise of autonomy and using coercion where deemed necessary. In fact, Raz believes that strict adherence to state neutrality would "undermine the chances of survival of many cherished aspects of our culture."[51]

NOTES

1. Plato, *The Republic*, trans. Desmond Lee, 2nd ed. (London: Penguin Books, 2003), VI, 508e–509b.

2. Aristotle, *The Nicomachean Ethics of Aristotle*, trans. D. Ross, rev. Lesley Brown (Oxford: Oxford University Press, 2009), I.7 1098a 15–17.

3. Id., I, 5 and 7.

4. Id., X, ch. 7.

5. *A Comment on the Commentaries and A Fragment of Government*, ed. J. H. Burns and H. L. A. Hart, in *The Collected Works of Jeremy Bentham* (London: University of London Press, 1977), p. 393.

6. See G. E. Moore, *Principia Ethica*, ed. Thomas Baldwin (Cambridge: Cambridge University Press, 1993).

7. But see Eldon Eisenach, *Mill and the Moral Character of Liberalism* (University Park: The Pennsylvania State University Press, 1998), ch. 8, regarding Mill's critique of Benthanism. Concerning controversies about the nature of the good and the debate between the mental-state or experience model and the desire-satisfaction model of utility, see Wendy Donner, *The Liberal Self* (Ithaca: Cornell University Press, 1991), ch. 3.

8. No living in a "City of Pigs" for Mill. See Mill (1998), p. xvi.

9. Mill (2004), p. 210.

10. John Gray, *Mill on Liberty: A Defence*, 2nd ed. (Oxford: Routledge, 1996), p. 141.

11. See Nicholas Capaldi, *John Stuart Mill* (Cambridge: Cambridge University Press, 2004), ch. 9. See also Joseph Hamburger, *John Stuart Mill and Control* (Princeton: Princeton University Press, 1999), in which Hamburger extends the self-discipline aspect in Mill's concept of liberty to one of control.

12. Gray (1996), p. 146. "Mill's ethical theory contains nothing which guides us in making choices among conflicting ingredients of happiness; if the general priority it accords, within the vital interests, to autonomy over security cannot be given a rational justification; and if Mill's doctrine cannot attach weights to different harms and rival liberties—then his revised utilitarianism does, after all, collapse."

13. John Stuart Mill, "On Liberty," in *John Stuart Mill on Liberty and other Essaya,* ed. John Gray (Oxford: Oxford University Press, 1998) p. 15.

14. See Christine Korsgaard, "Aristotle and Kant on the Source of Value," in *Ethics* (April 1986), pp. 486–505.

15. Id., pp. 502–505.

16. Immanuel Kant, *Critique of Practical Reason*, trans. and ed. Paul Guyer and Allen Wood (Cambridge: Cambridge University Press, 1997), pp. 62–64.

17. Immanuel Kant, *Groundwork of the Metaphysic of Morals,* trans. H. J. Paton (New York: HarperCollins, 2009), p. 88.

18. Underscoring how the Categorical Imperative differs from the Golden Rule ("So in everything, do to others what you would have them do to you"); the Categorical Imperative is based not on what an individual desires to do (or have done to her- or himself), but rather, what is necessary for any being to act rationally and *universally*, without consideration of self-interest.

19. In addition to such utilitarian challenges to Kant's ethical theory, environmentalists point to how his approach is anthropocentric, and hence, dangerous and wrong, since animals must also be taken into account when deliberating what justice is. Another contemporary approach critiques how Kant's theory has individuals adjudicate out of duty *a priori*, thus denying the importance of individual experience when working out what is right and thereby relying perhaps too heavily on certain socially accepted norms, which may not necessarily represent a majority of individuals. As a final example of contemporary challenges to Kant's approach, there is a question of motivation in his account. Realizing that something is irrational, that is, does not always motivate individuals to do the right thing. If it did, of course, we would have less need for laws and legal systems.

20. As an obvious example, in *The Republic,* Plato takes a metaphysical approach to the question of a moral universe. See also, Plato, *The Statesman,* trans. J. B. Skemp (London: Bristol Classical Press, 2002).

21. See Martha Nussbaum, *The Fragility of Goodness*, rev. ed. (Cambridge: Cambridge University Press, 2001), ch. 10.

22. George Crowder, *Liberalism and Value Pluralism* (New York: Continuum, 2002), p. 58. He also says that Isaiah Berlin usually associates Aristotle with value monism, but that he also refers to him as a pluralist "fox" rather than a monist

"hedgehog." Cf. Isaiah Berlin, *The Hedgehog and the Fox*, ed. Henry Hardy (Princeton: Princeton University Press, 2013).

23. See Elinor Mason, "Value Pluralism," in *Stanford Encyclopedia of Philosophy*, ed. E. Zalta (2006); http://plato.stanford.edu/valuepluralism.

24. See both studies by John Rawls: *A Theory of Justice* (Cambridge: Harvard University Press, 1971) and *Political Liberalism* (New York: Columbia University Press, 1993).

25. John Gray, *Two Faces of Liberalism* (Cambridge: Polity Press, 2000), p. 74.

26. Id., p. 92.

27. See Joseph Raz, *The Morality of Freedom* (Oxford: Oxford University Press, 1986), ch. 14, and chapter 4 *infra*.

28. Id., p. 133. "Moral pluralism asserts the existence of a multitude of incompatible but morally valuable forms of life. It is coupled with an advocacy of autonomy. It naturally combines with the view that individuals should develop freely to find for themselves the form of the good which they wish to pursue in their life. . . . But there is nothing here which speaks for neutrality. For it is the goal of all political action to enable individuals to pursue valid conceptions of the good and to discourage evil or empty ones."

29. How does one measure the lack of autonomy? Is autonomy a supervening value or a component of other values? Is autonomy an intrinsic good for Raz, instrumental in determining good choices, or both? See Gray (2000), pp. 96–104.

30. Joseph Raz, *Ethics and the Public Domain* (Oxford: Clarendon Press, 1994).

31. Joseph Raz, "The Practice of Value," in *Tanner Lectures on Human Value*, ed. Grethe B. Peterson (Salt Lake City: University of Utah Press, 2003), vol. 11, pp. 113–150.

32. See Gray (2000), pp. 96–99, regarding the conflict between the central role of personal autonomy in Raz' theory and value pluralism.

33. Joseph Raz, *Engaging Reason* (Oxford: Oxford University Press, 1999), p. 47. For Raz, "The will is the ability to choose and perform intentional actions. We exercise our will when we endorse the verdict of reason that we must perform an action, and we do so, whether willingly, reluctantly, or regretting the need, etc. According to the classical conception, however, the most typical exercise or manifestation of the will is in choosing among options that reason renders eligible."

34. For example, see Thomas Nagel, "The Fragmentation of Value," in *Moral Questions* (Cambridge: Cambridge University Press, 1991), pp. 128–141.

35. See Michael Sandel, *Liberalism and the Limits of Justice,* 2nd ed. (Cambridge: Cambridge University Press, 1998).

36. See Brian Barry, *Political Argument* (Berkeley: University of California Press, 1990), pp. 3–8.

37. Bernard Williams, *Moral Luck* (Cambridge: Cambridge University Press, 1981); see also chapter 4 *infra*.

38. Bernard Williams, *Ethics and the Limits of Philosophy* (Cambridge: Harvard University Press, 1985), p. 17.

39. Rawls (1971), p. viii.

40. Id., p. 62.

41. Id., p. 60.

42. See H. L. A. Hart, "Rawls on Liberty and Its Priority," in *Reading Rawls,* ed. Norman Daniels (Oxford: Blackwell, 1975), pp. 206–229. Hart also raises the question of whether there are secondary sets of principles for nonbasic liberties, id., pp. 238–239. Further, it is not clear whether Hart attributes a concept of negative liberty to Rawls, as part of his theory of justice as fairness, rather than the triadic one to which Rawls subscribes.

43. Hart (1975), p. 241.

44. John Rawls, "The Priority of the Right and Ideas of the Good," *Philosophy and Public Affairs* 17: 251–256 (1988).

45. Rawls (1971), p. 550.

46. Id., p. 574.

47. Michael Sandel believes that one version of the liberal-communitarian debate remains interesting, namely, the debate concerning the right versus the good. See Sandel (1998).

48. Mill (1998), p. 14.

49. See chapter 4 *infra.*

50. As Raz states, "If there is one common thread to the argument of this book [*Morality of Freedom*] it is its critiques of individualism and its endeavour to argue for a liberal morality on non-individualistic grounds." Raz (1986), p. 18. By individualism, Raz means, "the doctrine that only states of individual human beings, or aspects of their lives, can be good or valuable." Raz (1986), p. 18.

51. Id., p. 162.

Chapter 6

The Nature of the Polity

The political context for many contemporary accounts of justice is liberalism. Liberalism may be understood as a political tradition, a political philosophy, or a more general philosophical theory. Beyond category there is, of course, a variety of liberalisms, leaving the term with no one universal or commonly accepted meaning. That said, often the term *liberal* as used in political theory positions freedom or liberty, and equality or equality of concern and respect, as core notions. It is mostly the political theory that interests me here, and the liberal context I favor gives prominent place to equality, as well as including the concepts of tolerance and diversity.

In addition to a predominantly liberal context, many contemporary commentators on justice posit a version of democracy or democratic principles as the appropriate mode of government, although democracy as known today is per se a relatively recent political form. The word *democracy* (*demokratia*) derives from *kratos* (power or rule) and *demos* (people), and thus is intended to signify "rule by the people." Indeed, scholars have turned to the fifth and fourth centuries B.C. in ancient Greece, especially to the democratic *polis* of Athens, to examine the evolution of democratic institutions and ideals in city-states. Ancient Athenian democracy, however, was not a representative form of government. Further, although a political system that involved direct rule by citizens, citizenship was reserved to free males, aged eighteen or older, thereby excluding, for example, women, slaves, and most Greeks, from political life.[1] From third century B.C. to A.D. nineteenth century, democracies in Western states were only "momentary realities," with the word *democracy* coming into favorable use again only in the nineteenth century and coming to designate a state governed by a majority, who themselves are represented in the process of governance.[2]

Modern liberal political society is antithetical to Plato's ideal society, which envisions a closed system that is well ordered and hierarchal and ideally organized in a true constitution under the rule of a philosopher king.[3] Law-abiding constitutions are involved in the pursuit of knowledge, and the motive of their rulers is to seek the common good. In contrast, non-law-abiding constitutions are characterized by ignorant self-interest. As introduced in chapter 2, Plato delineates six imitative constitutions arranged in hierarchal order from most to least tolerable forms of governance.[4] He designates democracy as the third-best form of governance (after kingship and aristocracy) in law-abiding imitative constitutions, but also as the best of the three non-law-abiding imitative constitutions (the others being tyranny and oligarchy).

For Aristotle, "man is by nature a political animal" and his views of political justice differ deeply from those of Plato as to the organization and ends of political society.[5] Nonetheless, in his *Politics*, Aristotle adapts Plato's six forms of governance, as delineated in *The Statesman*.[6] While accepting Plato's taxonomy, Aristotle's vision of political society, critically, allows for less than perfect governance.

Modifying these classical views of citizens and the *polis*, the development of modern political theory may be traced to Thomas Hobbes, who foregrounds the state of nature and the human condition as in perpetual competition, where there exists a "war of every man against everyman."[7] With this view of nature and of humanity, Hobbes develops a social contract theory, a method of justifying political principles or arrangements, by appeal to the agreement that would be made among suitably situated, rational, free, and equal persons. Hobbes arrives, however, at the surprising conclusion that we ought to submit to the authority of an absolute—undivided and unlimited—sovereign power, so as to ameliorate life which would otherwise be "solitary, poor, nasty, brutish, and short."[8] In a sense, and contrary to Aristotle's moral viewpoint, Hobbes emphasizes the lack of virtue in the human enterprise, but arrives at both Plato's and Aristotle's conclusion that authority orders, organizes, and governs best.

In contemporary times, John Gray carries forward this Hobbesian view of the world in an indictment of the liberal project. He holds that liberal political theory either adopts an overly Eurocentric view of history in the formulation of its principles or, in deriving principles from practical reason, attempts to deny that history exists. It is from this standpoint that he views liberalism and value pluralism as rival doctrines, and in driving value pluralism to a logical conclusion defined in a Hobbesian manner, Gray argues that *modus vivendi* should be the order of the day.[9]

While also writing in the social contract tradition, in contrast to Hobbes, John Locke develops a rights-based account which heralds modern liberal political thought, thereby arguing more in the tradition of Aristotle than Plato.

In this tradition, as also developed by Jean-Jacques Rousseau, John Rawls, as one example, develops his influential theory of justice as fairness.[10]

CLASSIC LIBERALISM

Classic liberalism is said to be grounded in negative liberty, according to Isaiah Berlin, since negative liberty focuses on the removal of obstacles to liberty.[11] Berlin further advocates a negative concept of liberty, which would protect an individual from "deliberate interference of other human beings within the area in which he could otherwise act."[12] Berlin's well-known concept thus proposes freedom from governmental coercion or enslavement, and consequently, he views the liberal state as committed to ensuring that citizens do not coerce one another without compelling justification.

For liberal political theory, the burden of justification is placed on those who would limit freedom, underscoring the fundamental importance in determining whether political authority can be justified and under what circumstances. Ultimately, political authority must justify limits placed on the liberty of citizens.[13] Given this basic tenet's importance in liberal political theory, there is no consensus regarding the concept of liberty, which, not surprisingly, results in different conceptions of the proper tasks of government.

An extreme version of liberty-based liberalism, for example, may be found in libertarian thought. Opposed to a social contract theory as the political justification of government, Robert Nozick develops a libertarian account of justice in which there is the rise of a Dominant Protection Agency that leads to the development of a minimal state.[14] At another level, some classic liberals believe that individual persons are ontologically superior to social groups and that persons and their identities are distinct. Further, they believe that central to the concept of personhood is a capacity to choose among alternate ways of living. In such regard, they may be susceptible to the "communitarian critique of liberalism" since, by according the self as in some ways prior to the ends and substantive attachments of the person, they have "disembodied" themselves (implausibly so, say some communitarians) from their ends and values.[15] This level of inquiry presents the difficulty of defining what an individual is and what defines her or his purpose or end.

In spite of the various discussions on the concept of liberty and ensuing debates about the function of government, contemporary political discourse does generally agree that the liberal position includes the concept of equality or equality of concern and respect and, in fact, the dominant approach in recent liberal political theory, certainly in the past half century, is to hold the concept of equality as the core concept in liberal political thought.[16]

Liberty and the Harm Principle

While his essay "On Liberty" does not represent an account of justice as such, John Stuart Mill's political text probes the relationship between individual liberty and governmental authority. In doing so, Mill provides the political context for some contemporary theories of justice.[17] That is, even though many contemporary theories of justice focus on the equality element of liberalism, Mill's harm principle, in defining liberty (negative liberty, according to Berlin), has proven to be foundational in the political account of classic liberalism. Thus, Mill argues that "the only purpose for which power can be rightfully exercised over any member of a civilized community, against his will, is to prevent harm to others."[18] His famous harm principle further provides that "the sole end for which mankind are warranted, individually or collectively, in interfering with the liberty of action of any of their number, is self-protection."[19]

Theoretically, his "one simple principle" operates in two steps: (1) the inquiry is made as to whether liberty is restricted, and if so, (2) a calculus of harms is developed. Standing alone, the principle's restrictions on liberty resemble the kind of teleological rule proposed by Aristotle rather than forming part of an utilitarian happiness calculus. It also seems very much like a statement proposing liberty as an intrinsic good, reminiscent of Plato, rather than articulating a simpler instrumental justification. As such, the problem is whether the harm principle may subsist in a value monist view of utilitarianism.[20] Much criticized, as discussed in chapter 5, Mill's harm principle can in various ways be faulted for indeterminacy.[21]

The traditional criticisms and received opinion of Mill's liberalism focus on his attempt to derive a liberal political theory from utilitarian moral principles, an attempt to square the circle, as illustrated by his use of the utility principle. That is, Mill's harm principle applies a subsumed utility principle concerned with collective well-being grounded, however, in a strong principle of liberty, which is concerned with protecting the individual.[22] Such contradictory linkages draw criticism in other ways. Berlin, for example, regards Mill's account as incoherent, since Mill defended liberty as having intrinsic value while also claiming to ground his argument in utilitarianism.[23] Gray's view of Mill's attempt is that "such a principle [the principle of utility] can supply only a necessary, and not sufficient, condition for the just restraint of liberty."[24]

Likewise, although Mill intends the harm principle not to be morally dependent (and in that sense, anti-perfectionist), many judgments concerning harm depend on a rich, context-dependent concept of the good. Thus, what constitutes harm is seen as socially contingent and not a morally neutral idea, thereby subjecting the harm principle to further criticism with regard to its underlying concept of human interests.[25] Moreover, it is difficult to determine what is meant by harm. Thus, distinguishing between harm and mere offense, Mill's purpose in wielding the harm principle is to expand liberty and to exclude paternalism (although this *desideratum* does not hold in all cases), as exemplified in his views on birth control and the appropriateness for some women, given their circumstances, to have children. But, as easily imagined, the distinction between what constitutes harm or offense in any given situation is not always clear, and essentially, Mill would allow for instances of soft paternalism. The difficulty of determining what is meant by harm, then, obscures the application of Mill's concept of the permanent interests to be protected and consequently makes the application of the principle more troublesome.[26]

At times, Mill's attempts to square the circle prove useful, as seen in Mill's seemingly contradictory linkage of fallibilism with progress. Influenced by the Enlightenment tradition, fallibilists strongly reject the notion of skepticism, believe that all knowledge is revisable, and that there are therefore no foundations of knowledge. As Mill presents this view, his fallibilism is inductive, anti-skeptical, and anti-intuitive (i.e., there are no self-evident truths). Because he believes that knowledge is revisable and benign, for example, Mill has a very broad notion of free expression, limited only by incitement, and thereby reserving the harm principle's applicability only to actions and not to speech.[27]

While Mill argues that knowledge is constructive, he also argues that knowledge, contrary to a fallibilist perspective, does have foundations. Because knowledge has foundations, however, Mill can also bring in the idea of progress, which serves as a measure in the sense of cumulative improvements in ethics and politics. Indeed, for Mill, progress fits into a perfectionist theory of right action, promoting "utility in the largest sense, grounded on the permanent interests of man as a progressive being."[28] Moreover, allowing for foundational knowledge that is constructive and for progress that promotes utility comprises Mill's active happiness for individuals, which entails a pluralistic framework, since it involves different experiments in living for different people.

Gray relates Mill's views on progress to an indictment of the liberal project itself, whether grounded in a view of the priority of the good, as appear in Mill's and Raz' accounts, or in a view of the priority of the right, as with the accounts of John Rawls, Ronald Dworkin, and Brian Barry, among others. Yet, even while linking apparently contradictory ideas, Mill does provide valuable tools, as when he brings the notion of progress to bear upon decisions involving incommensurable moral values.[29] That is, believing in a fallibilist vision of progress makes the concept of choice important to Mill, perhaps more than instrumentally so. It appears that for Mill, an architecture of choices has independent, intrinsic value, although such a structure can also produce additional tensions, especially when faced with incommensurable belief systems of alternate lifestyles, as illustrated when a monk pursues acquisitive activities for personal gain. Importantly here, when faced with incommensurable values, Mill's concept of progress, though complicated and at times inconsistent with some of his other views, does provide tools with which to form a moral decision.

It is in this respect that Berlin argues that the concept of negative liberty is at the heart of Mill's liberalism.[30] Others, however, have emphasized instead how freedom from societal conventions and constraints and the "moral coercion of public opinion" inform Mill's concept of liberty.[31] Indeed, at the foundation of his thought, Mill bases his argument for the primacy of freedom on the good of developing individuality and cultivating individual capacities,[32] thereby extending his scope beyond political theory to articulate a substantive, perfectionist, moral theory of the good.

In this framework, Mill values the Aristotelian concept of the virtuous or excellent individual, which he links to his liberal political theory. In other words, Mill combines the excellence of individuality with the Greek emphasis on the active development of human powers, powers that will differ from individual to individual. Mill's morally informed political argument then leads to the conclusion that since liberal societies allow maximum scope for diverse modes of pursuing happiness, they are the most conducive to individuality. Indeed, since liberal societies rest upon individual freedom, they tend to promote the self-determination that is at the heart of individuality.[33]

Positive Liberty

Positive liberty—the freedom to do what one is supposed to do—has often been associated pejoratively with Plato. Thus, many liberals, including Berlin, have suggested that the positive concept of liberty carries with it a danger of authoritarianism and totalitarianism. In the case of a longstanding and oppressed minority, for instance, positive liberty may be especially insidious. Because members of an established minority may be said to participate in a democratic process defined by majority rule, they may be characterized as free simply on the grounds that they are members of a society exercising self-control over its own affairs. But the very fact that such members comprise a minority who, for all intents and purposes, have no access to power or participation in the configuring of power means that their "freedom" is of little practical value. In such a case, even majority members might be oppressed in the name of liberty.

Joseph Raz exemplifies contemporary thought on positive liberty, for which the conceptual touchstone is that good triumphs over right.[34] As discussed in chapter 5, Raz' analyses of value pluralism, his central concept of personal autonomy, and the idea of social forms mutually support his approach to a liberal perfectionist system of governance. His theory, however, fails to provide either assistance or method for making decisions involving conflicting moral values, since his strong value pluralistic views preclude his use of his own concept of autonomy, even in an instrumental fashion, as well as the ranking of social goods constituting his perfectionist scheme. Raz further fails to find a plausible solution to the problem of moral incommensurability and is left with the potential of sliding into subjectivism or the possibility of relativism.

More specifically, Raz' value pluralism seems ontologically unconnected to his account of social forms, thus depriving his account of fundamental resources. By not allowing his concept of personal autonomy to rise to the level of an overarching value, together with his radical reinterpretation of Mill's harm principle to support a conception of the good, Raz develops a liberal perfectionist political structure that seems curiously lacking in many of the characteristics expected in a liberal political order, namely, tolerance, diversity, and respect for other ways of life, regardless of whether, ultimately, an individual believes in the good over the right, which through extension, represents Raz' view on justice.

Tolerance and Diversity

Berlin is situated in the classical liberal view, and on the role of negative liberty Berlin reveals that he is a value pluralist who maintains that negative liberty derives from value pluralism. His argument begins by noting that value pluralism involves making choices "between absolute claims" and that the making of choices is an "inescapable characteristic" of the human condition.[35] From this platform, he infers that individuals place "immense value on the freedom to choose."[36] In other words, Berlin reasons that because individuals must choose, it follows that the freedom to choose is valued, and a political order that protects this freedom is cherished as well. For Berlin, a liberal political order based upon providing negative liberty yields the most legitimate kind of state, and value pluralism must consequently entail liberalism, thereby promoting tolerance and diversity.[37]

Among criticisms of his view is the observation that Berlin's argument suffers from a classic Humean "is-ought" error. Even granting that the inevitability of choice leads individuals to value strongly the freedom to choose, it does not follow that the state *ought* to provide or protect such freedom. Paradoxically, to do so would lead the state to recognizing an overriding value (free choice), thereby violating value pluralism. John Gray, who makes this point, further argues that value pluralism is consistent with a range of non-liberal political orders.[38]

Although Berlin's argument has been much criticized, several contemporary thinkers, including William Galston, have attempted to revive Berlin's project. The appeal in doing so is clear. A value pluralist liberalism, as Galston avers, would have the potential to "connect what one believes to be the best account of public life with comparably persuasive accounts of morality, human psychology, and the natural world."[39] Moreover, at least superficially, the inference from value pluralism to liberalism seems simple and natural. That is, value pluralism may be seen as a theory of the moral universe that provides for many kinds of goods and a plurality of valuable ways of life, thereby creating the possibility and conditions for tolerance and diversity. In this particular respect, value pluralism accords well with liberalism which, according to Mill, is a political order that attempts to provide the greatest possible freedom for individuals to "pursue [their] own good in [their] own way."[40] Moreover, Galston accepts the view that not all values are commensurable—they may neither be reduced to a single overarching value nor completely rank-ordered.

Beyond these points, however, Galston's basic view of value pluralism proves problematic in regard to those many forms of liberalism in which justice is viewed as the "first virtue of social institutions."[41] Likewise, his view can prove difficult for liberals who favor a lexical ordering among goods. In Brian Barry's liberal theory, for example, equality has a prime role,[42] and for Robert Nozick, liberty represents such an overarching value.[43]

Importantly here, in contrast to these and other thinkers who adopt the classical approach of making liberty central to liberalism, in his political theory, Galston foregrounds social diversity and tolerance; "[p]roperly understood, liberalism is about the protection of legitimate diversity."[44] Galston's approach to resuscitating Berlin's project is not to argue directly that value pluralism entails liberalism, but rather, that value pluralism defeats all non-liberal options. He thereby contends that it would be unreasonable for a state to impose a single way of life on its citizens. Indirectly, however, Galston does argue that value pluralism entails liberalism. That is, similar to Berlin, for Galston the inevitability of choice creates a presumption in favor of *expressive liberty*, by which term Galston means the liberty "of individuals and groups leading their lives as they see fit."[45] Galston consequently assumes that it is the mark of an illiberal regime to restrict or reject expressive liberty, and if value pluralism holds true, there could be no legitimate reason for such a restriction. Thus, he concludes that negative liberty derives from value pluralism in the absence of any legitimate reasons for restricting it.

Regardless of its merits, Galston's argument assumes that if value pluralism defeats all non-liberal views, it must support liberalism, an argument that proceeds by way of elimination. For his argument to succeed—even if he is only indirectly arguing that value pluralism entails liberalism—Galston must exhaustively cover the terrain of illiberal regimes that do not restrict negative liberty. One form of liberalism, libertarianism, offers a counterexample, however, since it functions as just such an illiberal regime that, in Galston's construct, would be clearly inconsistent with value pluralism. That is, while asserting the rights of individuals, libertarianism at the same time restricts them insofar as it denies government the power to protect multiple choices. In this manner, Galston's argument fails to develop an effective conceptual link between value pluralism and liberalism. Indeed, in his approach, even Plato's *Republic* may be seen as consistent with value pluralism.[46]

Berlin's and Galston's attention to what Galston terms expressive liberty, under the aegis of classic liberalism, has not settled the relationship of value pluralism to liberty or other political values. Focusing specifically on the argument of whether value pluralism entails liberalism, for example, Gray reasons that Berlin's value pluralism undermines liberalism's traditional claims to universal authority. As a result, liberalism is seen to occupy no more pride of place in Berlin's scheme than other legitimate political forms, and negative liberty does indeed form only one incommensurable good among others.[47] Consequently, for Gray, value pluralism asserts that illiberal societies are not necessarily inferior to liberal ones; indeed, value pluralism and liberalism comprise rival doctrines. This observation supports Gray's echoing of Hobbes' reliance upon the principle of *modus vivendi* to effect a state where conflicting parties may nonetheless coexist.[48]

In sum, Galston's argument that value pluralism necessarily leads to a liberal political order is flawed. However, the concepts of tolerance and diversity may be seen as a natural fit to a theory of political liberalism. In other words, while Galston's ontological argument portraying the diversion of such concepts into a liberal political formulation may be flawed, I favor integrating their presence into a formulation of liberalism as the proper political context for justice.[49]

EGALITARIAN CONCERNS

In his thoughts on justice, which he divides into individual moral virtue and justice in society, Aristotle articulates what has become a foundational view regarding the concept of equality, which he discusses as underlying particular justice. Focusing on Aristotle's examination of the concept of equality, many contemporary accounts of justice emphasize the equality component of liberalism, rather than the component of liberty, in their political theories.[50] Consequently, contemporary accounts often generate more granular discussions on what it means to treat individuals equally as well as to what equality references.

Fairness

In Aristotle's taxonomy, equality comprises two considerations, that of distributive justice and fairness. John Rawls' first principle of justice tackles fairness, for which the foundation is the equality of basic liberties. Writing in reaction to the then predominant theory of utilitarianism, which posits that the greatest good for the greatest number of people defines justice, Rawls begins *A Theory of Justice* with the statement that "justice is the first virtue of social institutions."[51] With this assertion, Rawls echoes both Aristotle and Mill and defines justice as fairness as based on a social contract. Engaging in a thought experiment, he further asks us to imagine ourselves in the original position, the position of rational, free, and equal persons who jointly agree upon and commit to principles of social and political justice. In other words, our operative ideas of justice should result from a hypothetical situation that incorporates all relevant moral and practical considerations. The original position, he explains, serves as the most effective place to apply the maximin rule—whereby the action whose worst outcome proves better than the worst outcome of all other alternatives. Rather than the principle of (average) utility, justice as fairness thereby argues for a conservative strategy of choice under uncertainty.[52]

Continuing the thought experiment, the critical and novel feature of Rawls' original position is the veil of ignorance, whereby individuals are deprived of all knowledge of their personal characteristics and social and historical circumstances. All that Rawls specifies is that all individuals are rational, free, and morally equal persons; moreover, they are autonomous and act from moral principles constructed from and expressive of the moral powers of agency that constitute our nature as free and equal, rational moral beings. As such, the veil of ignorance attempts to ensure impartiality in the autonomous choice of and agreement upon principles of justice. Rawls further imagines that parties in the original position are presented with a list of the main conceptions of justice drawn from the traditions of social and political philosophy, so that they can choose the conception of justice that best advances their interests. Thus, the selection process entails a reflective equilibrium, which has been interpreted as a coherentist method used to justify moral beliefs epistemically.[53]

Underlying the thought experiment, not unlike Aristotle's reliance on virtue, Rawls relies upon human beings to possess a sense of justice, which provides a source of moral judgment as well as a source of moral motivation. Beginning with considered judgments that arise from this sense of justice, parties are to engage in a deliberative process, reflecting upon and revising their considered beliefs until they are in equilibrium; that is, until the resultant principles of justice are stable and consistent with one another. Equilibrium, in other words, must be achieved as a consensus among different interests and needs. To posit this process of equilibrium as a workable mechanism, Rawls assumes social norms that would allow cooperation, which of course are both possible and necessary in a social contract.

Nonetheless, Rawls understands that society is also marked by members' conflicts of interest that lead to different conceptions of the good (the subjective condition of justice) as well as to different approaches to distributing resources (the objective condition of justice). Given these two conditions—the subjective and the objective conditions of justice—principles of justice are required to mediate between individuals' needs and desires and to divide the benefits and burdens of social cooperation, since "[a]ll social primary goods—liberty and opportunity, income, wealth, and the bases of self-respect—are to be distributed equally unless and unequal distribution of any or all of these goods is to the advantage of the least favoured" (Rawls 1971, 303). He thereby modulates his consideration of fairness through distribution concerns, recalling Aristotle's pairing of fairness with distribution responsibilities in his view of a type of particular justice.

To effect this approach to justice as fairness, Rawls contends that the most rational choice for parties in the original position yields two principles of justice, as follows:

> *First Principle*
>
> Each person is to have an equal right to the most extensive total system of equal basic liberties compatible with a similar system of liberty for all.
>
> *Second Principle*
>
> Social and economic inequalities are to be arranged so that they are both:
>
> 1. To the greatest benefit of the least advantaged, consistent with the just savings principle, and
> 2. Attached to offices and positions open to all under conditions of fair equality of opportunity.[54]

The first principle of justice as fairness, the basic liberty principle, guarantees the equal basic rights and liberties needed to secure the fundamental interests of free and equal citizens and to pursue a wide range of conceptions of the good, including these basic freedoms: liberty of conscience and freedom of thought, freedom of association, the political liberties, the rights and liberties constituting freedom of the person (including the right to hold personal property), and the rights and liberties of the rule of law.

These liberties, Rawls argues, are necessary to develop and exercise moral powers and to pursue a wide range of differing but reasonable conceptions of the good. Having staked the claim, Rawls formulates a second principle, the difference claim. Thus, his second principle regulates differences (inequalities) in primary social goods by providing fair equality of educational and employment opportunities and a guaranteed minimum of the all-purpose means (including income and wealth), so that all individuals can pursue their interests, powers, and prerogatives of office as well as maintain self-respect. Rawls views the individual's pursuit of interests as critical to distributive justice, while through his second priority rule, establishing the priority of justice over efficiency and welfare (the Pareto principle), as well as over the ideal of maximizing the sum of advantages in society.

Resources

In contrast to Rawls' focus on fairness in distributions, the account of Ronald Dworkin promotes a complex equality as the sovereign, indispensable political virtue of democratic sovereignty. To do so, he also evokes fairness and distribution principles in order to develop equality as a complex and multifaceted ideal. Thus, Dworkin begins *Sovereign Virtue* with his concern that equality is "the endangered species of political ideals," noting that even left-of-center politicians reject equality as an ideal.[55] In effect, Dworkin raises the question of whether we are under a duty of justice to help those responsible for the fact that they need help. Complications arise in distinguishing between matters of choice and matters of chance in his account, as well as with regard to justice for future generations in the redistributions of resources he advocates.

Although government must combat poverty, Dworkin argues, government seems not intent on making its citizens equal in any regard. He continues to argue against this stance in Kantian vein, as he asserts that no government may be legitimate that does not show an equal respect and concern for the lives of its citizens, and thus his account is in that sense similar to Robert Nozick's theory discussed later (see chapter 8). For Dworkin, however, the Kantian precept must inform the abstract and fundamental political ideal of treating all citizens as equals. Further unlike Nozick, Dworkin believes that a legitimate government must treat all its citizens as equals, and since the economic distributions of a society are largely a consequence of its system of laws and policies, this requirement imposes serious egalitarian constraints on such distributions.

In this framework, Dworkin views the concept of equality as foundational to all political and civil liberties and underscores that a political community cannot have legitimate authority unless it treats its members with equal respect. Importantly, equal respect entails that a government remain substantially neutral on questions concerning what makes a good life, thereby allowing individuals to formulate their own life plans. Intentions to the contrary, this political view may pose a theoretical conflict with Dworkin's own concept of liberty and its embedded notion of equality. That is, neutrality on what constitutes a good life may be intended as a guideline to respect the individual, but as such, it weakens the overarching structure through lack of definition.

For example, Dworkin does not recognize the conflict between liberty and equality that concerned Isaiah Berlin, arguing that no concept of liberty can reflect the value-free political process notion of negative liberty that Berlin proposes.[56] Instead, Dworkin develops a concept of liberty that includes elements of his own concept of equality, arguing that liberty must be conceptually based on some substantive concept of the good, of right and wrong. We cannot claim, for instance, that an individual's liberty is infringed upon when the individual is prevented from committing murder. In other words, liberty is not diminished when preventing harm, or for that matter, when no wrong has been perpetrated. Nonetheless, by defining liberty in accordance with some other value, Dworkin may be engaging, ironically, in precisely the type of exercise that leads to Berlin's account of positive liberty and the totalitarian dangers against which Berlin warns.

In support of his concept of equality of resources, Dworkin's distributive approach to justice articulates significant connections among the concepts of responsibility, justice, and equality. Fundamentally, underlying his theory is the liberal egalitarian concern with neutrality with regard to various conceptions of the good life. In order to allow for various conceptions of the good life, Dworkin creates an auction scheme supported by an insurance plan funded by means of the auction. The purpose of this thought experiment is to articulate a means by which individuals' choices and chance advantages might be leveled, and in this manner, allowing neutrality with respect to different definitions of the good life.

Jerry Cohen, however, rejects the simple contrast that Dworkin makes between choice and chance, along with the resultant distributive mechanisms of Dworkin's auction plus insurance scheme. Cohen's main contention is that the distinction between choice and brute luck is often not easily defined and that an individual's ambition-sensitive drives are, indeed, often matters of luck or chance.[57] Cohen further rejects Dworkin's theory of resource equality, arguing that the market outcomes that drive the theory are morally arbitrary.[58] Multiculturalists such as Will Kymlicka make similar arguments (see chapter 8), contending that an individual's cultural identity and affiliation are often not matters, strictly viewed, that are chosen.[59] Both Cohen and Kymlicka, that is, point to the arbitrariness of determining varieties of luck.

Dworkin's distinction is certainly controversial, but so too is Cohen's focus on economic matters. Moreover, both views point to the issue of where to draw the line between choice and chance, thereby also raising the question of whether a fuller theory of responsibility is necessary (see chapter 4), or whether any such position could be supported. This controversy is reminiscent of the indeterminacy issues associated with Mill's harm principle. As discussed earlier, in a given situation, it may be an intractably complex matter to determine whether an action constitutes harm or mere offense, since many judgments of harm depend on a rich, non-neutral, context-laden, socially contingent concept of the good.

The same is true when trying to distinguish between matters of choice and matters of chance. Putting aside practical questions such as the enormous administrative structure necessitated should Dworkin's hypothetical auction plus insurance scheme ever be actualized, the basic ability to distinguish between choice or chance situations in Dworkin's moral construct is especially difficult and subject to myriads of variables. While attempting to introduce individual moral responsibility into his conception of justice, Dworkin fails to provide sufficient tools or methods of deciding between choice or chance situations.

Real-World Comparisons

In *The Idea of Justice*,[60] Amartya Sen criticizes Rawls' account of justice as an idealized "transcendental" construct overly focused on the creation of just institutions, in contrast to his own comparative real-life approach to the question of justice. Unfortunately, though, Sen's comparative approach provides no guidance as to making decisions with respect to the real-world questions of justice he presents. That is, Sen provides no ranking, or criteria, in his comparative social justice account by which to make comparisons.

Sen's criticism of Rawls construct includes the contractarian nature of Rawls' model, based on a hypothetical social contract, and the creation of an "ideal theory"—justice as fairness—which generates principles through a veil of ignorance (and later in Rawls' revised account, through reflective equilibrium), principles for establishing just institutions in society. These institutions provide for such matters as equal liberty, fair equality of opportunity, and material differences justified only on the basis that they benefit the least advantaged. This last focus of Rawls, just institutions, perhaps constitutes an overly political answer to the question of justice, somewhat begging the normative question.

As an example of his real-world comparable approach to justice, Sen provides the flute example,[61] in which there are three children, Ann, Bob, and Carla, who argue over who should have a flute. Ann claims the flute on the basis that she is the only one who can play it. Bob claims the flute because he has no other toys to play with, while the others do. Carla claims the flute based on the fact that she made the flute in the first place. Sen's point is that one can produce intuitively plausible reasons for giving the flute to any of the children: utilitarians might favor Ann; egalitarians might favor Bob; and, libertarians might favor Carla. Unfortunately, though, Sen's comparative approach provides no guidance as to which child should be given the flute.

As another real-world analogy, and criticism of Rawls' ideal theory, Sen provides the *Mona Lisa* example.[62] In asking the question of whether a van Gogh or a Picasso is the better painting, it does not help to be told that the *Mona Lisa* is the best painting of all time. Sen's point is that pursuing justice is about making comparisons. Unfortunately, though, again Sen's comparative approach provides no ranking or criteria to determine, in this case, which is the better painting.[63] Further, the analogy itself may not be especially apt, as it seems to present questions of aesthetics, rather than questions of justice.

It appears that underlying Sen's comparative approach is a belief in the power of reason. Quoting from Ludwig Wittgenstein, Sen states that "what can be said clearly; and whereof one cannot speak thereof one must be silent."[64] For Sen, a smarter human being is a better human being, and a smarter world is a better world. An example of the belief in the power of rationality may be found in his discussion of capital punishment.[65] Unfortunately, though, while Sen appears not to favor a death penalty, even this example of his comparative approach provides no guidance as to what decision to make. Further, Sen's comparative approach does not effectively accommodate irrational decisions that may be made in comparative real-world situations.

The political context for Sen's views on liberty are pluralist and egalitarian.[66] His egalitarianism leads to a defense of democracy.[67] Interestingly, his defense of democracy appears based in part on the power of rationality ("depend[ing] on the contributions from discussion and discourse"[68]), and for rational help, he offers the concept of the impartial observer.[69] Further, he presents the observation that democracies seem immune from famine.[70] Here, I will not engage in a full-blown discussion of democracy, its merits and demerits, other than to suggest that perhaps a theory of justice should include provision for providing guidance in questions of justice, whether the underlying governmental model is democratic or not.[71]

NOTES

1. It has been estimated that in the fifth and fourth centuries B.C., the number of citizens fluctuated between 20,000 and 40,000, amid a population of 200,000 or

more inhabitants of Attica. See R. K. Sinclair, *Democracy and Participation in Athens* (Cambridge: Cambridge University Press, 1988), p. 114; generally, see P. Cartledge, *The Greeks* (Oxford: Oxford University Press, 2012).

2. Janet Coleman, *A History of Political Thought* (Oxford: Blackwell Publishing Ltd., 2000), p. 22.

3. See Plato, *The Republic,* trans. Desmond Lee, 2nd ed. (London: Penguin Books, 2003), and chapter 2 *infra.*

4. See chapter 2, note 26 *infra* and accompanying text.

5. Aristotle, *Politics*, trans. T.A. Sinclair, rev. Trevor Saunders (London: Penguin Books, 1992) I.1253a.

6. Id., I.7, and *Constitutions* in chapter 3 *infra.*

7. Thomas Hobbes, *Leviathan*, ed. J. C. A. Gaskin (Oxford: Oxford University Press, 1998), p. 76; "*Bellum omnium contra omnes*."

8. Id., p. 76, pp. 76–81.

9. See John Gray, *Mill on Liberty: A Defence*, 2nd ed. (Oxford: Routledge, 1996), pp. 130–131, and John Gray, *Two Faces of Liberalism* (Cambridge: Polity Press, 2000).

10. See John Rawls, *A Theory of Justice* (Cambridge: Harvard University Press, 1971); John Locke, *Second Treatise of Government*, ed. Crawford Brough Macpherson (Indianapolis: Hacket Publishing, 1980); Jean-Jacques Rousseau, *The Social Contract*, trans. Maurice Cranton (London: Penguin Books, 1968);

11. Isaiah Berlin, "Two Concepts of Liberty," in *Four Essays on Liberty* (Oxford: Oxford University Press, 1969), pp. 118–172.

12. Berlin (1969), p. 122.

13. Accordingly, disparate political theorists such as Hobbes, Locke, Rousseau, and Kant may all be grouped together as subscribing to a social contract theory of political authority, which provides one approach in response to the foundational problem of justification and limits on an individual's freedom.

14. See Robert Nozick, *Anarchy, State, and Utopia* (New York: Basic Books, 1974).

15. See Michael Sandel, *Liberalism and the Limits of Justice*, 2nd ed. (Cambridge: Cambridge University Press, 1998). Sandel targets "Kantian liberals," in general, and John Rawls in particular.

16. For example, see Rawls (1971); John Rawls, *Political Liberalism* (New York: Columbia University Press, 1993); Ronald Dworkin, *Sovereign Virtue* (Cambridge: Harvard University Press, 2000); see also Paul Kelly, *Liberalism* (Cambridge: Polity Press, 2005). These egalitarian thinkers share a rights-based deontological view, which is often concerned with the institutions and mechanisms in society that provide for a just distribution of social goods, and they subscribe to a liberal neutrality with regard to conflicting conceptions of the good.

17. John Stuart Mill, "On Liberty," in *John Stuart Mill on Liberty and Other Essays,* ed. John Gray (Oxford: Oxford University Press, 1998).

18. Mill (1998), pp. 14–15.

19. Mill (1998), p. 14.

20. As Gray notes, "the principal paradox of Millian utilitarian liberalism is that the Principle of Liberty actually disqualifies utility-promotion as a reason for restraint of liberty, unless such restraint also prevents harm to others." Mill (1998), p. xix. In

another aspect of political liberalism, that of private property and the market, Mill viewed the "so-called doctrine of Free Trade" as resting on "equally solid" grounds as the "principle of individual liberty" (Mill 1998, p. 105), but insisted that the justifications of individual and economic liberty were distinct.

21. See Jeremy Waldron, *Liberal Rights* (Cambridge: Cambridge University Press, 1993), pp. 117–120, and Gray (1996), pp. 133–158.

22. See chapter 5 regarding classic utilitarianism as a teleological moral theory.

23. Berlin (1969), p. 139, 161. Among those who deny any such contradiction, see John Rees, *John Stuart Mill's On Liberty* (Oxford: Clarendon Press, 1985); see also Jonathan Riley, *Mill on Liberty* (Oxford: Routledge, 1998), ch. 7.

24. Gray (1996), p. 136.

25. See Gray (1996), p. 140.

26. With regard to the moral coercion of public opinion, rather than negative liberty and freedom from governmental inference, a classic positive view of liberty posits autonomous individuals living in different ways (rather than with the same view of the good life), and in this sense living authentic lives. See Gray (1996), pp. 70–86.

27. See Mill (1998), ch. 2.

28. Mill (1998), p. 15.

29. See also Waldron (1993), ch. 5, regarding the contribution of ethical confrontation to Mill's notion of progress.

30. One question raised has been whether Mill was more concerned with the moral coercion of public opinion (arising from public reaction to Mill's affair with Harriet Taylor) rather than governmental interference. If so, then Mill's issue is not so much one of negative liberty, but rather, a concern about freedom of lifestyle.

31. See Nicholas Capaldi, *John Stuart Mill* (Cambridge: Cambridge University Press, 2004), ch. 9; see also Robert Devigne, *Reforming Liberalism* (New Haven: Yale University Press, 2006), ch. 6.

32. Mill (1998), pp. 62–82.

33. "He who lets the world, or his own portion of it, choose his plan of life for him, has no need of any other faculty than the ape-like one of imitation. He who chooses his plan for himself, employs all his faculties." Mill (1998), p. 65.

34. See Joseph Raz, *The Morality of Freedom* (Oxford: Oxford University Press, 1986).

35. Berlin (1969), p. 48.

36. Id., p. 52.

37. See Robert Talisse, "Does Value Pluralism Entail Liberalism?" 2007; http://ssrn.com/abstract=1005651.

38. See Gray (2000) and chapter 5 *infra.*

39. William Galston, "Must Value Pluralism and Religious Belief Collide?" in *The One and the Many,* ed. George Crowder and Henry Hardy (Amherst: Prometheus Books, 2007), p. 252.

40. Mill (1998), p. 17.

41. Rawls (1971), p. 2.

42. See Brian Barry, *Why Social Justice Matters* (London: Polity, 2005).

43. See Nozick (1974).

44. William Galston, *Liberal Pluralism* (Cambridge: Cambridge University Press, 2002), p. 47.

45. William Galston, *The Practice of Liberal Pluralism* (Cambridge: Cambridge University Press, 2005), p. 2.

46. Plato's triadic view of an individual's soul (reason, spirit, and appetite) is replicated and connected to three classes of the state (philosophers, auxiliaries, and producers); see Plato (2003). For value pluralists, if three ways of life are too few, one may increase the number. The fact that the state imposes a way of life on each citizen, however, is sufficient to render the state illiberal.

47. See Gray (2000).

48. See further discussion of Gray's thoughts regarding value pluralism and liberalism as rival doctrines in chapter 5 *infra.*

49. See Conclusion, *infra.*

50. See chapter 5 *infra* as to the deontological approach of a number of contemporary theories of justice, and a discussion of the priority of the right over the good.

51. Rawls (1971), p. 1.

52. While Rawls' use of the maximin rule to arrive at his two principles of justice as fairness has been criticized, parties in the original position might nonetheless arrive at and usefully apply his two principles. Rawls goes to some length to justify the maximin strategy over alternate strategies, such as a maximax strategy and the maximization of expected utility strategy. On critiques of his work, see, for example, John Harsanyi, *Essays on Ethics, Social Behavior and Scientific Explanation* (Dordrecht: D. Reidel, 1976), pp. 37–63; and R. M. Hare, *Essays on Political Morality* (Oxford: Oxford University Press, 1998), ch. 14.

53. Rawls himself confuses the issue in that he sometimes seems to argue that his theory of justice bypasses metaethical questions, including ones of moral epistemology and instead is intended to serve a practical function, that of linking together the cognitive and motivational aspects of the human "sense of justice" in an appropriate manner. For an effective overview, see Norman Daniels, "Reflective Equilibrium," *Stanford Encyclopedia of Philosophy,* 2011 http://plato.stanford.edu/entries/reflective-equilibrium.

54. Rawls (1971), p. 302.

55. Dworkin (2000), p. 1.

56. See Berlin (1969), pp. 118–172.

57. See G. A. Cohen, "Expensive Taste Rides Again," in *Dworkin and His Critics,* ed. Justine Burley (Oxford: Blackwell Publishing, 2004), pp. 3–29.

58. See Cohen (2004).

59. See Will Kymlicka, "Dworkin on Freedom and Culture," in ed. Justine Burley, *Dworkin and His Critics* (Oxford: Blackwell Publishing, 2004), pp. 113–133; see also chapter 8 *infra.*

60. Amartya Sen (2009). *The Idea of Justice.* London: Allen Lane.

61. Sen (2009), p. 12.

62. Sen (2009), p. 101.

63. Sen (2009), chapter 9 regarding moral reasons and pluralism.

64. Sen (2009), p. 31, quoting from Ludwig Wittgenstein's *Tractatus Logico-Philosophicus.*

65. Sen (2009), p. 403ff.
66. See Sen (2009), chapter 14 regarding liberty.
67. See Sen (2009), chapters 14–18.
68. Sen (2009), p. 89.
69. Sen (2009), drawing from Adam Smith in *The Theory of Moral Sentiments*; see pp. 124–135 regarding impartiality.
70. See also Ian Shapiro (2011). *The Real World of Democratic Theory.* Princeton: Princeton University Press.
71. See chapters 2 and 3 *infra* regarding Plato's and Aristotle's respective views of democracy, in the context of political constitutions.

Part III

DEBATES OF JUSTICE

Chapter 7

The Nature of Justice

As discussed earlier, I believe that the examination of justice should consider both moral and political aspects, thereby echoing the classical concept of *dikaiosune* in its micro- and macro-considerations. Now, imagine a number of individuals aboard a boat sailing on a largely uncharted ocean toward an unknown destination. The distribution of tangible and intangible goods among them is certainly a concern. However, how these individuals treat one another morally and how they interact politically on their journey more directly addresses the question of justice and just actions among them. In other words, I view the nature of justice as a relational matter rather than a distributive one. In this chapter, I examine both approaches to the question.

RELATIONAL JUSTICE

By relational justice, I mean a moral and political inquiry into the connections between and among individuals that focuses on their relations in society with respect to how these relationships are established and configured. I see the key to such a relational view as communication, both in a substantive sense as a rational, discursive method of resolving disparate conflicting views, but also in an instrumental sense of conveying ideas, and especially the transmission of values through time. In a normative perspective, relational justice includes an understanding of what these relations between and among persons should be. In a political perspective, this focus examines the method of organizing persons in society, including the formation of political institutions and attendant elements.

Formulating their considerations of justice in a moral framework, both Plato and Aristotle may be seen to have built relational elements into their accounts of justice. Thus, in Plato's metaphysical construct of an ideal society, there exists a common view of the Good, whereby individuals are arranged in hierarchal classes in relation to each other and associated with knowledge of transcendent or separated forms. This separation of forms from the mutable world is thought to be responsible for the relational character of Plato's theory, and Aristotle's rejection of such separation is sometimes thought to make Aristotle's account of justice non-relational.[1]

Aristotle develops the notion of distributive justice as a particular form of justice based on the concept of equality, with merit as the distributing principle. Such a distributing principle forces a comparative and relational view of the distributions entailed, especially when taking into consideration the concept of fairness, which in contemporary distributive justice comprises what may be known as a form of "social justice."[2] Moreover, while in his *Nicomachean Ethics*, Aristotle treats justice as a complete and perfect virtue, justice is not complete and perfect in an unqualified way, but in relation to other elements (1129b25–29). Thus, when moral virtues (such as justice) are exercised in accordance with the greater good, justice is perfect in relational terms, for instance, when an individual acts courageously for the good of the political community (1129b17–19).

While classical accounts of justice speak in terms of just persons and just actions, many contemporary accounts view justice as a function of political institutions, with government making just distributions of various social goods. Thus, many contemporary theories of justice are distributive by nature, and largely dominated by political concerns (especially the structuring of political institutions and attendant elements), thereby paying scant attention to moral aspects or to developing a moral framework for political considerations. In his influential *A Theory of Justice,* for instance, John Rawls conflates the moral with the political, as he stakes out the task for justice as configuring the distribution of primary social goods to benefit those worst off in society.[3]

However, Rawls' distributive scheme, and other distributive formulations, are not equipped to address critical moral and political issues that should be considered in a just society. For instance, none of the distributive schemes discussed in today's debates directly considers power relations between and among individuals, or between groups and institutional structures in society. Nor do they address important political considerations such as various structures of decision-making, such as in divisions of labor, culture, or the construction of social meanings. Likewise, important intangible goods cannot be said to be amenable or subject to distribution in society, not even Rawls' own basic value of self-respect.

Resolving Disputes

As stated above, the key to a relational approach to justice is communication, by means of which, I argue, matters of cultural contingency and the laws and customs of peoples come to play a prominent part in the setting or context for justice.

Plato may also be seen to feature communication as a critical element of his account of justice. In *The Republic*, for example, he declares dialectic to be the highest subject of study in the education of the philosopher. The purpose of Plato's communication and education system, however, is the search for knowledge, and more specifically, to understand intellectually the forms and especially the form of the Good. Nonetheless, Plato's various dialogues, and especially the mapping of progress in the intellectual education as presented in the analogies of the Sun (507a–509c), the Divided Line (509d–511), and the Cave (514a–521b), feature the concept of communication. Indeed, as described in chapter 2, the main treatment of the theory of forms in *The Republic* is presented in the context of defining the characteristics of the philosopher king and describing his special education. While such training requires that communication serve as a rational method for mediating disputes and as a means of transmitting values through time, fundamentally, Plato understands communication to be an epistemological method for discovering the truth and for acquiring knowledge.

Values and Cultural Influences

In theorizing communicative action, Jürgen Habermas develops a theory of communicative reason as part of his concepts of norms and procedures, whereby communication aims to further consensus among differing parties.[4] Although deontologically framed, discourse ethics in Habermas' framework also proves to be teleological, insofar as the successful resolution of conflicts is a necessary outcome of rational, deliberative discursive activity, a position that may be problematic.

More specifically, I do not believe that communication, through a deliberative process or otherwise, entails rationality. Rather, I accept rationality, together with individual autonomy, as formal components of moral agency. Further, while Habermas' theory attempts to escape relativism by providing necessary standards for critical evaluation, I choose to reference the external world along with experience and matters of cultural contingency, such as laws and customs of peoples, in order to provide moral resources for making determinations of just actions. In so doing, I remain mindful of Tim Scanlon's parametric universalism and Bernard Williams' morally thick concepts that can be seen to bear substantial cross-cultural ethical weight.[5]

The difference between the relationship of communication and reason in Habermas' theory and my views may rest in what we foreground. Thus, Habermas focuses on discourse, and specifically on argumentation, as the primary element of effective communication, which makes his approach close to Plato's. Indeed, the mechanics of finding consensus—to seek knowledge for Plato and to ameliorate difference in Habermas—is critical in both of their approaches, which are intended for rational, self-critical participants. While I certainly do not deny the possible efficacy of reasoned discourse, I do not foreground the mechanics of finding consensus, in part because mechanics do not provide guidance in establishing justice, in deciding upon right actions. Likewise, while Habermas requires rational, self-critical participants, I give primacy to the individual as rational and moral agent.

Political Aspects

With respect to the political aspects of justice, Iris Marion Young offers the insight that justice conceived as a distributive construct fails to take into account many of the demands of ordinary life, and thus justice is ill-served when viewed as a distributive paradigm. In *Justice and the Politics of Difference*, she consequently grounds a theory of justice on a relational understanding of differences among social groups.[6] This understanding is largely a political one, and includes acknowledgement of unjust power relations among individuals, groups, and institutional structures of society, further recognizing the oppression and domination of some groups in society.

For Young, it is the remit of justice to correct such unjust power relations and to respect differences among groups; moreover, justice is produced through cooperative behavior, through agreement and negotiation among the actors involved, thereby reminiscent of Habermas' focus on communicative action. As such, Young's underlying account of knowledge and power draws from feminist and critical theory. By critical theory, Young means an approach that generates critique through self-distancing from social reality, a "normative reflection that is historically and socially contextualized."[7] Thus, she states, "[C]ritical theoretical accounts of instrumental reason . . . and feminist critiques of the disembodied coldness of modern reason all converge on a similar project of puncturing the authority of modern scientific reason." The authority of scientific reason should be punctured, Young maintains, because of its "normalizing" effect that reduces "plurality of attributes to unity" and imposes a "dichotomy between subject and object."[8]

Young's epistemological use of theories has a phenomenological orientation, which allows her to view knowledge as plural and grounded in experience. Thus, a plurality of local kinds of knowledge based on plural experiences may be represented without being "objectified by science."[9] In lieu of objectifying science, Young attempts to evaluate epistemological claims in terms of functional and political criteria, meaning that the claim to validity of knowledge is judged according to political consequences, especially in terms of reinforcing or undermining relations of power and authority. Who may speak, who can be heard, and what discourse prevails—these are to some extent functions of epistemological choices. For Young, knowledge is always situated and relative to particular experiences and the social location of the knower.

In part, as mentioned above, this is why Young views distributive justice as an inadequate way of conceptualizing political justice—the standard distributive formulations take no consideration of the power relations among individuals, groups, and institutional structures. Because of the influence of its distributive paradigm, Young's critique focuses on Rawls' difference principle, based on the principle that it would be unjust to increase inequalities for the worst off in society.[10] Young attempts to show that while the difference principle, along with distributive justice more generally, condemns practices as unjust, it nonetheless fails to capture many of the standards of ordinary experience. She concludes that demands for justice in ordinary life often have little to do with distributive issues.

Young further contends that the discourse of distributive justice is used to sort phenomena that, even theoretically, may not be subject to distribution. For instance, the structures of decision-making—like the divisions of labor, culture, or the construction of social meanings—cannot properly be said to be distributable.[11] As mentioned earlier, while primary social goods may be distributable in Rawls' paradigm, his basic value of self-respect cannot be. Likewise, neither can ideals such as self-development and self-determination be distributed, nor, critically for Young, can power be distributed.[12] Since comparisons assume separate units, rather than examining the structured relations among them, Young concludes that power is relational, while distribution is only comparative. In the final analysis, while Young does not completely reject distributive approaches, her point is that justice is not essentially about distribution.

I also view the nature of justice as relational rather than distributive, and so, I also do not view the task of justice as the distribution of primary social goods or resources to those least advantaged in society. Young, however, moves from this largely political position to advocating group rights, at which point I disagree, since I view the task of justice as providing normative guidance in given circumstances, as further discussed in chapter 8. Preferring group rights over those of the individual, Young's view of relational justice differs from mine. In Young's approach, for example, the spokesperson for a group would likely speak for the group rights of its members, even if the spokesperson were a member of an illiberal group in a liberal order; in my view, the focus should be on the individual group member and her or his rights.

DISTRIBUTIVE JUSTICE

As discussed in chapter 3, Aristotle views distributive justice as a type of particular justice which is grounded in the concept of equality, itself comprising both distributive justice and fairness. In mapping out particular justice along the axes of distributive justice and fairness, Aristotle posits that an individual's fair share of a society's benefits and burdens should be determined according to merit. As such, this formula resembles the other universal aspect of justice, moral virtue as lawfulness, which provides the escape valve of equity in order to particularize moral virtue as far as generalizing allows. Moreover, in order to make operational distributive justice, Aristotle rejects mathematical equality for geometrical equality, since merit, and hence the distribution of goods, is not calculated as a simple distribution of equal amounts, but rather, proportionally, according to an individual's merits. Not treating the criteria for merit, his theory makes equality the fundamental principle to allow the pursuit of the good life, *eudaimonia*, for citizens. The problem of determining what merit in a social construct may be, however, persists in today's discussions.

Distributions

John Rawls' *A Theory of Justice,* which many credit with reviving interest in and generating numerous contemporary discussions of justice, owes its general distributive approach of justice to Aristotle.[13] Regarding the critical point of what is to be distributed fairly, to whom, and on what basis, Rawls answers that "[a]ll social primary goods—liberty and opportunity, income, wealth, and the bases of self-respect—are to be distributed equally unless an unequal distribution of any or all of these goods is to the advantage of the least favoured" (Rawls 1971, 303).

As discussed earlier, while Rawls views his theory as deontological, the question arises as to whether it is too outcome-oriented to qualify. Likewise, although Rawls intends his theory to affirm the priority of the right over the good, the various goods he acknowledges in his theory seem to compromise the priority of the right.[14] In similar vein, while Rawls holds a Kantian view of persons as owed due concern and respect, the individual as a moral agent tends to disappear in Rawls' account, as matters of morality are conflated with his largely political account of justice and just institutions.

In the final analysis, Rawls' definition of justice is largely political insofar as it results in a distributive scheme in which primary social goods are distributed to those least advantaged in society. Thus, distributive accounts like that of Rawls marginalize the individual, ignoring both poles of *dikaiosune,* the moral and the social, and reducing justice to one aspect of Aristotle's analysis of justice (itself comprising one of two fields constituting justice, the other being moral virtue). Indeed, in various distributive accounts, including Rawls' later articulation of his theory in *Political Liberalism,* justice is sought in mainly political solutions.[15] I argue instead that a relational view is inherent to justice, one which may lead to normative guidance in given circumstances.

Fundamentally, Rawls constructs his theory of justice for a society whose principles of justice directly structure society's basic institutions, institutions which anchor: a liberal constitutional democracy, including the political constitution; a system of markets and the regulation of economic relations; a legal system of trials, property and contracts; and the family. Rawls identifies these institutions as basic, since they provide rules that structure the lives of individuals in the larger framework of fundamental rights and duties, while they also determine how to divide advantages of social cooperation. As such, they have a profound influence on who we are as well as on our life prospects and form, accordingly, the first subject of justice. For Rawls, a just political constitution upholds the liberty principle, Rawls' first principle, through the claim that the state makes and enforces laws for equal citizens in a government with limited powers. Supporting the first principle, a just economic order upholds his second principle, the difference principle, providing equal opportunity with regard to education, culture, and income, while preventing monopolies.

In short, it is the justice of the basic structure of society that concerns Rawls. Subordinating fortune's claims to structure, Rawls would support distributions only when the basic structure of society is fair, and only if such claims meet legitimate expectations of the parties involved. For instance, as Robert Nozick sees it, Rawls' position is far from uncontroversial.[16] Evoking the static nature of models articulated by Plato and Aristotle, Rawls embraces the ideal of a well-ordered society, one which is perfectly just and in which all citizens openly agree upon the same conception of justice. Postulating such a society allows justice to be enacted in its laws and institutions, while citizens have a sense of justice and a basic willingness to comply with these terms. Indeed, heeding deliberations made in his thought experiment of the original position (see chapter 6), individuals engage in and desire to seek a conception of justice that will remain stable in a well-ordered society and that proves generally acceptable to all reasonable and rational persons, thereby leading to government as a representative democracy.[17]

Distributing Mechanisms

In *Sovereign Virtue*, Ronald Dworkin answers the question of what is to be distributed as resources, in a theory of justice based on a complex view of equality.[18] That is, while Dworkin expresses a Kantian view of equality, he reinterprets the concept to mean an equality of resources to be distributed through a hypothetical set of conditions. That is, as introduced in chapter 6, Dworkin develops a hypothetical auction and insurance scheme to distribute resources, a mechanism intended to treat people fairly and with an equality of due concern and respect. In the process, Dworkin's hypothetical distribution mechanism is intended to further balance ambition sensitivity with endowment insensitivity.

By including an echo of Aristotelian fairness along with the Kantian notion equality of respect and concern, Dworkin informs the structural aspects of his theoretical mechanism with the liberal position that overall outcomes should reflect the choices and actions of individuals. To effect his distribution, he further relies upon two fundamentally liberal principles: that every individual's life is per se and equally valuable, and that each individual has personal responsibility to realize his or her own potential. Dworkin's focus then turns to what kind of distribution of a society's goods results in equal respect and concern for all. If all should flourish and individuals are responsible to make the most of their lives, the second of these principles enacts the first through impact or challenge responses, as it also provides his solution to the fundamental quandary.

That is, Dworkin ultimately decides that true equality means equality in the value of resources that each person commands, not in the success an individual may achieve. Underlying this view is the second fundamentally liberal principle—individuals are responsible for developing and implementing their visions of the good life—leading to what Dworkin thinks it would take to execute this principle. Informing his approach is the belief that the natural endowments of intelligence and talent, or their absence, are morally arbitrary and should not affect the distribution of resources in society. Thus, Dworkin intends the concepts of equality, freedom, and individual responsibility not to conflict, but rather, to combine and proffer different aspects of a fundamentally humanist conception of life and politics. His political views arise from this concept of equality and may be seen as a monistic egalitarianism that is, at its core, anti-pluralist.[19]

In order to achieve resource equality in society, Dworkin assumes a universal value system. Thus, he first develops a hypothetical test, his so-called "envy test," as the criterion for determining whether distributions in society are just. Using this test, a distribution of goods is not satisfactory if after the distribution a person envies another because of the bundle of resources that individual has received. To solve the problems presented by the envy test, Dworkin develops the above-mentioned mechanism of an auction, which also serves to address the proper basis for assessing an individual's condition. For Dworkin, the auction reveals what others would pay for the resources they control in an ideal market economy.

In Dworkin's auction procedure everyone receives the same initial amount of money, with which they all engage in bidding for resources that are available within the political community. If all proceeds as expected, the bidding process would result in one individual paying more of her or his initial allocation of money in order to obtain goods that are highly valued by others and paying less for goods that are not as popular. The choices that people make in using their resources during the auction affect the value of their holdings. Economic inequalities such as these prove justifiable since they derive from an individual's own values and tastes. Importantly, a properly regulated market is essential to Dworkin's construct, as it provides the only appropriate (market) measure of value for the resources that an individual holds. As such, Dworkin's scheme reveals the opportunity costs of denying resources to others.

Although Dworkin includes both material goods and internal resources in items to bid upon, the scheme is not without its problems. Thus, when a person bids to purchase internal resources, another's of one's own—for instance, hours of time belonging to the person who has the resource or labor power—such an auction can lead to the "slavery of the talented."[20] For example, imagine a person who has a great talent for singing and that her talent commands a high price in a given society. Other people at the hypothetical auction are willing to bid for many hours of her labor just to hear her sing. Consequently, she will have to work by singing, her most lucrative employment, to satisfy the owners (or purchasers) of her time. Her free time has become a scarce commodity, and she herself has to bid for hours of her own time at the high auction price. Now imagine another person with no such valuable talent. It turns out that his most lucrative employment is as a common laborer. Since few are willing to pay a high price for his services, the auction sets his labor time at a low price. Consequently, he may purchase many of his hours for his own recreational or other use. In such a scenario, the common laborer has more use of his own time than does the talented singer, who is enslaved by her talent.

In response to just such a scenario, Dworkin articulates the proviso of the envy test. For the envy test to function effectively, great differences in the personal abilities and talents of the persons involved cannot exist. Since such a condition cannot be guaranteed and since Dworkin believes it to be important that no one suffers or profits by reason of what he views as the individual's undeserved natural abilities,[21] an additional procedure must also be introduced, one based on an insurance scheme.

That is, Dworkin heuristically introduces a Rawlsian veil concept, whereby no one knows whether anyone present has some sort of mental or physical disability or whether the talents that the gathered individuals possess are in demand or not. In such circumstances, it would be rational, argues Dworkin, for everyone to buy insurance against such risks. Thus, a portion of the initially allocated equal sums of money intended for use at the auction is collected from each individual and used to establish an insurance fund to provide support for the disabled or for insufficiently talented persons. To Dworkin, this insurance model looks less like welfare than the Rawlsian model does, which also attempts to care for the least advantaged in society.[22] Be that as it may, the re-allocations entailed in the insurance scheme do raise the question of disincentive effects along with the problem of "second-best efficient egalitarianism."

The central ambition of Dworkin's insurance scheme is to remove any negative impact of the distribution of resources along with factors not under individuals' control, while allowing influence only of factors that are under personal control. In this manner, Dworkin also introduces a sense of moral responsibility into his model for just distributions in society, because he believes that it is appropriate to hold individuals morally accountable for matters of choice or auction luck (for such matters as the value placed by others on a distributable resource), but not so for matters of brute luck such as a person's natural endowments.[23] Thus, his theory of resource equality may also be seen as a form of luck egalitarianism.

The combination of the hypothetical auction with the hypothetical insurance scheme is designed to provide a theory of distributive justice that treats individuals as equals and that is both ambition insensitive and endowment insensitive. Interestingly, Dworkin's theory of resource equality appears to rest upon at least a thin concept of the good (or alternatively, his thin concept of the good flows into his concept of the right), rather than presenting the disinterested liberal neutrality to which Rawls subscribes. This raises the question of how to categorize Dworkin's liberalism, which in turn raises questions about the place of liberty in his liberal political theory, as well as about the relationship of liberty to his concept of equality.

Endowments and Welfare

The question of how, or if, natural endowments should play a role in justice theories has been asked since ancient times. Aristotle considers them minimally, when he suggests that virtues are not reducible to natural endowments. Thus, in the *Nicomachean Ethics*, he identifies virtue not with natural endowments granted at birth, but rather with the flourishing of individuals possessed of practical wisdom (1145a1). He does grant, however, that except for theoretical wisdom (*sophia*), intellectual virtues are "natural," or bestowed by nature, making them natural endowments (1142b8–9).

In contrast, Plato clearly posits inequality as an important mythic element to be used in order to undergird a stable social structure. As discussed in chapter 2, his Noble Lie claims that the metals divinely placed in an individual's body determine their stations in life: rulers have gold, auxiliaries have silver, and producers have bronze. Movement from one class to another, upward or downward, depends upon whether or not another metal intermingles with the predominant metal (414–415). With such a myth firmly in place, Plato seems to think, people will conform to expectations and occupy their "proper place" in society, thereby ensuring a stable social structure. Of course, in developing the Noble Lie, Plato reveals his belief that most people either are not intellectually capable of looking after their own and society's best interest, or perhaps they are too much in Thrasymachus' camp and thus would be too unbalanced to apprehend the need for a stable social structure. Only a few qualified people of the world, the rulers, intellectually apprehend forms including the form of the Good, and thereby are capable of leading the rest of the flock.

Comparing Rawls and Dworkin reveals that they too recognize natural endowments in their theories of justice, but not in the manner of either Plato's use of them to place people in appropriate stations or Aristotle's marginalization of them in favor of developing virtue. Instead, for Rawls and Dworkin, natural endowments become a point of economically and politically framed contention. Yet, underlying all four approaches is the working assumption that those with natural endowments have an advantage over others. Plato would distribute such advantages in the best interest of the state, Aristotle would have them tempered by the cultivation of virtue, Rawls would minimize them so that all can share equally in the state, and Dworkin looks to support those disadvantaged by the lack of natural endowments. In this array, Plato is the odd man out, as the three other thinkers seem to challenge the fairness of natural endowments.

In contrast to Dworkin, then, Rawls attempts to generate a disinterested liberal neutrality, dependent upon his conception of justice as fairness. Thus, his original premise proposes that each member of society has an equal claim to society's goods and that an individual's natural abilities should not affect this claim. Any inequalities in the distribution of a society's material wealth may be justified under his second principle of justice as fairness, the difference principle, only if such inequalities benefit the least advantaged in society. In other words, for Rawls, justice as fairness concerns individuals' means rather than their use of them. In considering just distributions, for example, there is no reason to consider income and other primary goods produced by individuals. Instead, what should be considered are the unproduced primary goods. In partaking in an equitable sharing of primary goods, as well as their free exchange, an individual is involved in the process of freedom rather than the substance of exchanges.

Here is where Dworkin parts most sharply with Rawls. Criticizing Rawls' difference principle as being insufficiently endowment insensitive, he argues that Rawls' difference principle is conceived to distribute only social primary goods (liberty and opportunity, income and wealth, and the bases of self-respect). In doing so, Dworkin continues, Rawls' difference principle overlooks the claims of those who are unequally endowed with natural primary goods, especially the disabled, whose actual needs would require more resources to compensate for unequal natural endowment.

In addition to being endowment insensitive, Dworkin argues that Rawls' difference principle is insufficiently ambition sensitive. To illustrate this point, consider the oft-cited example featuring a tennis player and a gardener.[24] Both have equal natural endowments in terms of strength and intelligence, and both receive equal distributions of primary social goods under Rawls' difference principle. The tennis player uses her resources to support her interest in playing tennis, while the gardener cultivates his plot of land to produce flowers and vegetables that he enjoys and is able to sell to others. Both have made choices about how to use their resources, but the choices that the gardener makes result in his being better off than the tennis player. Consequently, the ambition-sensitive choices of the two have resulted in a new pattern of distribution. Moreover, for the initial distribution to be justifiable in Rawlsian terms, there would have to be a transfer from the industrious gardener to the tennis player in order to validate any inequality that would emerge between the two. The tennis player's lifestyle may prove to be very expensive, so that although she gets fulfillment from playing tennis, she makes little by way of income. Further, under the Rawlsian scheme, the gardener, who also finds fulfillment from his choices, finds himself subsidizing the tennis players of society as well as his own consumption choices.

In other words, if the Rawlsian difference principle cannot distinguish between inequalities that result from unequal natural endowments or from different consumption ambitions or decisions, then it runs up against the primary intuition concerning fairness residing at the heart of social justice. That is, for many, compensating for expensive tastes is not properly a matter of distributive justice.

Generally, in objecting to supposed objective theories of welfare and equality of welfare, Dworkin believes that any attempt to make people equal in welfare aims to make them equal in something that they value differently. In fact, he notes that "an objective ranking (of activities) would be controversial even one with a generous helping of indeterminacy, and basing distribution on such a ranking is not compatible with equal concern for all."[25] In his argument against the distributive approaches suggested by proposing equality of welfare, Dworkin generally notes that the concept seems vulnerable to the problem of expensive tastes and varying ambitions.[26] Does justice, in other words, demand that those satisfied with beer and burgers are entitled to less than those satisfied only with champagne and steak? Dworkin continues by arguing that the problem of expensive tastes, and compensation for tastes, is at the core of the distributive schemes that flow from the concept positing equality in welfare. Thus, if the notion of compensating for champagne and steak proves offensive, the distributive scheme emerging from the equality of welfare concept itself is at fault and must be discarded.

Rawls, however, rejects the criticism of the difference principle on such grounds since he views questions of responsibility and choice, concerns of moral agency, as outside the parameters of a fair distribution of goods. Rawls also objects to Dworkin's focus on how distributions emerge. The purpose of the difference principle for Rawls is to maintain a distribution of primary goods that secures fair equality of opportunity and advantage for those who are the worst off in society. Indeed, from this perspective, the question of how the distribution comes about is irrelevant. For Rawls, introducing the issue of ambition sensitivity makes an unnecessary concession to the concepts of desert and merit.

THE TASK OF JUSTICE

Both Rawls and Dworkin place distribution schemes at the core of their political views of justice. Some iteration of a distribution scheme is present in any system of governance, but as can be seen from these critiques, they do not provide normative guidance in ambiguous situations. Indeed, asserting that a person had an "unjust" amount of resources has a quite different meaning for Dworkin than for others. Dworkin would likely inquire as to whether the distribution and redistribution of resources to the individual were obtained, optimally, through a fair auction and with the backing of insurance. For instance, alternatively, one could inquire whether the resources were obtained by lying, or cheating, or in violation of applicable laws or customs. If not, one could further inquire as to what extent conflicting values are represented and decide in favor of the value that best adheres to a priority rule.[27]

I do not mean that a society should not adopt distribution and redistribution schemes, such as taxation and welfare systems. Such schemes are acceptable as long as they do not raise questions of value above that appropriate for a thin theory of the good underlying a deontological approach of the justice question. More directly, with respect to distributive approaches, when a society imposes duties upon its citizens through laws to abide by distributive schemes, if such schemes are not attendant to the notion of equal respect and concern for individuals, for instance, such laws may be viewed as unjust. Likewise, my view of justice would also assess whether, in the political formulation of distributions, the scheme would be offensive to the negative liberty component of political liberalism.

I view justice not as a distributional matter—which would ignore individual responsibility—but rather as a relational matter. Thus, I view the task of justice not as the distribution of social goods to those least advantaged in society, or otherwise, but rather, I view the task of justice as providing normative guidance in an individual's relations to others, with the key to such a relational view of justice being communication, both in a substantive sense as a rational, discursive method of resolving disparate conflicting views, but also in an instrumental sense of conveying ideas, and especially the transmission of values through time.

Further, I argue that a person owes a duty of justice when her or his actions may affect others. This responsibility for intentional actions, as I see it, should be limited by consideration of how others might act in response to one's actions. This second condition may be seen as a reference to the external world and experience, thus providing resources and guidance for moral decision-making, as it empirically reaches into particular communities in which individuals are situated along with the laws and customs of such communities. This egalitarian concern may also provide the touchstone for a priority rule in situations involving conflicting values.

NOTES

1. Gail Fine, *Plato on Knowledge and Forms* (Oxford: Oxford University Press, 2003), ch. 13.
2. See chapter 1, note 11 *infra.*
3. John Rawls, *A Theory of Justice* (Cambridge: Harvard University Press, 1971).
4. See Jürgen Habermas, *Between Facts and Norms*, trans. William Rehg (Cambridge: MIT Press, 1996).
5. See T. M. Scanlon, *What We Owe Others* (Cambridge: Harvard University Press, 2000); Bernard Williams, *Moral Luck* (Cambridge: Cambridge University Press, 1981); and chapter 5 *infra.*
6. Iris Marion Young, *Justice and the Politics of Difference* (Oxford: Oxford University Press, 1990), p. 5.
7. See also Iris Marion Young, *Inclusion and Democracy* (Oxford: Oxford University Press, 2000), p. 10.

8. Id., p. 125.
9. Young (1990), p. 145.
10. See Rawls (1971), and later in this chapter.
11. Young (1990), p. 22ff.
12. Id., p. 30.
13. See Rawls (1971), and chapter 6 *infra.*
14. See discussion of The Right and the Good in chapter 5 *infra.*

15. Rawls moves from the idea of a person having a moral personality to one of the person as a citizen, with political structures and social stability achieved through "overlapping consensus." See John Rawls, *Political Liberalism* (New York: Columbia University Press, 1993).

16. See Robert Nozick, *Anarchy, State, and Utopia* (New York: Basic Books, 1974) and discussion of The Individual in chapter 8 *infra.*

17. Among the vast multitude of works on Rawls' theory of justice, the following provide excellent insights: Samuel Freeman's examination in *Rawls* (New York: Routledge, 2007); the essays of various authors in Norman Daniels, ed., *Reading Rawls* (New York: Basic Books, 1975); and Chandran Kukathas and Philip Pettit, *Rawls* (Cambridge: Polity Press, 1990).

18. "Equality of resources, as described here . . . aims to provide a description of (or rather a set of devices for aiming at) equality of resources person by person, and the considerations of each person's history that affect what he should have." Ronald Dworkin, *Sovereign Virtue* (Cambridge: Harvard University Press, 2000), p. 114.

19. See Arthur Ripstein, "Liberty and Equality," in *Ronald Dworkin,* ed. Arthur Ripstein (Cambridge: Cambridge University Press, 2007), pp. 82–108.

20. See John Roemer, "Equality of Resources Implies Equality of Welfare," *Quarterly Journal of Economics* 101 (1986): 751–784.

21. Contrast Robert Nozick's view that the natural lottery in respect to an individual's abilities and talents is not unjust. See Nozick (1974), p. 226; also see chapter 8 *infra.*

22. However, in imagining the implementation of Dworkin's theory of equal resource allocation (market auction plus insurance scheme), there must be many of the complexities of tax and money-transfer systems found in a welfare state.

23. See Bernard Williams, *Moral Luck* (Cambridge: Cambridge University Press, 1981).

24. The example appears in Will Kymlicka, *Contemporary Political Philosophy* (New York: Oxford University Press, 1990), pp. 73–76. Jonathan Wolff describes this example as "[Kymlicka's] retelling of Dworkin's objection to Rawls." Jonathan Wolff, "Fairness, Respect, and the Egalitarian Ethos," *Philosophy and Public Affairs* 27; 2 (1998): 99.

25. Dworkin (2000), p. 300.

26. "Equality of welfare seems to recommend that those with champagne tastes, who need more income simply to achieve the same level of welfare as those with less expensive tastes, should have more income on that account. But this seems counterintuitive." Dworkin (2000), pp. 48–49.

27. See conclusion *infra.*

Chapter 8

Individual Rights and Responsibilities

Over time, the individuals on the boat introduced in the last chapter, those taking a long uncharted voyage, start to form groups, making voluntary associations with other individuals through friendships or common interests. At times, however, some may be marginalized and involuntarily relegated to various smaller groupings. Having been unwillingly cordoned off into non-majority status, and due to lack of numbers without a powerful voice, the question emerges whether these minority groups should have special rights along with appropriate attendant responsibilities accorded to them. After all, these individuals are all on the same boat, so it seems unfair that those in the majority have the best picks of all the sailing boat's amenities.

The complexities involved in determining whether individual rights should be given priority over group rights are explored in this chapter. An often polarized discussion grounded in differing views of liberal principles, the focus on the individual is examined here by means of two distinct views that give a sense of the range of the intricacies involved: self-ownership and the matter of luck. Thus, I examine Robert Nozick's libertarian approach to individual rights as generated from a Lockean view of self-ownership, before interrogating Ronald Dworkin's proposal to interject the question of choice and chance into a liberal egalitarian framework.

To give a sense of the theoretical approaches to the concept of group rights, I have chosen an array of perspectives that focus on power and distribution in attempting to make groups the defining bearer of rights. I start the discussion of group rights with Iris Marion Young's political focus on multiple forms of oppression within a society, before treating Susan Okin's selection of one criterion—oppression against women—to highlight the multiple perspectives that must be brought to bear on power dynamics across a society. From power, I turn to two efforts to interpolate distribution concerns in group rights theory. For this, I examine Michael Walzer's use of an economic model to probe social goods and how they should be distributed among groups, before considering the debate between Will Kymlicka and Brian Barry on the multicultural distribution of social goods.

THE INDIVIDUAL

The concept of individual rights in modern political society is often traced to Thomas Hobbes and John Locke. Indeed, in the modern sense, neither Plato nor Aristotle considers the concept of individual rights in political society. Plato's discussion may nonetheless be seen to foreshadow the possibility in his functional argument about individuals working in society as appropriate to their class. Further, some scholars link Aristotle to the natural rights tradition, while additionally claiming that Aristotle's teleological view of human nature and his ethical theory of *eudaimonia* can serve as a foundation for a theory of individual rights akin to Locke's.[1]

In basically arguing that government should not be a matter of brute force, John Locke echoes Plato's rebuke of Thrasymachus. In placing the individual at the center of fundamental analyses, Locke theorizes more in the direction of Aristotle. With this focus, Locke has influenced classic political liberalism, whereby individual liberty (negative liberty in Isaiah Berlin's terminology) is the key political value to be preserved. Within this framework, I argue that the individual is the proper bearer of rights and responsibilities, rather than groups, one reason being that awarding rights to groups denies moral responsibility.

In exploring the issue of individual rights and responsibilities in this chapter, I examine the extreme views of Robert Nozick, who provocatively begins *Anarchy, State, and Utopia* with the statement that "individuals have rights . . . so strong and far-reaching . . . that they raise the question of what, if anything, the state and its officials may do."[2] With this declaration, Nozick launches a rights-based approach to justice, one which is grounded on his concept of Lockean self-ownership and which leads to an entitlement theory of justice accompanied by the preference for a minimal state. While his concept of individual rights is amply developed, his attendant view of individual responsibility appears undernourished.

As a proponent of strong political liberalism, Nozick argues that liberty must trump all other values and may be tempered only by the bounds of hypothetical natural rights and voluntary agreements. Problematically, however, the belief in liberty as the highest value in this manner does not allow for concerns of the common good, social welfare, or equality, concerns that when not addressed may indeed restrict an individual's freedom. In other words, for

Nozick, protecting basic rights to life, liberty, and property exhausts the scope of politics. Indeed, he argues that if liberty were in some manner restricted by measures of equality or social justice, these latter values must give way to liberty. Thus, Nozick explicitly acknowledges that his approach has "no presumption in favor of equality."[3] With this statement, he proposes that rather than viewing how wealth may be distributed more equally in society, the proper inquiry would turn attention to examining whether the distribution in question came about in accordance with rules of acquisition, transfer, and rectification, or whether they involved coercion. Only in complying with such rules, that is, would a distribution be just.

The concept of liberty nonetheless proves complex for Nozick, especially with respect to coercion. Unlike Friedrich von Hayek, for instance, Nozick does not take the position that all actions that are coercive infringe upon liberty.[4] Rather than coercion per se, it is interference with individual choice that infringes upon liberty. Further, interference is broken down into threats and offers, whereby only threats comprise the category of coercive intervention that restricts an individual's freedom. This distinction underscores Nozick's concept of liberty as based on an individual's rights as foundational. That is, Nozick argues that individuals morally own themselves and have the full right to control the use of their persons, in just the same manner as they can fully own and control the use of inanimate objects. For him, the concept of self-ownership would even extend to include voluntary noncoercive enslavement contracts between adults.

In critiquing Nozick's concept of liberty, Jerry Cohen focuses on this very point, characterizing Nozick's approach as proffering a moralized notion of freedom that categorizes only illegitimate actions as capable of violating liberty. This allows Nozick, Cohen continues, to ignore situations in which people may be forced by circumstances, such as poverty, to take or forgo certain actions.[5]

Extremely put, Nozick postulates that an individual's rights exhaust the ethical terrain of contested moral and political issues. More concretely, Nozick argues that basically, an individual has the right to self-ownership, to own and control the use of her- or himself and of her or his own property. In this respect, Nozick argues from a libertarian, moral point of view,[6] one in which negative liberty occupies the field, without the contribution or restraint of equality. This version of libertarianism is sometimes referred to as "self-ownership" libertarianism.[7]

For John Rawls, by contrast, self-ownership is a morally arbitrary matter and we are not automatically entitled to what we may procure or amass on the basis of our talents. What Nozick disagrees with in Rawls' account is how Rawls' difference principle centers his view of equality, which proves inimical to Nozick's concept of self-ownership.[8] Nozick does argue as a Kantian in the sense that he views individuals as separate and morally valuable, as ends unto themselves, and thus not to be used simply as a means for others. From here, however, he reasons that if individuals are inviolable and ends unto themselves, it follows that they have certain rights, including rights to their lives, liberty, and the fruits of their labor.

Influenced by John Locke, he constructs a Lockean natural rights theory arguing not only that the individual is inviolable, but also that a person's property rights become nonnegotiable.[9] As Locke asserted, "every man has a 'property' in his own 'person.' This nobody has any right to but himself. The 'labour' of his body and the 'work' of his hands, we may say, are properly his."[10] For Nozick, natural rights are "natural" in the sense that they are not legal rights established by legislation, but rather, they constitute moral rights, which legislation and government should respect.

In spite of his adaptation of Lockean self-ownership, whether the notion of natural rights is actually compatible with privately held property, as Nozick claims, is questionable, especially in situations where the property is a natural resource and not produced by persons, by the work of their hands. Nozick does not entertain the question, however; for him, property is a pre-political right, not subject to state interference or considerations of social justice. In fact, Nozick uses Locke's ideas of self-ownership and combines an individual's right to her or his own labor with the question of natural resources to categorize private property as a natural right, to form what he terms the Lockean Proviso, which governs the initial acquisition of property in a society. That is, by means of his Lockean Proviso, Nozick asserts that although every appropriation of property is a diminution of another person's rights, it is acceptable as long as it does not make anyone worse off than if he or she would have been without any private property.

How Nozick's Lockean Proviso would play out in practice is not actually clear, and he himself raises the question of what the baseline would be for making such determinations (Nozick 1974, 177). It certainly remains a controversial proposition, challenged by many theorists, as patently evident in the exercise of trying to identify a suitable baseline. Although concerned with the appropriation of property, that is, Nozick's Lockean Proviso does not represent a positive theory of acquisition. In spite of such ambiguities, Nozick affirms that the Lockean Proviso would be clearly violated if a person appropriates something necessary to others' lives, or if circumstances concerning the property should change so as to effect harm, as exemplified by the drying up of watering holes (Nozick 1974, 180).

In fact, Locke viewed natural resources, initially unprotected by any property rule (no consent is needed for use or appropriation), as protected by a compensation liability rule. Further, his original formulation itself goes beyond the measure articulated by Nozick to suggest that a limit be placed upon the amount of a resource that may be extracted from nature by any individual. Those who use natural resources or claim rights over them owe compensation to others for any wrongful costs imposed. Defining what is "enough and as good," however, is to be left to others. Given Nozick's vaguely articulated measure of usage violation, he bases compensation on what he terms each person's reservation price, which is the lowest payment that would leave the individual indifferent with nonuse or non-appropriation. At issue, however, remains the fact that use or appropriation of natural resources typically produces significant benefits even after providing such compensation. There is little reason to hold that those who first use or claim rights over a natural resource should reap all the excess benefits that those resources provide.

While ignoring baseline considerations as well as consequences with respect to natural resource claims, Nozick also perseveres in accounting for what is already universally established. Thus, he argues that Lockean rights serve as side-constraints on the actions of others, setting limits on how others may treat a person. For example, since you own yourself others may not kill you (destroying your property) or force you to work against your will, even if the purpose is judged to be a good one. Indeed, Nozick has rather famously claimed that taxation for the purpose of distributive justice constitutes a form of forced labor (Nozick 1974, 169). His analysis as to why these three examples—murder, slavery, and taxation—are not just, exemplifies rather tortured logic.

Indeed, Nozick's fundamental view of ownership and exchange seems to emerge from marginalizing the human dignity at the core of Kantian principles, whereby an individual is not to be used simply as a means for others—or put another way—from ignoring, as Cohen has argued, that given an individual's impoverished circumstances, coercion may exist beyond what the law defines. That is, what Nozick treats as normatively axiomatic presents problems not only with respect to the ownership of natural resources and the use of one's own property, but also with respect to his fundamental view of ownership and exchange.[11] Aligned with Locke's state of nature, individuals have the "perfect freedom to order their actions and dispose of their possessions and persons as they think fit, within the bounds of the law of nature, without asking leave, or depending upon the will of any other man."[12] His position has led to a significant array of critiques.

Thus, for Bernard Williams, any application of Nozick's formal treatment of the concept of rights proves suspect since it is impossible to talk meaningfully about rights or when a moral boundary may be crossed without supplying the rights in question with normative content.[13] Likewise, other critics challenge Nozick's views, since his moral intuitions claim that the nature of rights is absolute rather than *prima facie*. In defining rights, that is, Nozick ignores both their ontology and relational aspects, and he fails to examine the values in whose pursuit they set limits. Perhaps most egregiously and fundamentally, Nozick argues without a critical understanding of the basis of rights; any theory of rights must explain the relation between the possessor of a right and the actor and not simply focus on the intrinsic nature of the possessor and her or his life.[14]

Choice/Chance Considerations

One question raised in Nozick's exegesis is how to treat individuals who are placed differently in political society, a question of chance and circumstances. For Kant, matters of morality are viewed as matters of good will and are not susceptible to luck.[15] As discussed in chapter 4, however, contemporary philosophers often pose the question of whether we should be morally responsible for only those matters that are within our control, and further, whether two persons should be morally assessed differently, if the only differences between the two are outside of their control. Thus, the problem of moral luck and the correlation of moral responsibility with voluntary action generate discussion on when a moral agent is assigned moral blame or praise for an action or its consequences, even when it is clear that the agent did not have full control over the act or its consequences.[16]

In presenting an egalitarian and distributive construct of justice, John Rawls asserts that natural talents and abilities are morally arbitrary. He argues that "[T]he existing distribution of income and wealth, say, is the cumulative effect of prior distributions of natural assets—that is, natural talents and abilities—as these have been developed or left unrealized, and their use favored or disfavored over time by social circumstances and such chance contingencies as accident and good fortune. Intuitively, the most obvious injustice of the system of natural liberty is that it permits distributive shares to be improperly influenced by these factors so arbitrary from a moral point of view."[17]

In contrast, as discussed in chapters 6 and 7, Ronald Dworkin moves beyond such considerations to propose that an adequate theory of justice addresses moral luck or egalitarianism as he attempts to distinguish between brute luck and auction luck by means of the hypothetical mechanism of an auction plus insurance scheme to administer just distributions of resources. Starting with the view that individuals are due equal respect, for Dworkin it follows that it is inappropriate to expect some individuals to subsidize or to bear the burdens of choices made by others. His resultant theory of resource equality is intended, then, to balance the concerns of ambition sensitivity with those of endowment insensitivity.

Fundamentally, underlying Dworkin's theory is the liberal egalitarian concern with neutrality among various conceptions of the good life, while also maintaining the choice-and-chance distinction. However, as treated later in this chapter, Will Kymicka and other multiculturalists underscore how an individual's cultural identity and affiliation are not, strictly speaking, a matter of choice.[18] Likewise, Jerry Cohen argues not only that Dworkin's focus on market outcomes is morally arbitrary, but also his approach is too simplistic since, for example, an individual's ambition-sensitive drives are often matters of luck or chance.[19] Both Kymlicka and Cohen, that is, point to the arbitrariness of determining varieties of luck. But Dworkin's distinction between choice and chance and his underlying theme delineating the extent of an individual's moral responsibility prove critical for his theory, and consequently, he defends his views against particularly Cohen's criticisms along two primary lines: (1) by presenting a defense involving moral intuitions, and (2) by invoking an argument from identification.[20]

First, Dworkin launches his defense by resorting to what he designates as ordinary moral intuitions without, however, articulating a likely decision-making procedure in the case of conflicting views, especially necessary in complex cases. To make his case, he distinguishes between kinds of luck. Thus, Dworkin asserts that there are matters of luck that raise questions of fairness and those that do not. In the latter case, for instance, it is a matter of luck that the planet Earth has the necessary conditions to support human life. As such, luck that does not raise questions of fairness is morally neutral. On the other hand, the luck of being born into a particular social position may indeed generate issues of fairness that could be addressed in a distributive scheme that allocates resources based on equality. Drawing from ordinary moral intuitions as to what constitutes fairness in particular situations, Dworkin questions whether a condition or disposition is a matter of choice or chance, thereby responding to the expensive tastes challenge that claims an individual should not be penalized for expensive preferences since such preferences are a matter of luck.

Secondly, in order to address complex cases, Dworkin considers the manner by which we identify or endorse choices and preferences by providing two illustrations. The first case concerns a man who finds the taste of tap water unbearably sour and therefore has to spend more of his resources on bottled water. The second case involves a man who is driven by ambition to become a photographer and thereby has the need to buy expensive photographic equipment. In both cases, it can be assumed that the agents did not choose their preferences. On the other hand, how they relate to them ought to be viewed and treated differently. In the first instance, Dworkin argues that the man's tastes are a matter of brute bad luck. If he could take a pill to change his sense of taste, then he would be presented with a choice. In the second case, however, Dworkin contends that the man's ambition to become a photographer creates a much more complex matter, even though the preference was also not chosen. His ambition nonetheless came about through an interconnected web of beliefs and judgments about things that have societal value. In this case, it may be less likely that the photographer could take a pill to change his preference just because his ambition proves to be more expensive. Especially in this second example, by referencing an interconnected web, Dworkin may indeed recognize the complexity of the situation, but he nonetheless proceeds as if it were a monolithic construct allowing for a universal response.

Dworkin's distinction is certainly controversial, but so too is Cohen's focus on economic matters. As discussed in chapter 4, they both point to the issue of where the line between choice and chance should be drawn. That is, it may be an intractably difficult matter to distinguish between matters of choice and chance. Indeed, while attempting to introduce individual moral responsibility into his conception of justice, Dworkin fails to provide sufficient tools or methods of deciding between such choice or chance situations.[21]

GROUP THEORIES

Plato, of course, recognizes groups in his vision of an ideal society, identifying three classes of persons organized in a hierarchal, orderly social structure so as to ensure the stability of political society, with each individual doing work appropriate to his class. In more limited fashion, Aristotle also recognizes groups, via his ethical theory of *eudaimonia* as applied to political constitutions. Thus, he identifies the *aristoi*, the best group of persons, as the most appropriate to rule in a society. Neither thinker promotes group rights as such, since they both regard groups from the other direction: those that are the best in society, virtuous persons pursing the good life, should govern.

In contemporary times, Iris Marion Young develops a theory of group rights that could be said to focus on those who are omitted from the classical philosophers' analyses. In other words, she does not focus on promoting the best in society, but rather, her concern is for those minority groups that suffer oppression and domination. In doing so, she takes a relational approach to questions of justice rather than a distributive one, while her orientation toward organizing a just society is political, rather than moral.

Young defines injustice as oppression and domination,[22] and delineates five forms or faces of oppression: exploitation, marginalization, powerlessness, cultural imperialism (invisibility, silencing), and systematic violence.[23] She examines these five faces of oppression as a structural problem, describing them as a condition of social groups and as a comprehensive as well as irreducible set of the various aspects of oppression experienced by social groups.[24]

At the heart of her analysis, Young insists that the rights held by a group, rather than by its individual members, obtain—a position prompted by her views of a pluralistic human condition in which ways of life and commitments significantly differentiate one group from another. She supports, for example, affirmative action programs not to compensate for past discrimination, but rather, as an important means for undermining oppression, in particular the oppression that results from unconscious aversions and stereotypes.[25] In supporting affirmative action, Young is not blind to its problems, such as the supposedly impartial merit distribution of positions as well as the hierarchical division of labor in the workplace between task-defining and task-executing positions. Nonetheless, Young gives primacy to group rights, recognizing and advocating rights for groups involved in debates about equality and difference in women's liberation, bilingual education, and Native American rights.[26]

When Young refers to a social group, she means "a collective of persons differentiated from at least one other group by cultural forms, practices, or way of life."[27] With this definition in mind and in order to overcome the difficulties created by oppression and domination, Young recognizes group rights, whether organized by gender, ethnicity, race or sexual orientation. This view may be objectionable on a moral basis, however, to those who view moral agency, including the notions of responsibility and intentional actions, as properly based in the individual rather than in groups. The power granted to groups, for example, can be wielded over its individual members, thereby diminishing their individual rights and responsibilities, as is most evident in the situation of illiberal minority groups and their practices (discussed later in this chapter). Moreover, as mentioned above, membership in a minority group may be involuntary and not a true case of free association, since individuals may not be able to exit such groups easily, as is possible with a club or association. If the group's authority is oppressive or its way of life intolerable, group members may not have the array of options available to them that other citizens in a liberal society may have.

Beyond these objections, an ontological argument against group rights concerns the social groups themselves. That is, to attribute rights to groups supposes that groups have a being and integrity matching those of individuals. This cannot be the case. Groups aggregate individuals and do not themselves simply form a human-like being to whom it would be appropriate to ascribe moral agency, values, reasoning, and moral decision-making.[28] Adjustments have to be made to account for important differences. Indeed, members of a group who should benefit from specific measures may actually criticize or oppose them. This last observation suggests another essential point. While an individual's proclivity for ethical thought and action can and is also attributed to governments per se, the basic difference between Young's group model and a government is that these groups do not act, even in theory, for the common good, as liberal governments are intended to do.[29]

While diversity and pluralism reside easily within a liberal societal construct, the claim of equal recognition for groups proves problematic, since the two linchpins of the liberal account, liberty, and equality, focus on the autonomous individual as the relevant moral agent. While cultural or religious groups may be allowed special exemption from a duty to obey, the reasons for such exemptions, as some liberal theorists claim, are based on political prudence or on an estimate of the balance of advantages, not on the diminishing of individual rights.[30]

Group rights prove fundamentally problematic to a liberal view then, because when moral standing is accorded to groups, individuals within the group disappear from view. Indeed, social groups are not static, since the individuals comprising them all but guarantee constantly changing and unclear boundaries. Moreover, any social group that may be demarcated may be further subdivided into smaller groupings. Thus, the indeterminacy inherent to social groups and their membership not only creates a problem at the margins, but it also challenges the usefulness of the group concept itself. In other words, an indeterminacy challenge can be directed at the core concept of Young's group approach to, and theoretical conception of, justice, as has been aimed at Mill's harm principle and at Rawls' first principle of justice as fairness as well.

For these reasons, the disconcerting arbitrariness characterizing the defining of groups and their membership makes them difficult theoretical units to work with. Young herself acknowledges the analytical porosity in her approach, but insists nonetheless that social groups are real, preferring the position that group rights attempt to achieve equality of opportunity.[31]

Gender

Contemporary discussions of gender and justice have moved beyond feminism in the narrow sense to include gender identity and sexual orientation issues, some of which have been associated with human rights arguments.[32] Nonetheless, the term *feminism* itself has a broad range of meanings, ranging from the attempt to attain equal legal and political rights for women to any theory which views the relationship between genders as one of inequality, subordination, or oppression, and which aims to identify and remedy the sources of oppression.

As to views about women in *The Republic*, interestingly, Plato states that the function of guardianship is to be performed by men and women alike (451c–457b). He observes that the only distinction between male and female guardians is that women give birth to children and are physically weaker than men; thus, there is no justification for barring women from the guardian class. Further, for guardians the private household and therefore the institution of marriage is to be abolished (457b–466d), since the guardians do not own property and the care of children is to be a communal responsibility.[33] In contrast, Aristotle develops a model of political community as the city-state in the *Politics*, which is composed of citizens who have the right to participate in deliberative or judicial office, presenting a more direct involvement of citizens in governance than in the representative democracy model (I.1.1252a1–7). Restricted from citizenship, however, are women, slaves, foreigners, those of the working class, and others.

Aligned with her premises concerning group theory, Iris Marion Young examines how gender defines women as oppressed and dominated, thereby necessitating special representation and rights, including the appropriate institutional mechanisms and public resources to exercise these group rights. In contrast to Young, Susan Okin develops a liberal feminist account grounded in the autonomous individual.[34] As I described in chapter 7, while Young seeks to replace the liberal-communitarian debate with the politics of difference, Okin examines different cultural groups mainly to ensure that no gender discrimination persists. While contrasting in approach, both feminist thinkers point to the challenges of maintaining group rights without reducing the agency of the individual and to the problems resulting from theorizing on the basis of a homogenous society, such as presented in Plato and Aristotle, which marginalizes the complexities attendant to diverse or pluralistic societies.

For Okin, problems multiply as the question of how to assess patriarchy in different cultural contexts is played against defining what constitutes harm.[35] In balancing between cultural accommodation and other social costs, the role of intention becomes critical. In such situations, Okin explores the dilemma of what should be done when the claims of minority cultures or religious groups clash with the norm of gender equality, conceding that the claims of feminism and multiculturalism are often not easily reconciled. Nonetheless, while Okin argues that the state should support the liberal priority with respect to the feminist charge that women should not be disadvantaged because of their gender and that they should have the opportunity to have lives as fulfilling and freely chosen as men's lives, she also argues for the multicultural claim made in liberal democracies as ensuring the individual rights of members in minority cultural groups, and that these rights should be protected by special group rights or privileges.

Thus, in an example regarding the balancing of multicultural preferences, in 2014, the Ontario Premier ruled that in spite of their religious and cultural preference, Sikhs cannot wear only turbans, they must also wear safety helmets when operating motorcycles.[36] An analogous but contrary decision made by the United Kingdom treats Sikhs' rights to wear turbans on construction sites. Based on the Employment Act of 1989, it was decided that Sikhs can indeed wear turbans on construction sites in the U.K., but employers must at the same time provide for sufficient protection.[37] Okin would likely support the latter decision.

With respect to feminist concerns, Okin argues that cultures are suffused with practices of gender, with some cultures endorsing the control of men over women in various ways, often informally in the private sphere of domestic life. If more powerful male members of a culture determine or articulate the group's beliefs, practices, and interests for the good of the group, the group rights are anti-feminist. The multicultural thesis, Okin contends, does not take cognizance of this problem because it treats culture as monolithic, without taking into account the broad differences within particular minority cultures and because multicultural concerns play out in the public rather than the private sphere.

This lack of attention to the private sphere, however, proves to be a significant concern since personal, sexual, and reproductive life functions frequently constitute the dominant theme and central point of contention. Indeed, many cultural and religious groups demonstrate a great deal of concern with personal law, such as is the case with Islamic Sharia laws, pertaining to such matters as marriage, divorce, child custody, gender propriety, as well as the division and control of family property. Consequently, with respect to power, cultural practices have a much greater negative impact on women than on men.

In this framework, Okin argues that one of the principal aims of culture is to control women. The drive to control women remains particularly strong in various fundamentalist versions of many religions. Citing examples, she contends that sometimes culture and tradition are so closely linked with the control of women that they are equated. Okin recognizes that Western liberal democracies depart more from patriarchal models than is the case with many other nations. However, pointing to Will Kymlicka (whose account of justice is treated later in this chapter) as a representative multiculturalist,[38] Okin contends that multiculturalism still does not examine the relation between gender and culture or the tensions between feminism and multiculturalism.

Okin recognizes that Kymlicka accords various group rights based on individual rights, but confines such privileges and protections to cultural groups that are internally liberal. Consequently, he would not allow such rights to oppressive groups. However, as Okin further argues, Kymlicka fails to acknowledge that the subordination of women is often informal and private and that, critically, his public sex discrimination test, if applied to the private spheres of the world's cultures, would pass in few cultures. She concludes that minority group rights are not part of the solution of the endemic problem of gender discrimination and may, in fact, exacerbate it.[39]

Communities

Some contemporary thinkers on justice have posited hypothetical communities, as do Plato and Aristotle, according them power and raising questions regarding competing values within the political framework of differing visions of the good life. While both Plato and Aristotle propose comprehensive, political visions of the good life, their envisioned societies exhibit what Okin identifies as a lack of understanding for the complexities within groups, especially as originated in the private sphere, with their power-shaping repercussions in the public sphere.

Historically, classic liberalism, with its focus on the individual, has been termed a product of the Enlightenment. Communitarianism, with its emphasis on groups or communities, has been seen as an outgrowth of the Reformation. In contrast to the atomic individualism characteristic of both libertarian and welfare liberal strands of political liberalism, communitarians emphasize our social nature, underscoring that individuals belong to groups or communities.[40]

As part of the contemporary liberal-communitarian debate, I examine here the distributive account of Michael Walzer, a strong value pluralist who constructs a communitarian theory of justice. In *Spheres of Justice,* Walzer engages in a moral inquiry focusing on the concept of equality for purposes of determining what makes a just society.[41] The answers Walzer articulates are grounded in an understanding that "the aim of political egalitarianism is a society free from domination" (Walzer 1983, xiii) and that the nature of society and various social meanings of the good are pluralistic.

As its core notion, Walzer's argument proffers complex equality which, for him, has to do with the autonomy of various spheres of justice in which diverse societies may have distributions of different social goods for different internal reasons by different agents to different people, all of which may be different at different times.[42] These spheres may also reflect social meanings within a society, and in so doing, they have a bearing on Walzer's conception of the nature and the point of political society. By implication, his views additionally represent a critique of the Rawlsian distributive paradigm. Fundamentally, in Walzer's view the presence or absence of complex equality within a society serves as an index of whether or not the society is just. His ideal proves complex, as Richard Arneson notes, "by virtue of registering the moral import of distinct and autonomous distributive spheres."[43] It is patently intricate and its usefulness as the centerpiece of a positive theory of distributive justice is attenuated in part by its complexity, but also due to basic theoretical problems in its formulation.

Walzer's political construct may be seen as part of the communitarian critique of the universal claims of liberal theory, and especially of Rawls' formulation of the original position in *A Theory of Justice*. Walzer's view is that effective social criticism must derive from and resonate with the traditions and habits of actual people particularly located in time and space. His baseline thus diverges in focus from other communitarian criticisms of the devaluation of community by liberal political thinkers, criticisms that focus on ontological or metaphysical claims about the social nature of the self, as well as on normative claims about the value of community.[44] In contrast, Walzer's claim may be seen as a methodological one, concerning the importance of social context and human traditions in moral and political reasoning. Indeed, Walzer states that the central process in his theory of distributive justice comes from his view that "[p]eople conceive and create goods, which they then distribute among themselves."[45]

Walzer's main concern thus focuses on how to prevent the dominance of one particular social good—and thereby of the individuals whose power is based on their possession of this particular social good—over a wide range of other goods. In attempting to reduce such dominance, he develops a notion of complex equality, which in his view better satisfies the diversity of social goods than criteria used in other distributive justice schemes that focus on free exchange, desert, and need (Walzer 1983, 21–26). In the course of his deliberations, his answer to the problem of dominance becomes political pluralism, suggesting at the same time that a capitalist society cannot agree that all goods are translatable into cash values. His political pluralism, however, is premised upon and exhibits an understated value pluralism. And yet, one does not necessarily entail the other.

Just as critically, the political context in which Walzer's distribution of social goods operates needs to be examined too, since it seems that unlike other goods within a society which may be distributed according to some social meaning, membership in the polity appears to be a unique good for Walzer, and accordingly, not so distributable. Problematically, this membership principle seems to be a condition precedent to the operation of Walzer's distributive scheme. In contrast, Rawls solves the problem of membership in *A Theory of Justice* by assuming a closed society as the political context for the operation of his two principles of justice as fairness. Not satisfied with Rawls' theoretical construct, in *Spheres of Justice,* Walzer specifically discusses issues of immigration and citizenship, thereby evaluating membership in the polity as a necessarily unique and primary good.

Before examining Walzer's concept of complex equality in more depth, it may be useful to understand what it is not. With Walzer devoting an entire chapter in *Spheres of Justice* to the topic, Jeremy Waldron contends that Walzer's theory of justice is all about money, since Walzer argues that various social goods and their distribution must be viewed in terms of their exchangeability or non-exchangeability for cash.[46] Waldron attributes this preoccupation with wealth to Walzer's concern that currency may become a dominant good, a good whose possession enables individuals to command a wide range of other goods.[47]

Waldron is correct in highlighting Walzer's preoccupation with one social good dominating others in order to guard against an individual or group who may, by controlling or monopolizing that good, control political society. Waldron is further correct in identifying money as a social good that has been a primary object of various theories of distributive justice. Nonetheless, Waldron's reading of Walzer may be extreme. A more charitable reading would interpret Walzer's project as integrating a theory of distributive justice—and such theories are often concerned with the distribution and redistribution of money and wealth and concomitant opportunities—into notions of social equality.

Nonetheless, in his critique of the concept of "blocked exchanges" (Walzer's term for those social goods that are not exchangeable for money), Waldron does correctly demonstrate the category confusion that Walzer perpetrates in his development of a list of fourteen goods (Walzer 1983, 100–103), many of which are better seen as rights rather than goods. Included in Walzer's list of goods, for example, are the basic liberties of the freedoms of speech, press, religion, and assembly. Waldron underscores his point with the analogy that although Walzer describes the American Bill of Rights as a "series of blocked exchanges" (Walzer 1983, 100), the Founding Fathers did not word the First Amendment thus "Congress shall not *accept money as an inducement for* abridging the freedom of speech."[48] Consequently, the goods/rights confusion in Walzer's account raises the further questions of whether political pluralism can exist without value pluralism, and what motivation impels his theory of goods.

Regarding Walzer's concept of complex equality, Richard Arneson claims (as Walzer himself acknowledges[49]) that Walzer sets up a concept of simple or literal equality as a foil to identify a society "in which everything is up for sale and every citizen has as much money as any other."[50] In the course of his argument, Walzer objects to the equality of money in particular, because attempting to maintain it leads to state tyranny. After an initial equal distribution of money, individuals within a society—because of their different desires, plans, talent, luck, and ambition—would increasingly develop inequalities in their wealth and incomes. In order to maintain equality of wealth, a large and powerful state that frequently redistributes resources would prove necessary. For Nozick, this would constitute an unjustifiable constraint on personal liberty.[51] This is where Walzer parts company with Nozick—that is, Walzer gives less credence to the inviolability of an individual's rights.

For Walzer, goods in a society are socially constituted, and these distinct social goods are each associated with distinct social practices and a shared understanding of the goods as well as of the proper criteria for their distributions. Contrary to Nozick, then, Walzer believes that a liberal state may intervene to make practices conform to a communal understanding of the goods circulated in various spheres. Thus, it would appear that Walzer would subscribe to the rejoinder made to Nozick that if people care about equality and conceived of it as a public good, they should be allowed to assume restrictions to their liberty in order to maintain that egalitarian condition.[52]

Anchored in an implicit assumption that everyone recognizes the same goods and the same sense of communal life, for Walzer the proper, just, distribution of a good constitutes part of that particular good's social meaning. Complex equality obtains then, when distribution in all spheres in a society is autonomous, and further, distribution is autonomous when goods are distributed according to their social meanings. Asserting that a just society prevails when complex equality exists, however, Walzer's basic formulation of the concept of complex equality and its core place in his positive theory of distributive justice is problematic, generating questions stemming from the defects of his theory, such as:

1. What spheres exist within a society?
2. Who are its members?
3. Who and by what authority are "shared understandings" of goods and their proper distribution developed within a given sphere?
4. How is the product of such autonomous distributions within autonomous spheres determined? This should be important in his approach, because such distributions function as markers that indicate whether a society is just or unjust.
5. How useful is a concept of equality in formulating the complex equality calculus?
6. In the final analysis, does a just society result from a hitherto questionable complex equality distributive calculus?

Much of Walzer's discussion of complex equality and distributive justice in *Spheres of Justice* raises more questions than it answers. Nonetheless, Walzer's intuition that certain distributive justice schemes based on such notions as exchange, desert, or need provide inadequate accounts of the pluralistic social meanings and goods found in society is indeed valuable.

His positive theory of distributive justice based on the notion of complex equality, however, suffers from defects in its conceptual construction and formulation. As he himself suggests in his "Response," written a dozen years after *Spheres of Justice* to address various criticisms of his account, perhaps complex equality may best be viewed as a metaphor and his negative argument in *Spheres of Justice* taken most appropriately as interpretative social criticism (Walzer 1995, 282). We are left with the problem of evaluating how useful his social critique may be.

Culture

While *Multicultural Citizenship* is written primarily as a political text, it also presents some of Will Kymlicka's views on human nature and cultural diversity, social values, and goods, along with discussion of the proper ends of the social enterprise. Although he does not present a comprehensive moral theory, he does express some of his ethical views, including thoughts on moral agency, actions, and outcomes. His starting point is the observation that most countries today are culturally diverse: there exist about 200 independent states containing over 600 living languages and 5,000 ethnic groups. This cultural diversity gives rise to important and potentially divisive questions involving regional autonomy, political representation, land claims, education curriculum, language rights, integration, and immigration and naturalization policies, just to list some of the obvious problems.

Grounded in societies' multicultural realities then, *culture* designates a nation or a people, which he conceives of as "an intergenerational community, more or less institutionally complete, occupying a given territory or homeland, sharing a distinct language and history."[53] As an empirical observation, Kymlicka notes that in the modern world, just as societal cultures are almost invariably national cultures, so too nations are almost invariably social cultures. Further, with the term *multicultural*, Kymlicka designates a state in which the "members either belong to different nations (a multination state), or have emigrated from different nations (a polyethnic state), and . . . this fact is an important aspect of personal identity and political life."[54]

In isolating common threads found in both Kymlicka's multicultural thesis and other proponents of multiculturalism, Paul Kelly identifies two roles of culture:

1. In terms of a methodological argument, similar to the arguments of communitarians regarding liberalism and social atomism, multiculturalists view culture as the context that shapes an individual's identity and is inseparable from who we are as persons.
2. In terms of a social thesis, multiculturalists view culture as providing a moral resource, in addition to providing a context for personal and moral identity.[55]

Indeed, for Kymlicka, culture provides the moral resources (values, beliefs, and obligations) from which an individual may construct an autonomous and valuable life. By providing the moral resources to make choices and thus promote an individual's autonomy, Kymlicka argues that culture constitutes part of a liberal platform from which an individual may engage the world.[56] From identifying the problem set, Kymlicka moves on to setting himself the task of "finding morally defensible and politically viable answers to these issues [which pose] . . . the greatest challenge facing democracies today."[57] The political solution he devises in his account of justice is to supplement traditional human rights with minority cultural rights.

Perhaps overstating his disagreement, Brian Barry avers that, on the contrary, with regard to modern liberal societies "the notion that membership in some community is a constitutive element in anybody's identity is vastly implausible."[58] In addition to contesting whether culture is constituent or not of the self, also at the conceptual level of cultural rights, Kymlicka and Barry part ways as well in their broader liberal frameworks. Thus, Barry advocates a difference-blind approach to culture in the political realm, and more generally, he rejects group-based rights as antithetical to the universalist liberal project, which he views as based in the individual. Consequently, he claims that Kymlicka's views are not liberal at all, since they are not universalist in nature and allow for cultural relativism. More narrowly, Barry believes that the task of a just society is to provide for a fair and equal distribution of social goods.[59] In contrast, Kymlicka ascribes to a rights-based, distributive account of justice whereby rights are distributed equally to citizens within a multicultural political order, unless one is a member of a qualified minority culture, in which case additional rights obtain.[60] In a classic liberal response, in which the concept of negative liberty occupies much of the political terrain, Barry further accuses Kymlicka of posing a false choice between liberalism as autonomy and liberalism as tolerance, asserting that claims for cultural rights and for equality of treatment are incompatible.[61]

Kymlicka and Young share the view that, psychologically, individuals develop in an influence-generating social context. However, Barry argues against politically transferring identity development into group rights; rights should be defined as situated in the individual, rather than groups. Currently, for instance, while it is now commonly accepted that European recruits of ISIS became radicalized through negative encounters with their societal contexts, this does not mean that justice is achieved by acceding European for radical values. In other words, politically awarding group rights or limited cultural rights to persons is antithetical to the formulation of liberalism. Based in the individual, rights thrive in a political context furthering the components of liberty and equality, along with the concepts, I argue, of tolerance and diversity (See Conclusion). As discussed below, these latter two concepts respond to Kymlicka's initial concerns about persons situated in oppressed minority cultures.

In Kymlicka's taxonomy of minority cultural groups then, a national minority or minority nation comprises a people present at the establishment of a new nation, who had a prior history of self-government, as effected through institutions, and who were bound together by a common culture and language.[62] He proffers the nation of Canada as an example to illustrate his criteria, in which two such minority nations exist: the First Nations population and the Quebecois. Kymlicka argues that such minority groups deserve unique rights granted by the state by virtue of their particular role and history within the newly formed nation state, unique rights that include the right of self-government. In contrast, for polyethnic groups who come to a state voluntarily, such groups must accept some responsibility for integrating into the norms of their new nation and thereby prove less deserving of special rights. Kymlicka further specifies that other rights, such as the protection of a distinct culture and language, may be granted to immigrant groups so that integration into the dominant culture does not require abandoning all previous ways.

In response, Young criticizes the dichotomy that Kymlicka creates between nation and ethnicity as "creat[ing] too rigid and even contradictory an account of multicultural citizenship. Loosening this distinction and creating a continuum would better serve Kymlicka's purposes."[63] By way of example, she points to the case of African-Americans, who are neither an incorporated national group nor an immigrant group, but descendants of slaves, who had been "transported to a new land by the most brutal force, violently deprived of their original cultures, but also forced to remain segregated from the new culture."[64] Young's point is that a rigid choice vs. chance principle used to generate the category of a minority nation confuses the notion of multiculturalism. Cultural minorities "vary along a continuum . . . in the degree and manner in which they wish to integrate into a larger society and the degree they wish to separate, and the degree to which the larger society welcomes their participation also varies."[65]

While Young articulates reservations regarding Kymlicka's characterization of multiculturalism, Barry attacks his account along the lines of category confusion. He accuses Kymlicka of equating nationhood with cultural distinctiveness by definitional fiat.[66] Moreover, with regard to Kymlicka's multination concept, Barry takes him to task specifically over his Canadian example of Quebec and the rest of Canada (ROC), in which Kymlicka promotes an "asymmetrical federation . . . [that follows] . . . almost necessarily from the idea that Canada is a multination state."[67] With respect to this example, Barry points to the obvious inequity inherent in allowing Quebec to opt out of institutions that operate in all other provinces. While the notion of asymmetric federalism may indeed allow Quebecois to determine their own future without interference from outsiders the concept does not, however, allow the ROC to do likewise, nor does it permit common issues (such as foreign policy or defense) to be decided in a forum in which Quebec, as the minority nationality, may be outvoted.[68]

With regard to Kymlicka's second concept of polyethnicity, where members of a polyethnic state (the United States, Canada, and Australia) emigrated from different nations, Barry remains uneasy. He considers Kymlicka's cultural conception as inapposite, and perhaps more damning, as lacking explanatory power in the case of the United States, where discrimination against African Americans has not occurred along cultural lines at all.[69]

Further, with regard to the taxonomy of Kymlicka's cultural communities, Barry points to the slipperiness and arbitrariness of the immigrant-national communities typology in three of Kymlicka's examples involving Hispanic immigrants and Spanish-speaking national minorities in the United States.[70]

As discussed earlier, while some commentators continue to view liberty as the key concept fueling liberalism, others claim that the core value of liberalism is articulated in equality rather than liberty. Further, among liberal egalitarians, some emphasize the substantive moral value of the concept (equality of concern and respect), while others concentrate on the political nature of the concept, focusing on the fair distribution of rights and the economic resources necessary to protect individuals.

Kymlicka is an egalitarian in the Dworkian sense, since he accepts the idea of equality of concern and respect as the basis of any viable moral and political theory.[71] For a multicultural society, the problem of a distributive approach to justice remains in determining what should be distributed in order for a just society to provide each person equal concern and respect. Here, cultural rights provide Kymlicka with the theoretical underpinning for opportunity egalitarianism. For Kymlicka, that is, respect for an individual's culture provides a significant platform allowing for the requisite equal concern and respect for the individual. In this context, Kymlicka defines culture as a building block integral to how he views equality of concern and respect for the individual, thereby providing the basis for his positing of cultural rights in a liberal political framework.

Barry further accuses Kymlicka of confusion, when arguing for making an individual's exit from a group as painless as possible since Kymlicka does not draw distinctions between different kinds of costs when leaving a group. Referring in particular to religious bodies, Barry examines Kymlicka's statement that liberal principles preclude non-liberal minorities from imposing "internal restrictions which limit the right of individuals within the group to revise their conceptions of the good."[72] Barry believes it overly intrusive of a liberal society to interfere with how a person may think about the truth or value of constitutive beliefs or norms of a group. Regarding Kymlicka's concern of "what a group may legitimately do to those whom it defines as heretics or apostates,"[73] Barry suggests exclusion from the group, as he continues to claim that Kymlicka's suggestion to make exits from a group in such a situation as costless as possible is wrong-thinking, since such an exclusion could very well be deeply disturbing for the individual. Instead, Barry argues that legal relief may be sought by the individual. Easy exits, Barry believes, stem from an overly paternalistic government engaging in a view of positive liberty, a situation that he rejects.

Here, however, Barry appears to argue the wrong side of the question. He acknowledges that exclusion from a minority cultural group, whether membership in the group is a matter of freedom of association or stems from more complex cultural identity issues, may be deeply disturbing to an individual, an acknowledgement that seems to argue for easy exits from the group rather than for reliance on legal remedies. Consequently, the existence of any such legal remedies seems a greater indication of governmental paternalism in place of easy exits.

Ultimately, multiculturalists regard Barry's faith in the robust enforcement of classic difference-blind liberal principles as wanting. In developing his thesis, Barry does minimize the problematic nature of multicultural concerns, especially with respect to questions of customs practiced by illiberal religions in liberal societies, thereby evoking a situation reminiscent of the difficulties encountered when trying to apply Mill's liberty principle to determine what distinguishes harm from mere offense. Indeed, Barry appears to be somewhat oblivious to the depth of multicultural issues.

As may be derived from this discussion, the complexities involved in any group approach stem in large part from its intermediate positioning between individuals and states. Like a state, a group can exercise some sort of control over individuals, and like individuals, a group can act to effect ethos-based guidance. However, unlike a state, a group is neither geopolitically circumscribed nor acting in the best interests of its members based on law within that territory, and unlike individuals, a group does not have the flexibility to make moral decisions.

Such views provide support for the designation of the individual as the proper bearer of rights in political society, and not groups. As lodged in the individual, the question of just or unjust actions can be most effectively determined along moral lines, with cultural contexts and traditions including those of both groups and states, functioning as critical touchstones. Issues regarding the oppression of groups—whether by race, religion, gender, or culture—may be addressed by integrating the concepts of tolerance and diversity in the formulation of the liberal context for these discussions, shoring up the elements of negative liberty and equality of concern and respect, as the political context for justice.

NOTES

1. See Fred Miller, *Nature, Justice, and Rights in Aristotle's Politics* (Oxford: Oxford University Press, 1995); John Gray, *Liberalism* (Minneapolis: University of Minnesota Press, 1985).

2. Robert Nozick, *Anarchy, State, and Utopia* (New York: Basic Books, 1974), p. ix.

3. Id., p. 223.

4. See Friedrich von Hayek, *Law, Legislation and Liberty* (Chicago: University of Chicago Press, 1978), vol. II. Von Hayek attempts to make the distinction that only those actions of other individuals which are coercive restrict freedom, while the law (and therefore obedience to the law) never restricts freedom.

5. See G. A. Cohen, ed. *Self-Ownership, Freedom, and Equality* (Cambridge: Cambridge University Press, 1995). To the extent that Nozick's views may be seen as further representing Lockean self-ownership, a term that Nozick does not expressly use as other libertarian writers do, Cohen has written an oft-cited critique of the principle including its deployment in defense of libertarianism. Also see Jonathan Wolff, *Robert Nozick* (Stanford: Stanford University Press, 1991).

6. In addition to Nozick, influential modern proponents of libertarianism include such writers as Murray Rothbard, *Ethics of Liberty* (New York: New York University Press, 1998). See, generally, Peter Vallentyne and Bas van der Vossen, "Libertarianism," *Stanford Encyclopedia of Philosophy*, 2014. http://plato.stanford.edu/entries/libertarianism/.

7. Interestingly, although libertarianism is often seen as a right-wing political doctrine, with regard to social rather than economic issues, libertarianism tends to be left-wing when it opposes laws that restrict consensual and private relations between adults, restrict drug use, impose religious practices, and demand compulsory military service. Further, there is both a right-libertarian and left-libertarian approach to the issue of the initial appropriation of unowned natural resources.

8. See Cohen (1995).

9. See John Locke, *Second Treatise of Government*, ed. Crawford Brough Macpherson (Indianapolis: Hackett Publishing, 1980).

10. Id., p. 12.

11. See T. M. Scanlon, "Nozick on Rights, Liberty, and Property," in *Reading Nozick,* ed. Jeffrey Paul (Totowa: Rowman and Littlefield, 1991), pp. 107–129.

12. Locke (1980), p. 2.

13. See Bernard Williams, "The Minimal State," in *Reading Nozick,* ed. Jeffrey Paul (Totowa: Rowman and Littlefield, 1991), pp. 27–36.

14. E.g., see Thomas Nagel, "Libertarianism Without Foundations," in *Reading Nozick,* ed. Jeffrey Paul (Totowa: Rowman and Littlefield, 1991), pp. 191–205.

15. See Immanuel Kant, *Groundwork for the Metaphysics of Moral,* trans. J. J. Paton (New York: HarperCollins, 2009), p. 62.

16. See Thomas Nagel, *Mortal Questions* (New York: Cambridge University Press, 1979); Bernard Williams, *Moral Luck* (Cambrisge: Cambridge University Press, 1981).

17. John Rawls, *A Theory of Justice* (Cambridge: Harvard University Press, 1971), p. 72.

18. See Will Kymlicka, "Dworkin on Freedom and Culture," in *Dworkin and His Critics,* ed. Justine Burley (Oxford: Blackwell Publishing, 2004), pp. 113–133.

19. See G. A. Cohen, "Expensive Taste Rides Again," in *Dworkin and His Critics,* ed. Justine Burley (Oxford: Blackwell Publishing, 2004), pp. 3–29.

20. See Ronald Dworkin, "Ronald Dworkin Replies," in *Dworkin and His Critics,* ed. Justine Burley (Oxford: Blackwell Publishing, 2004), pp. 339–350.

21. Alternatively, the choice/chance distinction of how individuals are situated in society and whether there exists a duty of justice to help those responsible for the fact that they need help may be dealt with in two ways. As to the underlying individual responsibility issue (see chapter 4 *infra*), intentions may comprise a key factor to consider. Then, as to a duty of assistance, a principle of due concern and respect may be applied, and if circumstances present a conflict in values, the laws and customs of the society involved may help guide determinations. See Conclusion *infra.*

22. Iris Marion Young, *Justice and the Politics of Difference* Oxford: Oxford University Press, 1990), p. 39.

23. Id., ch. 2.

24. Id., p. 42. It is worth asking whether these five faces of oppression may be reduced to her third category of powerlessness.

25. Id., ch. 7.

26. Id., ch. 6.

27. Further, "members of a group have a specific affinity with one another because of their similar experience or way of life, which prompts them to associate with one another more than with those not identified with the group, or in a different way. Groups are the expression of social relations; a group exists only in relation to at least one other group. Group identification arises, that is, in the encounter and interaction between social collectives that experience some differences in their way of life." Id. at 43.

28. For instance, for the view that only individual human beings may be of ultimate value, see Chandran Kukathas, "Are There Any Cultural Rights?" *Political Theory* 20; 1 (1992): 105–139.

29. As I argue in chapter 9 *infra*, it seems appropriate to attribute moral agency to nations and states, discussions of which often devolve into questions of the political legitimacy of the nations or states involved.

30. See Brian Barry, *Culture and Equality* (Cambridge: Harvard University Press, 2002).

31. Young (1990), p. 173.

32. For example, see United Nations Universal Declaration of Human Rights (1948), and the United Nations Convention on the Elimination of all Forms of Discrimination against Women (1979).

33. See Julia Annas, "Plato's 'Republic' and Feminism," *Philosophy* 51; 197 (July, 1976): 307–321; Gregory Vlastos, "Was Plato a Feminist," in *Plato's Republic: Critical Essays,* ed. Richard Kraut (Lanham: Rowman & Littlefield Publishers, Inc., 1997).

34. See Susan Okin, *Is Multiculturalism Bad for Women?* (Princeton: Princeton University Press, 1999).

35. See discussion of John Stuart Mill's harm principle in chapter 6 *infra*, and of Joseph Raz' radical reinterpretation of Mill's harm principle into a harm prevention principle based on autonomy in chapter 5 *infra.*

36. See the CBC news account, on http://www.cbc.ca/news/canada/toronto/sikhs-on-motorcycles-must-wear-helmets-ontario-government-says-1.2742185, last accessed on May 18, 2017.

37. See the account on the UK Health and Safety Executive website, http://www.hse.gov.uk/foi/internalops/og/og-00003.htm, last accessed on January 24, 2015.

38. See Will Kymlicka, *Multicultural Citizenship* (Oxford: Oxford University Press, 1995).

39. Other scholars exploring both multiculturalism and women's rights have interrogated and attempted to adjudicate the tensions between minority group recognition and oppression within groups, when laws and practices within such groups violate central values of political liberalism such as individual human rights, democracy, and social justice. See, for example, Ayelet Shachar, *Multicultural Jurisdictions* (Cambridge: Cambridge University Press, 2001). Likewise, Sarah Song has explored the relationship between liberal values and legal and informal accommodations for religious and cultural minorities, further tracking the tensions between such accommodation and the pursuit of gender equality. See Sarah Song, *Justice, Gender, and the Politics of Multiculturalism* (Cambridge: Cambridge University Press, 2007).

40. Some have made the connection between Aristotelianism and communitarianism, e.g., see Charles Taylor, *Sources of the Self* (Cambridge: Cambridge University Press, 1989), while others see them as opposing doctrines, e.g., see Alasdair MacIntyre, *After Virtue*, 3rd ed. (Notre Dame: University of Notre Dame Press, 2007).

41. Michael Walzer, *Spheres of Justice* (New York: Basic Books, 1983).

42. See Michael Walzer, "Response," in *Pluralism, Justice and Equality,* ed. David Miller and Michael Walzer (Oxford: Oxford University Press, 1995), p. 283.

43. Richard Arneson, "Against Complex Equality," in Miller and Walzer (1995), p. 231.

44. See Michael Sandel, *Liberalism and the Limits of Justice*, 2nd ed. (Cambridge: Cambridge University Press, 1998); see also Stephen Mulhall and Adam Swift, *Liberals and Communitarians*, 2nd ed. (Oxford: Blackwell, 1996).

45. In abbreviated form, the principles of his theory may be stated as follows: (1) All the goods with which distributive justice is concerned are social goods. (2) Men and women take on concrete identities, because of the way they conceive and create and then possess and employ social goods. (3) There is no single set of primary or basic goods conceivable across all moral and material worlds. (4) It is the meaning of goods that determines their movement. (5) Social meanings are historical in character, and so distributions, just and unjust, change over time. (6) When meanings are distinct, distributions must be autonomous. Walzer (1983), p. 4.

46. See Jeremy Waldron, "Money and Complex Equality," in Miller and Walzer (1995), pp. 144–170.

47. Id., p. 146.

48. Id., p. 156.
49. Walzer (1995), p. 283.
50. Walzer (1983), p. 14. Arneson (1995), pp. 227–228.
51. Id., ch. 3.
52. See G. A. Cohen, "Robert Nozick and Wilt Chamberlain: How Patterns Preserve Liberty," in *Self-Ownership, Freedom and Equality,* ed. G. A. Cohen (Cambridge: Cambridge University Press, 1995), pp. 19–37.
53. Kymlicka (1995), p. 18.
54. Ibid.
55. Paul Kelly, "Introduction," in *Multiculturalism Reconsidered,* ed. Paul Kelly (Cambridge: Polity Press, 2002), pp. 5–9.
56. Kymlicka (1995), pp. 80–81.
57. Kymlicka (1995), p. 1.
58. Brian Barry, "Second Thoughts," in Kelly (2002), p. 223.
59. Barry (2002), p. 148: "The fundamental liberal position on group rights . . . is that individuals should be free to associate in any way they like, as long as they do not in so doing break laws designed to protect the rights and interests of those outside the group."
60. "A comprehensive theory of justice in a multicultural state will include both universal rights, assigned to individuals regardless of group membership, and certain group-differentiated rights or 'special status' for minority cultures." Kymlicka (1995), p. 6.
61. Barry (2002), p. 48.
62. See Kymlicka (1995), ch. 2.
63. Iris Marion Young, "A Multicultural Continuum," *Constellation* 4; 1 (1997): 49.
64. Id., p. 50.
65. Id., p. 51.
66. Barry (2002), p. 308.
67. Kymlicka (1995), p. 143.
68. Id., pp. 310–314.
69. Id., p. 306, Barry quotes Kwame Anthony Appiah: "It is not black culture that the racist disdains, but blacks. There is no conflict of visions between black and white cultures that is the source of racial discord. No amount of knowledge of the architectural achievements of Nubia or Kush guarantees respect for African-Americans. No African-American is entitled to greater concern because he is descended from a people who created jazz or produced Toni Morrison. Culture is not the problem, and it is not the solution."
70. Kymlicka (1995), pp. 217–220. In reviewing Kymlicka's examples, the following problems emerge: First, Mexican citizens who resided in Arizona, California, Colorado, New Mexico, and Texas were granted citizenship when those territories were annexed by the United States. In Kymlicka's typology, their descendants should constitute a national minority. Contrary to Kymlicka's approach, many of these descendants early on challenged their lack of equal protection of the law in court, based on their dependence upon segregated educational facilities. Their demand, in other words, was to be integrated into the larger society. Second, post-Castro Cubans

in Miami satisfy all of Kymlicka's criteria to qualify as a national minority, and yet many choose to assimilate linguistically. Third, Kymlicka identifies Puerto Ricans as a national minority. They are not, however, national minorities in Puerto Rico, a self-governing commonwealth, or on the mainland. Thus, if they were to be counted as an immigrant group on the mainland, how would their strong bicultural and bilingual education goals be accounted for?

71. See Ronald Dworkin, *Sovereign Virtue* (Cambridge: Harvard University Press, 2000).

72. Kymlicka (1995), p. 161. Cf. pp. 162–165.

73. Id., p. 163.

Chapter 9

International Relations

As the boat introduced in chapter 7 sails across vast oceans, docking in various locales to replenish its resources and otherwise engage its passengers, it comes across other boats of varying sizes filled with diverse individuals organized socially in different manners. As contact between passengers of our boat and those of other boats takes place, the constraints of justice governing individuals and groups living on different boats and under different moral and political conditions become more manifest, especially when interaction is sought.

For such interaction of passengers of different boats to proceed harmoniously, there needs to be agreement upon rules of conduct, on how to interact, further including such questions as the basis passengers may move to other boats, if at all. Possible conflicts between passengers of different boats may also need to be addressed.

Thoughts on what we now call international relations have been articulated since at least since the fifth century, B.C. Thucydides' *History of the Peloponnesian War*, Book I, for example, describes human nature's priority of self-interest over morality as a foundational concern, associating the absence of government with anarchy (5.97), and expressing security as an especial concern (1.23).[1] In expressing skepticism about the relevance of morality on international politics, Thucydides relates the Melian Dialogue, the classic debate between idealist and realist views, exploring whether what may now be called international politics should be based on a moral order derived from principles of justice, or whether such matters merely provide the arena for conflicting interests and power.[2]

In their roughly contemporary accounts of justice, both Plato and Aristotle occupy the position of political idealists, in that they believe that there are universal moral values on which political life can be based. While idealism in international politics has no commonly accepted meaning, generally, such idealism seeks to advance certain ideals or moral goals such as peace and stability, to make the world a more just place. Ontologically, the concept may be interpreted to promote a more cosmopolitan and harmonious world order.[3] In contrast, the realist stripe of international relations emphasizes the role of power in the development of norms of justice. Its theoretical roots are found in the tradition including Machiavelli and extending at least as far back as Glaucon's challenge to Socrates.[4]

Whether from the positioning of idealism or cosmopolitanism or from realist concerns, to consider what political justice might mean internationally, a series of conditions should be established. A first task, for example, is to sort out what political order among nations may obtain. Put another way, assuming that a Hobbesian state of nature does not adequately define international relationships, the task is to identify the appropriate political conditions for justice among nations to flourish. However, outside of the United Nations, which has significant limitations with respect to meting out global justice,[5] there is no single existing supranational cooperative scheme that regulates relations among nations, including questions of war and peace.

Suggested by the United Nations's limits, neither a realist nor a cosmopolitan view can suffice. I argue that the concept of due concern and respect may help guide just international relations. Further, communications in the substantive sense of a method of resolving disputes, as well as an instrumental sense of conveying values of international institutions through time, may play a key role in establishing and maintaining a peaceful, stable world order. For instance, in this manner, a liberal political order with components of liberty and equality, as defined through tolerance and diversity, may be mapped onto an international format in questions of justice among nations, perhaps even onto existing institutions, like the UN's International Court of Justice, as well as more limited international governance structures.

In this chapter, in discussing an appropriate ethical and political model for the operation of justice internationally, I interrogate the account of Charles Beitz, who presents a contractualist view of international relations, along with John Rawls' principles of justice, which Beitz adapts. In discussing the possibility of international justice, I follow the well-known distinction between nations and states developed by Max Weber, whereby a nation is seen as a group that views itself as "a people," often with such shared matters as ethnicity, language, culture, historical experience, ideals and values, habitat, cuisine, and the like. In contrast, a state refers more narrowly to the machinery of government that organizes life within a given territory.[6] The distinction becomes apparent when, for example, natural disasters evoke state (or government) assistance to aid the people of a nation in distress.

POLITICAL REALISM

Charles Beitz contends that in a realist view, international relations between states exist in a Hobbesian state of nature, a state of anarchic war where might makes right. Such a view of international relations is realist in the sense that it advocates viewing states as they "really are," rather than portraying them in idealistic circumstances or according to their purported ideals. States are given, in effect, an exemption from the moral constraints that apply to individuals. As a result, the rulers of states are guided by and morally bound to only the interests of their own nations without regard to the rights and interests of other nations. In other words, states defend and promote domestic national interests in an anarchic international arena, thereby echoing a Hobbesian view.[7]

Arguing against such Hobbesian anarchy, Beitz develops a contrasting and normative view in order to provide a moral basis for guiding international relations. He begins his project by postulating that for the Hobbesian state of nature analogy to work at the level of international relations, four propositions must obtain, as follows:

1. The actors in international relations are states.
2. States have relatively equal power (the weakest can defeat the strongest).
3. States are independent of each other in the sense that they can order their internal (i.e., non-security matters) affairs independently of the internal policies of other actors.
4. In the absence of a superior power capable of enforcing rules of cooperation, states cannot count on reciprocal compliance to such rules. (Beitz 1999, 36)

Beitz then makes the case that none of these Hobbesian conditions obtain in contemporary international relations. By successfully making the point, Beitz believes he defeats the basis of realist claims and its pervasive view that international relations should be treated as in a constant state of war.

Indeed, current prevalent geopolitical conditions do deny the applicability of these four elements. First, it is clear that states are not the only international actors in global governance. There are alliances and coalitions between and among states, and while some, as Hobbes allows, may be unstable and actually increase the chances of war, others including regional, political, and economic alliances may actually promote peace and stability. Second, and critically, in Hobbes' claim, the actors would have roughly equivalent power; otherwise, an empire formed by the dominant actor would emerge. In contemporary international relations, however, it is clear that there are vast disparities of relative national power.

Third, and fundamentally important for Beitz' argument, in contemporary international relations, rather than Hobbes' self-sufficient actors all pursuing their own self-interests, what characterizes the international geopolitical scene is a large degree of interdependence, both in areas of security as well as with regard to economic and welfare concerns. This interdependence and cooperation, for example, helps to explain the rise of such international institutions as the United Nations, the World Bank, and the International Monetary Fund. Such interdependence of states is foundational to Beitz' cosmopolitan view of justice even though, clearly, such a foundation is contingent and may not at times provide the normative platform desired. To support his position from another perspective, in later works, without changing his conclusions, Beitz shifts his ground to rely more upon the Kantian notion detailing the capacities of individuals to act as moral agents in order to provide a moral grounding for his cosmopolitan theory.[8]

With respect to Beitz' fourth necessary Hobbesian condition, even while lacking a superior supranational force that may enforce compliance, many international institutions exhibit high degrees of voluntary compliance with expected norms and institutionalized rules established by agreement, as witnessed in the international postal service, the World Health Organization, and even at the level of regional associations such as the European Union. Although Beitz does not make the following argument, the Hobbesian point loses effect when considering that even without physical coercive power or expectations of benefits for obedience, such factors as identity, role, habit, and convention—as suggested by Weber—may also play a part in explaining such compliance.[9] Indeed, supranational institutions, often following a cooperative model, place greater weight on reasoned discourse, compromise, and consensus, thereby offering a better empirical understanding of international relations than does Hobbesian competition. This cooperative model would accord both with the communicative key essential to the relational goals of justice discussed in chapter 6.

War

In developing his theory of global political justice, Beitz explains that he does not focus on questions of war and peace, one of the central concerns of international relations. He accounts for this omission on two grounds: first, scholarship on just war theory, *ius ad bellum*, has received considerable philosophical attention in recent years. Second, any just war theory must rest upon a more general theory of international right, which is what he prefers to discuss (see below). Thus, Beitz points out that when rallying for justice in war, arguments "often turn on claims that particular rights (e.g., to land) have been infringed or that rules of international conduct (e.g., those defining a balance of power) have been broken" and that such claims furnish a justification for resorting to war in part because they "rest upon principles that distribute rights to international actors and define a structure of international life that actors have duties to promote or uphold" (Beitz 1999, 10).

Although Plato does not discuss the matter in depth, in *The Republic* training in war is required of the guardians and thus constitutes a necessary part of a just *polis* (467b). Critically, occupying the idealist position, war is subservient to justice and may be controlled as Plato argues in the *Statesman* (305e) and *Laws* (628d). Since war stems from the aggressiveness of human nature, the key to controlling such aggressiveness, and placing it in balance, is rationality. Further, while not endorsing all-out devastating wars, *The Republic* allows the waging of wars to protect a state, to train its guardians, and to ensure that the state has enough resources to provide for luxuries (373d). He thus outlines on what occasions the *polis* should go to war (*ius ad bellum*), and how it should fight wars, in a controlled manner (*ius in bello*).

Aristotle also links war with justice, but unlike Plato, he states in his *Politics* that war should always be fought for the sake the peace (1333a30). Nonetheless, his view of proper causes for war (*ius ad bellum*) is broader than those traditionally cited in modern times; for instance, beyond the acquisition of property and the establishment of proper leadership and peace, Aristotle includes war for the sake of enslavement and for obtaining resources. Further unlike Plato, Aristotle does not see war as necessary for the cultivation of the *polis* or the soul, but he does mention two aspects of the soul as origins of war: spiritedness and acquisition. The spiritedness that Aristotle portrays is not the same as the appetite of Plato's triadic soul, but rather, it is a "commanding and an unconquerable thing" (1327b36). Likewise, the need for acquisition that Aristotle refers to exhibit his teleological orientation as he describes acquisition in terms of domestic affairs: "Accordingly, if nature makes nothing purposeless or in vain, all animals must have been made by nature for the sake of men. It also follows that the art of war is in some sense a natural mode of acquisition" (1256b15).

Plato and Aristotle articulate ideas about war that serve as precursors to just war theory, which was more fully developed in the framework of the Christian theological tradition. Just war theory accepts the notion that while war is evil, under certain conditions, it may represent the lesser of two evils. Understood as an actual, intentional, and widespread armed conflict between nations war, according to Carl von Clausewitz, constitutes an extension of politics. Looking beyond this dictum, however, it can be argued that war is concerned with the creation of policy; in other words, war entails governance. Consequently, the goal of just war theory is to develop criteria to determine whether a war is morally justifiable, including whether there is a right to go to war (*ius ad bellum*), the right conduct in war (*ius in bello*), and more recently, the morality of postwar settlement and reconstruction (*ius post bellum*).

Consideration of whether a war constitutes a just war (*ius ad bellum*) includes a variety of moral, political, and pragmatic considerations, such as: Will the war be fought for a good cause or out of good intentions? Will war be declared by a lawful authority? Have all other ways of resolving the conflict been explored? Is there a reasonable chance of success in conducting the war? Are the means of the conduct of war commensurate with its goals?

In contemporary times, and as self-professed Kantians, John Rawls and Michael Walzer support the concept of a just war. In reviewing Kant's own views on the topic, however, debate ensues, with some commentators referring to "The Doctrine of Right," Part One of the *Metaphysics of Morals* to argue that Kant embraced the concept, while others point to Kant's *Perpetual Peace* as evidence that he rejected the notion and rejected the views of just war proponents Hugo Grotius (1583–1645), Samuel von Pufendorf (1632–1704), and Emer Vattel (1714–1767) as "sorry comforters."[10]

Taking into consideration the Kantian notion of due concern and respect, from a moral perspective there is no imperative to engage in war, although the principle does leave open the possibility of a just war. Thus, in the case of competing values, an argument for war may prevail if engaging in war adheres more closely to or better promotes due concern and respect for others. Thus, the concept of due concern and respect itself weights the scale more heavily toward peace rather than war, since it supports the idea that all other ways of resolving conflict should be properly explored first.

In lieu of parsing questions of war and peace, as mentioned above, Beitz attempts to provide a more general theory of international right in his *Political Theory and International Relations*. Thus, what he might have said about the problem of *ius ad bellum* needs to be extrapolated from his exegesis on international politics. Doing so, it is not difficult to surmise that Beitz approaches the problem of just war differently than how a realist might suggest. In a realist's view, the central issue is not really the amoral international context, but rather, the responsibilities of rulers, who are bound to their own subjects and fellow citizens. This obligation means that rulers must take actions, or be excused in taking actions, to guarantee the security of their subjects and advance their well-being.

In contrast, Beitz argues that nothing should be enacted for others that they could not do themselves, a moral argument that must similarly apply to rulers with respect to their responsibilities toward their fellow citizens. Rulers are thereby constrained to act only with the consent of their nations' populace; in the case of war, a state may not determine that people may be killed on behalf of the nation. Nonetheless, Beitz would not repress all war, since he does countenance the concept of just and unjust wars. It remains unclear, however, whether his version of cosmopolitanism would lead him to discuss war in terms of a domestic analogy, so that unjust wars, for instance, would be treated as criminal acts, and just wars as police actions and instances of law enforcement.

COSMOPOLITANISM

In recent years, interest in the liberal political tradition in international thought has been revived. Beitz notes that this interest stems from several sources, but most prominently from doubts concerning the adequacy of political realism in explaining international collaboration, as well as from the examination of the neo-Kantian idea of a democratic peace.[11]

From this philosophical vantage point, Beitz poses the question of whether the obligations of justice stop at the borders of one's country or whether they are international in nature, to then respond that nations do indeed have global obligations of justice. Positioned against a realist approach and advocating a cosmopolitan view of international relations, Beitz would allow, however, only limited political intervention between the individual nation and the world community.[12]

Although Beitz does indeed demonstrate the failure of realism in the absence of a Hobbesian state of nature, his answer, cosmopolitanism, is not the only better response. To sketch briefly one counterexample, Michael Walzer, whose account of justice is referred to in chapter 8, makes a case for the moral autonomy of states and thus proffers a norm of nonintervention.[13] That is, in developing what he calls a "Legalist Paradigm," Walzer defines nonintervention as the norm and aggression as a crime that justifies war as an act of self-defense. Rather than presenting nonintervention as an empirically observed account of the state of current international law, Walzer thus ascribes to it a morally defensible position.

More specifically, Walzer asserts that political communities have moral rights, such as the right to exist through time, and are entitled to defend such rights by whatever means necessary including, in the case of "supreme emergencies," the performance of acts that would otherwise be illegal. It is not difficult to imagine, unfortunately, how the proviso for supreme emergencies might be used in defense of such actions as large-scale murder. Be that as it may, such a position has been included in views of communitarianism as well.[14] Indeed, in his *Spheres of Justice*, Walzer analyzes the challenges posed by immigration and national borders, and in so doing, he raises the question of whether communitarianism, with its emphasis on political communities, may have a longer reach than cosmopolitanism.[15]

In addition to such responses to the question of international justice, the liberal political tradition generates concepts emphasizing the rights and interests of individuals. As these relate to international relations and cosmopolitanism, such concepts are often intertwined with questions of the political legitimacy of nations. By political legitimacy, I mean the justification of coercive power and the creation and/or sanctioning of political authority or the right to rule. In such regard, Weber's famous delineation of three sources of political legitimacy (traditional, charismatic, and rational-legal) is seen as a descriptive account.[16] Other accounts introduce normative concepts into the acceptability or justification of political authority,[17] or the moral justification of political authority.[18] Still other accounts develop concepts of political legitimacy that are both descriptive and normative. For instance, David Beetham criticizes Weber's purely descriptive account as not treating people's second-order beliefs concerning legitimacy; that is, their beliefs are not only concerned with the actual legitimacy of a political institution, but also with the justifiability of the institution. He states that a "power relationship is not legitimate because people believe in its legitimacy, but because it can be *justified in terms of* their beliefs."[19]

In extending a normative concept of legitimacy, some authors define legitimacy as a criterion of justice. For instance, in focusing on the rights and interests of individuals, rather than those of nations (as does Beitz), Allen Buchanan advocates a moralized conception of legitimacy in which entities are legitimate if they are morally justified to wield political power.[20] He understands political legitimacy as requiring a minimal standard of justice. For Buchanan, that standard of justice includes an internal requirement of protecting basic human rights and improving democratic accountability, procedural justice, and an external requirement specifying how political entities should interact with each other.[21] In this approach, a much contested question raised in discussions of political cosmopolitanism, one which is not addressed here, is the extent to which international or global legitimacy requires democracy, either at the level of nations and states or at the level of global governance institutions.[22]

Beitz identifies two types of cosmopolitanism in the international context: institutional cosmopolitanism and moral cosmopolitanism. Institutional cosmopolitanism is concerned with the political structures and institutions of the world along with such matters as world government. Moral cosmopolitanism is concerned less with the institutions themselves and more with the basis on which such institutions should be justified or critiqued. It is the second kind of cosmopolitanism that occupies Beitz' attention.

Thus, Beitz maintains that moral cosmopolitanism is the natural offspring of the individualist moral egalitarianism associated with the Enlightenment. Importantly, it "applies to the whole world the maxim that choices about what we should do or what institutions we should establish should be based on an impartial consideration of the claims of each person who would be affected" (Beitz 1999 article, p. 9). Here, Beitz understates the novelty of what emerges as a kind of cosmopolitan liberalism.

Liberalism, for example, may be easily mapped onto a realist international view, when the liberal model recognizes the claims of rightly organized states that have a just constitution and basic structure. Beitz, however, prefers to dismantle received notions of liberalism. For him, the core of liberalism comprises a set of universal moral commitments to, and respect for, an individual's concerns with regard to equality. Liberalism in this view is thus seen to constrain how domestic political power may be exercised. Further, liberalism addresses the appropriate set of principles and institutions to secure the equal status of individuals, in order to provide a basic structure and a state with constitutional constraints on power, together with redistributive mechanisms. In such an approach, tensions arise because the set of moral commitments which tracks with Beitz' views of moral cosmopolitanism is universal in scope and therefore does not apply solely to those with whom we are bound in social cooperation.

Human Rights

Fault lines in Beitz' approach to justice on an international scale can be detected in how he attempts to accommodate the issue of human rights. Although Beitz concedes that there may be some pragmatic reasons why state autonomy might be desirable, he holds that there is no principled reason for a norm of nonintervention in international affairs. More specifically, no principled reasons with respect to nationality can justify different treatment in matters such as human rights. Beitz reaches this conclusion on the basis of the interdependence of nations or peoples. He does recognize that such a contingent argument proves unsatisfactory and later shifts his ground to focus more on the Kantian notion of the capacity of individuals to act as moral agents (see Beitz 1999 article).

While a significant development in the concept of universal human rights emerged in the latter part of the twentieth century—as captured, for instance, by the United Nations Declarations—serious challenges to the scope and content of the concept have erupted as well. Specifically debated is whether universal human rights should include economic and social basic rights, rather than merely political rights as defined in the Western liberal tradition. Likewise controversial, views differ as to whether freedom of religion should also be included as a universal human right.[23] Importantly here, raising such questions in and of itself brings attention to the cultural contingency of Beitz' approach.

Rather than through empirically based and normatively contextualized guidelines, both Rawls and Beitz attempt to solve the difficult question of human rights through abstracted rules. Indeed, the very fact that human rights purport to have near universal agreement demands that individual cultures and their laws and customs be ignored in favor of authoritative pronouncements on moral issues. On the one hand, in *The Law of Peoples*, Rawls attempts to address the problem of neutrality in human rights by arguing that some human rights are fit to serve as minimum standards for institutions of all decent societies, whether liberal or not.[24] Beitz, on the other hand, is more concerned about the scope of the ideal of human rights, particularly "insofar as it implicates questions about the material minimum that should be upheld by any decent society and the extent to which the wealthy, whatever their location, have responsibilities to contribute to its achievement" (Beitz 1999 article, 13).

Further, in Beitz' view, any plausible form of international liberalism should include an interpretation of the doctrine of human rights, since human rights serve as terms of reference for foreign policy, as normative standards for international financial and development policy, and as a basis of appeal for intercession in cases of irresolvable domestic dispute. Unfortunately, Beitz must concede that despite their centrality in contemporary international life, the doctrine of human rights lacks a widely accepted underlying theory. Further, as things now stand, the attempt to apply justice to the question of human rights could lead to Western liberal political views clashing with the religious views of Islamic nations, including various Islamic traditions and practices, and even with the structure of some Islamic states, both of which could be found to be unjust.

INTERNATIONAL JUSTICE

For Beitz, as demonstrated above, the four elements necessary for a Hobbesian state of nature do not currently obtain. In addition, Beitz believes that a Hobbesian state of nature does not explain how to justify the regulative principles of international politics. He acknowledges, however, that rejecting a Hobbesian state of nature approach to international relations does not mean that the international realm should be analogous to a domestic society for all purposes. Rather, he contends that it would be better to understand international relations as "occupying a middle ground . . . there are, in international relations, both shared and opposed interests, providing a basis both for cooperation and competition. But effective institutions for exploring bases of cooperation are insufficiently developed" (Beitz 1999, 50).

Rather than accepting a Hobbesian state of nature framework, that is, Beitz looks to the natural law tradition of John Locke and Samuel Pufendorf, for whom moral obligations exist even within a state of nature,[25] as he seeks to articulate a normative basis for international politics. Beitz fails, however, to provide a sufficient foundation in his resulting account for why nations should be viewed as moral agents in his interdependency of nations argument. He comes closer to the mark in his later shift to a Kantian view of rational moral agency as attributable to nations. If nations do have moral obligations to other nations then, what type of political order allows nations to fulfill such moral obligations with regard to questions of justice?

Global Resource Equality

As a proponent of international cosmopolitanism, Beitz is primarily concerned with economic distributions and redistributions, rather than with distributive justice per se. Thus, the first-order question that he seeks to answer is: What are our global obligations of justice? From a more particularized perspective, this question can be restated as follows: Should the radical inequalities of resources in international society be accepted as the norm, or should they be addressed in some manner, and if so, in what manner? Beitz responds that such resource inequalities should be addressed as a matter of justice, and through extending the Rawlsian difference principle, Beitz argues that they should be addressed globally. Importantly, the resources that Beitz seeks to redistribute are especially natural resources and not the broader category of societal goods (including such matters as talent) found in the Rawlsian domestic scheme. In his choice of distribution territory, Beitz thus recognizes the scale of matters to be addressed. Under the difference principle extended globally, natural resources, behind a veil of ignorance, would be distributed to the advantage of those least well off in the world.

In making his argument, however, Beitz also attempts to marginalize Rawls' first principle of justice, the greatest liberty principle, as well as the political aspects of Rawls' paradigm. Consequently, both Rawlsian principles only obtain under Beitz' theory in the special condition of justice and not in the general condition of justice. That is, when applied to the special condition of natural resources that centers Beitz' concern, the basic liberties encompassed in Rawls' first principle of justice have lexical priority over others, including the Rawlsian difference principle.

This analysis leads Beitz to the second-order problem raised, that of compliance, which seeks to understand what mechanism could accomplish this distribution and redistribution of natural resources. Put another way, since states have no appropriate international governance structure, the problem to solve is whether their duties to promote justice and to redistribute resources should be directed to their own citizens and not to those outside their borders. One way to respond to the problem could be to develop a new world order, a new political entity that would embrace all individuals and replace the global structure of individual sovereign states, treating all individuals with equal respect and concern as rights-possessing individuals in a global state. A more measured and realistic approach would obtain if international organizations, such as the United Nations, the International Monetary Fund, and the World Trade Organization would be allowed to act in the interests of international distributive justice.[26]

The international resource distributions and redistributions called for in Beitz' theory are what have attracted the most criticism, and include the following:

1. Although not purely a Hobbesian state of nature, the international realm does not function in a cooperative scheme. Problematically, Rawls' principles of justice, including the difference principle that Beitz would extract and apply, are based upon a cooperative scheme. Moreover, compounding difficulties, Beitz attempts to apply the difference principle in the international realm, not domestically as Rawls proposes. Rather than relying on reciprocity and social cooperation as the foundation for applying the difference principle, it is fair to consider whether it would be more effective to use a less contingent principle, such as a principle of impartiality.
2. Another set of critiques involves the difficult relationships between nation-states and universal moral obligations. In suggesting that there are universal moral obligations, for example, the cosmopolitan thesis may actually generate confusion with respect to empirical-moral arguments. For example, cosmopolitanism seems to ignore the power of national self-identity and hence the right, perhaps, to distributions. Likewise, but on another scale, also given short shrift in the cosmopolitan scheme are pluralistic and localized identities as well as the moral obligations of individuals.[27]
3. Focusing once again on the particular, some critiques further claim that cosmopolitan theory under-theorizes the mechanisms necessary to effectuate the distributions that are called for along with the redistributions of resources. In other words, more than the interdependence of states seems to be required for the effective distributions and redistributions of resources, such as, for example, a political basis for an international distributive scheme. Not to be underestimated, in focusing on the mechanisms for effecting such a scheme, the problem of authoritarian regimes needs to be addressed as well.

4. Finally, some critiques aver that Beitz' focus on natural resources is antiquated since, for example, he does not seem to take into account that the distributive mechanisms for such efforts must be massive.

As previously argued, I do not view the primary task of justice as distributional, even in an international structure (see chapter 7). Rather, for international purposes, I view global justice as focused on the relations among nations, including questions of international collaborative efforts as well as self-interested competition, and matters of regulation and governance in the relations of nations with each other, emphasizing communication and rational discourse as a means of clarification and resolution of disputes, as well as for the transmission of values through international institutions.

Laws and Customs of Peoples

By advocating the extension of the difference principle of justice as fairness to an international context, at times Beitz seems more Rawlsian than Rawls. That is, Beitz ignores that the basic liberty principle in Rawls' formulation of justice as fairness obtains domestically only under special conditions. Even Rawls himself does not advocate the exporting of the difference principle globally. Instead, in *The Law of Peoples*, Rawls takes a position on global justice somewhere between the realist and cosmopolitan approaches to international relations. While domestically, his concern is indeed to develop a theory of justice; internationally, Rawls' arguments revolve about concepts such as legitimacy and the laws of peoples.[28]

Beitz, on the other hand, contends that the existing resource endowment of states is, to use a Rawlsian phrase, "morally arbitrary," and therefore not an issue to which states would willingly wish to devote their energies. Further, Beitz argues that the interdependence among nations actually means that the idea of a self-contained, insular society must be abandoned. This leads to Beitz' above-stated conclusion that distributive justice must apply among nations, and the Rawlsian difference principle should privilege the least advantaged globally, culminating in a radical redistribution of resources. As also indicated above, at this point, Beitz grounds his reasoning less on the contingent notion of the interdependence of peoples and more along Kantian lines.[29]

Interestingly, as Beitz' initial attempt to fit international distributive justice into a Rawlsian formulation suggests a weakness in Rawls' theory resides in the attempt to base the requirements of justice in the special conditions where justice as fairness would obtain, on contractual foundations of mutual advantage, since such conditions are morally contingent. For Rawls, the difference principle articulated in *A Theory of Justice* expresses a relatively egalitarian concept of distributive justice characteristic of liberal political theory, one that has no international analogue.

Rawls does, however, provide for a duty of assistance in *The Law of Peoples,* which would require a greater level of international transfers than currently exist, but importantly, he sees the global extension of the difference principle as incorrect. Instead, in *The Law of Peoples*, Rawls develops principles to guide a liberal society in the conduct of its foreign policy, including relations with other states, the policy's contributions to forming and interpreting international law, and its views about the structure and policies of international organizations. These principles are intended to direct and limit a liberal society's concept of its own national interest.

The Law of Peoples then, may be seen as an extension of Rawls' *Political Liberalism,* with the same emphasis on politics and institutions transferred to the international realm. In effect, his law of peoples presents an analogue in foreign affairs to his concept of social justice in a society's domestic affairs. Indeed, by *The Law of Peoples*, Rawls seems to mean a society with a common political culture organized as a state by means of a social contract doctrine, with "peoples" replacing the "persons" in his earlier formulation. Principles of *The Law of Peoples* thus result from a hypothetical agreement among representatives of various peoples meeting in what Rawls postulated as an original position. In the international original position, Rawls includes representatives of both liberal and hierarchal societies, provided that in both cases, the societies are well ordered.

Centrally, the problem that Rawls addresses in *The Law of Peoples* is the fact of pluralism, specifically the pluralism of cultural and religious conceptions of the good society as found internationally. Rawls further delimits global pluralism to reasonable pluralism, whereby a peaceful international life is one in which liberal societies may flourish. Given the fact of pluralism, he argues there must be a basis upon which reasonable and decent peoples can cooperate willingly. He thus articulates eight principles to provide a solution to the problem, and he contends that representatives in an international original position would agree to a similar list of principles, as pertaining to nations:[30]

1. Peoples are free and independent, and their freedom and independence are respected by other peoples.
2. Peoples are to observe treaties and undertakings.
3. Peoples are equal and are parties to the agreements that bind them.
4. Peoples are to observe a duty of nonintervention.
5. Peoples have the right of self-defense but no right to instigate war for reasons other than self-defense.
6. Peoples are to honor human rights.

7. Peoples are to observe certain specified restrictions in the conduct of war.
8. Peoples have a duty to assist other peoples living under unfavorable conditions that prevent their experiencing just or decent political and social governance.

As such, Rawls' law of peoples essentially divides into ideal and nonideal theory. Consisting of principles that apply in an idealized political society of well-ordered domestic societies in which the principles are fully complied with, ideal theories (also like those of Plato and Aristotle) depict societies that operate in conditions that favor just (or decent, hierarchically structured) institutions. Nonetheless, the principles of ideal theory, Rawls contends, also apply to conduct in the nonideal world in two ways: (1) by regulating relations among well-ordered, liberal, and hierarchical societies; and (2) by establishing goals for such well-ordered, liberal, and hierarchical societies to pursue with societies that are not well ordered. The most general such goal is to "bring all societies eventually to honor [the law of peoples] and to be full and self-standing members of the society of well-ordered peoples, and so secure human rights everywhere."[31] This goal also serves as the foundation for international distributive obligations of well-to-do societies, as such actions fall under Rawls' principle to provide assistance, specifically to those societies facing unfavorable conditions, for developing institutions capable of satisfying their own peoples' needs and human rights.

Beitz attempts to develop a normative approach to international relations that results in a moral cosmopolitan theory that reaches back to a Lockean natural law tradition in which moral obligations exist even in a state of nature. By linking the moral basis of his cosmopolitan doctrine to a universal feature of political liberalism—equal concern and respect for the individual—Beitz nuances the approach to develop a brand of cosmopolitan liberalism. In addressing the question of global obligations of justice, however, Beitz seems primarily focused upon the redistribution of natural resources from wealthier nations to the least advantaged nations. His distributive concern seeks to eliminate the political (states and institutions) from the resultant scheme, creating problems, especially with respect to his theory's efficacy in regard to the subject of distributions (natural resources) as well as with respect to the mechanisms deployed to effect such distributions. Related to these pragmatic infelicities, problems emerge on the theoretical level as well, with his attempted extraction and deployment of the Rawlsian difference principle out of its original domestic political context and with the moral universality of his claims.

Both Beitz and Rawls are drawn to the concept of distribution in order to level the playing field for the most disadvantaged in their explication of justice as fairness. Regardless of problems on a domestic level, internationally such an approach necessitates an authoritative declaration of what is moral, what is fair, and what should be distributed and redistributed.

Having previously addressed the debate of whether distributions of social goods or resources constitute the proper task of justice (see chapter 7), a relational view of international justice focuses instead on the concept of due concern and between and among nations, with communication serving in a substantive sense, through reasoned discourse, as a method of resolving disputes, and instrumentally, though the transmission of values over time via international institutions. Politically, this approach resides in the Western secular humanist tradition. Nonetheless, this context may be usefully mapped onto an international political order, with international institutions of governance arising through the express agreement and consent among nations, thereby formulating a cooperative foundational model.

NOTES

1. Thucydides, *History of the Peloponnesian War*, trans. Martin Hammond (Oxford: Oxford University Press, 2009).
2. Id., 5.85–5.113.
3. In a narrow sense, the term idealism in international relations is often understood as tied to the interwar period (1919–1939), and theoretically looks to interdependence and unity of mankind; viz., the League of Nations. But see the critique by E. H. Carr, *The Twenty Years' Crisis* (Houndmills: Palgrave, 2001).
4. See Plato, *The Republic*, trans. Desmond Lee, 2nd ed. (London: Penguin Books, 2003), Book II; see also Niccolò Machiavelli, *The Prince*, trans. W. K. Marriot (London: Penguin Books, 2004).
5. For example, in 1986, when the UN's International Court of Justice (World Court) decided against US military activities in Nicaragua as being in violation of international law, the US simply withdrew from UN jurisdiction.
6. The systems of contemporary nations, in American usage of the term, are seen to include variants of republics, monarchies, and single-party states.
7. See Thomas Hobbes, *Leviathan*, ed. J. C. A. Gaskin (Oxford: Oxford University Press, 1998), ch. 13.
8. See Beitz, "International Liberalism and Distributive Justice," *World Politics* 51; 2 (1999): 269–296 (hereafter, Beitz 1999 article).
9. See Max Weber, *Political Writings*, eds. Peter Lassman and Ronald Speirs (Cambridge: Cambridge University Press, 1994).
10. See Howard Williams, *Kant and the End of War* (New York: Palgrave Macmillan, 2012), and Pauline Kleingeld, *Kant and Cosmopolitanism* (New York: Cambridge University Press, 2012).
11. "The view that ethics based on enlightened self-interest is inadequate . . . fails to account for certain principles that intuitively seem to impose requirements on our actions regardless of considerations of actual or positive benefit to ourselves." Charles

Beitz, *Political Theory and International Relations* (Princeton: Princeton University Press, 1999), p. 56; see also Beitz 1999 article.

12. See also Thomas Pogge, *World Poverty and Human Rights* (Cambridge: Cambridge University Press, 2002).

13. See Michael Walzer, *Spheres of Justice* (New York: Basic Books, 1983).

14. Walzer himself rejects this term, as he views the rights of communities as grounded in a liberal concern for the rights of individuals, as exemplified in Mill's approach to self-determination. See chapter 8 *infra.*

15. See Walzer (1983), ch. 2.

16. Max Weber, *The Theory of Social and Economic Organization*, ed. and trans. Alexander Henderson and Talcott Parsons (New York: Free Press, 1997), pp. 324–406.

17. See John Rawls, *Political Liberalism* (New York: Columbia University Press, 1993).

18. See Joseph Raz, *The Morality of Freedom* (Oxford: Oxford University Press, 1986).

19. David Beetham, *The Legitimation of Power* (Basingstoke: Palgrave, 1991), p. 11.

20. Allen Buchanan, *Justice, Legitimacy, and Self-Determination* (Oxford: Oxford University Press, 2003).

21. Buchanan (2003), p. 266ff.

22. E.g., see Beitz (1999); Buchanan (2003); Allen Buchanan and Robert Keohane, "The Legitimacy of Global Goverance Institutions," *Ethics and International Affairs* 20; 4 (2006): 405–437; David Held, *Democracy and the World Order* (Palo Alto: Stanford University Press, 1995); but see, John Rawls, *The Law of Peoples* (Cambridge: Harvard University Press, 1997), who requires only that peoples and their states are "well-ordered."

23. By way of example, Saudi Arabia, a member of the United Nations, abstained from signing the Universal Declaration of Human Rights on the grounds that Article 18 thereof, which provides for a right to change religions, articulates a view offensive to Islam.

24. See Rawls (1997).

25. See John Locke, *Second Treatise of Government*, ed. Crawford Brough Macpherson (Indianapolis: Hackett Publishing, 1980), and Samuel Pufendorf, *On the Duty of Man and Citizen According to Natural Law,* ed. James Tully, trans. Michael Silverthorne (Cambridge: Cambridge University Press, 1991).

26. See Pogge (2002).

27. See David Miller, *On Nationality* (Oxford: Oxford University Press, 1995).

28. See also Allen Buchanan, "Recognitional Legitimacy," *Philosophy and Public Affairs* 28 (1999): 46–78.

29. See Immanuel Kant, "Perpetual Peace," in *Kant's Political Writings,* ed. Hans Siegbert Reiss, trans. Hugh Barr Nisbet (Cambridge: Cambridge University Press, 1970), pp. 93–130.

30. Rawls (1997), p. 37.

31. Rawls (1997), p. 75. Rawls has an unconventional understanding of human rights.

Chapter 10

Future Lives

Over time, the communities on the various boats described in chapter 9 increase in population. While interactions are complex enough in any moment in time, it seems nonetheless advisable for these communities to consider their journeys' long-term goals and attendant concerns. In addition to, and in conjunction with, material concerns like ensuring supplies, and matters of governance such as who will captain the boat, and how supplies will be distributed, the moral calculus with which the boats have hitherto more or less successfully navigated the waters needs to be reviewed in order to secure an acceptable quality of life for persons in the future, given the limited space and growing population of the boats. As new passengers are born, duties and provision for future lives require planning and understanding at both the micro- and macro- levels of *dikaiosune*.

Both Plato and Aristotle explored ideal states with static models, leaving no need to consider future lives as such. Indeed, as discussed in chapter 2, Plato's entire conceptual framework is grounded in the concept of an immortal soul and universal, eternal forms,[1] obviating the need to design a state responding to the needs of the mutable world. Nonetheless, Plato does concede that even if a state were organized politically according to the lines that he advocates, it would eventually decay.[2] On the other hand, Aristotle does not review the soul in terms of the question of justice, since for him justice belongs to the domain of practical reason.[3]

At the micro-level of *dikaiosune*, the concept of personal identity is actually fundamental to the question of justice over time. Typically, the question of personal identity presents a basic ethical concern, for example, in terms of moral responsibility or such self-regarding practical concerns as the nature and grounds of survival, as well as in practical concerns such as population ethics, the macro-level of *dikaiosune*.[4] Many problems of personal identity are located synchronically, in a moment of time, and address a subject's consciousness as central. Thus, questions of identity, origin, personhood, and death anchor how personal identities are moored in any individual life, but also in any given culture. The anchoring of personal identity over time is often referred to as the identity persistence question.

Derek Parfit has developed two kinds of responses to the persistence question: the psychological approach and the somatic approach. In the psychological approach, some psychological relation is necessary (or sufficient) for one to persist over time. Thus, an individual's future being inherits mental features from her or his present being. Memories, the capacity for rational thought, beliefs, and preferences, for example, persist over time, which is especially true for memory.[5] In contrast, the somatic approach (Aristotle's approach) answers the question of personal identity in terms of physical relations without regard to psychological facts; that is, an individual's future being persists in her or his present body, the same biological organism.[6]

PERSONAL IDENTITY

Parfit takes the psychological approach to the question of personal identity, generating problems that I discuss below. Simply put, in Part III of *Reasons and Persons*, Parfit examines the relation between personal identity and ethics, ultimately concluding that personal identity does not matter in developing our moral and prudential commitments. By concluding in this manner, Parfit expresses a reductionist view of human beings in which personal identity is seen as not much more than a bundle: a series of experiences, thoughts, and feelings tied together by various causal relations, especially those of memory and character (Parfit 1984, 210–211).[7] In subscribing to this bundle theory of personal identity, Parfit rejects what he terms "ego theories," which are based on the notion of a metaphysical ego (Plato's approach) or what it means to be a person: some single ego (substance, subject of experiences, and the like) persisting over time. Consequently, rather than claiming that personal identity is important per se, Parfit asserts that what matters is Relation R, the psychological connections (memory and character) in an individual, and continuity (overlapping chains of strong connectedness). As such, Relation R proves central to his moral account of future lives.

Parfit poses the central question in this manner: given the choice of whether to maintain personal identity *or* psychological continuity, would an individual prefer to die—thereby experiencing a loss of character, but maintaining personal identity—*or* to retain character (or personality) while losing or undergoing fragmentation of personal identity? This choice leads to his Non-Identity Problem, in which a scenario is tested: if a change in the identity of the parties involved in two possible morally framed outcomes occurs, how should the change affect the moral evaluation? Parfit subscribes to a No-Difference View to argue that the change in identity should not change the answer (Parfit 1984, 367).

To support his No-Difference View, Parfit poses the fission case (Parfit 1984, 254–255). One of a set of triplets has been in an accident and is about to die. Both of his brain hemispheres are functional duplicates of the other, and each of his other two brothers has suffered irreversible brain damage. A brilliant neurosurgeon can transplant one of the dying brother's brain hemispheres into each of his other brothers' skulls, and so each survivor will be fully psychologically continuous with the dying brother upon emerging from anesthesia. Without Parfit's no-branching clause, we might be led to conclude that, because both brothers are psychologically continuous with the deceased, they are both him. Given the transitivity of identity, however, both survivors would also have to be identical to each other, which would seem even more implausible and false. Thus, to avoid violating the transitivity requirement, Parfit posits Relation C: we may simply have to stipulate in our criteria of personal identity that, if the relations in which identity consists may include one-to-many situations, they must obtain uniquely for identity itself in order to prove valid. The stipulation itself, however, appears to make the no-branching response implausible and, moreover, articulates a construction by definitional fiat.

In addition to these considerations, the problem remains of how to describe what has happened to the deceased brother. Parfit seems to argue that he cannot survive in the same manner as the two remaining triplet brothers, so the identity relation does not obtain between him and them. In addition, there is no rational reason why the identity relation should obtain between him and just one of the two survivors, so the only remaining option is that he does not survive fission.[8] Still another question remains: how does his situation differ from more conventional exits from the mortal. Parfit indicates that both surviving brothers will remember his thoughts and experiences, and they will fulfill intentions he had in action. They will have the same beliefs, desires, and goals as the deceased, and their characters will be exactly like his. Indeed, it will be just as if he had survived in them.

For Parfit, then, most everything that matters in ordinary survival is preserved in fission, despite the fact that the identity relation does not. This must mean, Parfit continues, that the identity relation is not what matters in survival; instead, what matters must be psychological continuity and/or connectedness, Parfit's Relation R. As long as that relation holds between me-as-I-am-now and me-at-some-other-person-stage, then what happens to me is just as good as ordinary survival. In other words, for Parfit personal identity does not matter—*Q.E.D.*, Parfit's No-Difference View.

While I subscribe to a psychological approach to the question of personal identity, and to Parfit's bundle theory (experiences, thoughts, and feelings tied together by various causal connections, especially those of memory and character), along with the importance of his Relation R, I think that his no-branching treatment of fission cases is unsatisfactory. I offer no alternate psychological solution to problems posed by the fission cases, however, nor to the issue of uniqueness. Rather, I simply point out here that even with Parfit's resultant No-Difference View to personal identity, there are no necessary negative implications to our moral and prudential commitments, including the moral and political inquiry into the question of justice.

POPULATION CONCERNS

As seen in the last chapter, internationally conceived distribution theories of justice prove exceptionally difficult to realize, for example, when attempting to move from a single nation with a legitimate political authority, itself problematic on its own, to multiple nations with additional problems concerned with the legitimacy of political entities. Distribution theories prove to be limited as well when projecting how justice can be secured over time, which the ideal of justice demands. After all, if justice prevails only for short periods of time (as Plato fears), then moral and political chaos is programmed to ensue.

As Parfit illuminates, one of the focal points for securing justice over time is the issue of continuous population growth. Indeed, Rawls' formulation of justice as fairness may well be troubled by the possibility of overpopulation, as the question of lexical priority with regard to his liberty principle and the distributions required of his difference principle prove more and more difficult to realize. Key to examining the reach of justice over time depends, in part, on: what values are to be transmitted into the future, what mechanism exists for their transmission, and what provisions are made for future justice.

The Repugnant Conclusion

In contrast to a liberal view, in *Reasons and Persons*, Parfit extracts numerical metrics from the classic utilitarian account. Since increasing the happiness of human beings forms the single value worth pursuing, he explores this *desideratum* in the framework of an increasing global population. His approach leads to what he terms the Repugnant Conclusion, whereby for any possible population of minimally ten billion people, all with high qualities of life, there must be some much larger population whose existence, *ceteris paribus*, would be better off through the sheer gains in the aggregate quantity of good, even though its members have lives barely worth living.[9]

By bringing numbers into sharp focus, Parfit forces a calculus that, perhaps unintentionally but certainly necessarily, pushes issues of quality of life and personal identity into a less prominent space. Henry Sidgwick, an ethical hedonist in the tradition of Jeremy Bentham, proffered an earlier formulation of the problem in *The Methods of Ethics,* when he argued that "the point up to which, on utilitarian principles, population ought to be encouraged to increase, is not that at which the average happiness is the greatest possible—as appears to be often assumed by political economists of the school of Malthus—but that at which the happiness reaches its maximum."[10]

More aggressively, Parfit posits a series of worlds that he labels with letters of the alphabet. Terming the first population the A-population, Parfit then works through the alphabet to a vast Z-population, with increasing population levels and decreasing levels of happiness at each letter. The Repugnant Conclusion, he posits, is inevitable if a loss in quality is outweighed by a sufficient gain in the quantity of well-being.

To undergird his calculations, Parfit delineates two types of reasons, normative reasons and motivating reasons. With normative reasons, the question raised is: "What do we have most reason to want, and do?" In contrast, motivating reasons elicit this question: "What is the most rational for us to want, and do?" An individual may have normative reasons without being motivated, and vice versa, posing still other questions regarding the relations between the two types of reason. Since the first question represents a belief aimed at truth, while the second merely tests whether it is rational to respond to reasons, it is the normative question that proves fundamental in Parfit's view.[11]

Consequently, in citing Bernard Williams, Parfit notes two types of theories to explain normative reasons, an internalist theory and an extrernalist theory,[12] whereby such theories, spanning a wide variety of positions, may also be reductionist or non-reductionist. Put somewhat simplistically: an internalist theory focuses on internal deliberation to arrive at normative reasons, while an externalist theory seeks facts outside internal deliberations to provide reasons.

Parfit believes that reasons for acting must be external, and further, that if we are rational, they should provide a motivating force as well,

> Reasons for acting, I believe, are all external. When we have a reason to do something, this reason is not provided by, and does not require, the fact that after some Internalist deliberation we would want to do this thing. This reason is provided by the facts that also give us reason to have this desire. We have reason

> to try to achieve some aim when, and because, it is relevantly worth achieving. Since these are reasons for *being* motivated, we would have these reasons even if, when we are aware of them, that awareness did not motivate us. But, if we are rational, it will.[13]

Thus, Parfit builds upon his views of normative reasons to reject self-defeating theories of ethics—by which he means theories of ethical egoism, in which agents ought to do what is in their own self-interest[14]—along with self-interest theories of rationality.[15] Without himself developing a full ethical theory, he does posit the need to develop an ethical framework that combines common sense morality with consequentialism; that is, the consequences of an individual's actions are the proper basis for moral judgments about such conduct, a view commonly stated in the aphorism, *the ends justifies the means*.

Returning to Parfit's theory, another way of modulating the No-Difference View is by examining Parfit's Impersonal Total Principle which holds that, *ceteris paribus,* the best outcome provides the greatest quantity of whatever makes life worth living.[16] Problematically, this position implies that any loss in the quality of lives in a given population can be compensated for by a sufficient gain in the quantity of a population. Parfit terms this counterintuitive situation the Mere Addition Paradox, which functions as a quantitative argument contesting that no matter how many worthwhile lives a world contains, another world contains more and hence articulates a better world, thus leading to the Repugnant Conclusion: "For any perfectly equal Population with very high positive welfare, there is a population with very low positive welfare which is better, other things being equal."[17]

Jesper Ryberg and Torbjörn Tännsjö, editors of the *Repugnant Conclusion*, a collection of essays addressing Parfit's question, both pessimistically "bite the bullet" and accept the Repugnant Conclusion, arguing in different ways that it is not known what life in the A-world would be like and that perhaps life in the Z-world does not differ very much from what a normal privileged life could be.[18]

Nonetheless, the Repugnant Conclusion presents a serious obstacle to normative population theories which attempt to configure the optimal global population. From a utilitarian perspective, the tension emerges in whether to attempt to bring about the greatest total happiness or the highest level of average happiness. Such positions in effect debate whether a rights-based or a Rawlsian approach would prove more effective in providing just solutions. In addition to contesting which quantitative metrics to apply to achieving happiness, the Repugnant Conclusion puts moral principles under investigation as well. In *Reasons and Persons,* for example, Parfit's main challenge is to develop a theory of beneficence, Theory X, which is positioned to solve the Non-Identity Problem and not lead to the Repugnant Conclusion, while blocking the Mere Addition Paradox, without leading to other morally unacceptable conclusions. Parfit himself concludes that he did not succeed in developing such a Theory X. Similarly, many traditional moral principles also appear not to provide an answer to the conundrum regarding a change in identities between outcomes, or they provide solutions that are implausible.

Among the various solutions to the problem that Parfit himself does offer is to suggest that a discontinuity between values in the loss of things that make life worth living cannot be made good by any gain in a quantity of inferior values.[19] In other words, moving from the A-world to the B-world can be blocked by discontinuity. This approach sounds similar to Mill's concept of higher and lesser pleasures and may offer a similar Mill-like twist to the utilitarian presentation of the problem.[20]

Critically, however, from a similarly structural perspective, Parfit's notion of total utility as a trumping value does not necessarily obtain in a system where values are incommensurable. Positing a situation of value pluralism in the context of a communitarian orientation toward the cultural traditions and habits of particular communities then, we can block progress toward the Repugnant Conclusion, while also constructing a platform for future generations with the communitarian's conservative cultural bias.[21] As Clark Wolf suggests, rather than accept the utilitarian premise of maximizing happiness, the emphasis should be placed on the converse, on minimizing suffering.[22] Thus, it would be obligatory to reduce ill-being and praiseworthy to promote well-being. According to Wolf, neither the A-world nor the Z-world would necessarily be preferable to the other since the unit of significant value is not happiness, but rather, the reduction of suffering.

Instead of contesting Parfit's quantification of happiness, several thinkers, including Ingmar Perrson, have challenged Parfit's teleological framework by noting that the measurement of "better than" (in the sense of the A-world is better than the B-world) comprises a transitive relation. By removing the transitive relation, a controversial move, Perrson understands, there exists no further obligation to follow the steps of Parfit's moral alphabet.[23] Larry Temkin and Stuart Rachels agree that the Repugnant Conclusion may be avoided by denying the transitivity axiom with regard to the all-things-considered-better-than relation.[24]

As a final example of critical responses to Parfit's approach, Tim Mulgan, in a Rawlsian, distribution approach to the problem, proposes the counter idea of a minimal threshold of liberties and primary social goods for individuals, whereby societies must ensure that everyone lives above that critical level, a critical level should be context-dependent.[25] That is, the more affluent a society is, the higher the critical level of liberties and primary social goods is set. This approach has attendant problems, of course, if extended to global considerations of justice.

Parfit's insistence on applying quantitative metrics to the utilitarian problem of maximizing happiness effects a transition from Rawls' deliberations on justice as fairness to justice as statistically realizable, a perspective that will almost certainly become more and more contested as the world's population increases. As such, Parfit's approach also reflects recent trends in other fields that, in a sense, similarly move from qualitative to quantitative measurements, such as psychology's focus on the inner psyche to neuropsychology's shift to measuring brain functions.

Importantly, both the shift in discussions of justice effected by Rawls' study as well as the transition foreshadowed in Parfit's work clearly demonstrate that justice may indeed be relational, albeit in Parfit's case, in an impersonal sense. The challenge remains, it seems to me, as to whether or not we can formulate models that integrate all concerns formulated over time and cultural modalities, or whether justice, since it occupies such a complex space accommodating both individuals and larger societal configurations, must be viewed from just one or more perspectives at a time. In my own view, I believe that we may develop models or theories to provide normative guidance over time, with the political context formulating a liberalism that foregrounds components of liberty and equality, as well as the concepts of tolerance and diversity.

NOTES

1. See Plato, *Phaedo*, trans. David Gallop (Oxford: Oxford University Press, 1993). Also see Plato, *The Republic*, trans. Desmond Lee, 2nd ed. (London: Penguin Books, 2003), Appendix II, for a discussion of the Spindle of Necessity.
2. See *Polis and the Soul* discussion in chapter 2 *infra.*
3. See Aristotle, *De Anima*, trans. Hugh Lawson-Tancred (London: Penguin Books, 1986), Book I. See also Aristotle, *The Nicomachean Ethics of Aristotle*, trans. David Ross, rev. Lesley Brown (Oxford: Oxford University Press, 2009), 1102b11–12.
4. See generally, David Shoemaker, "Personal Identity and Ethics," *Stanford Encyclopedia of Philosophy* (2008), http://plato.stanford.edu/entries/identity-ethics/.
5. Derek Parfit, *Reasons and Persons* (Oxford: Clarendon Press, 1984), p. 388.
6. See Ingmar Perrson, "The Root of the Repugnant Conclusion and its Rebuttal," in *The Repugnant Conclusion,* eds. Jesper Ryberg and Torbjörn Tännsjö (Norwell: Kluwer Academic Publishers, 2004), pp. 187–200 (hereafter, Ryberg and Tännsjö 2004). Compare with Gustaf Arrhenius, "The Very Repugnant Conclusion," in *Logic, Law, Morality,*

eds. Krister Segerberg and Rysiek Sliwinski (Uppsala: Uppsala University, 2003), pp. 167–180.

7. See also David Hume, *A Treatise of Human* Nature, eds. David Fate Norton and Mary J. Norton (Oxford: Oxford University Press, 2001), I. IV. vi, 4.1, 2 regarding personal identity as a loose cohesion of one's personal experience.

8. See Parfit (2001), p. 42.

9. See Parfit (1984), Part IV.

10. Henry Sidgwick, *The Methods of Ethics,* 7th ed. (Indianapolis: Hackett Publishing Company, 1980), p. 418.

11. See Parfit (1984), Part I.

12. See Bernard Williams, *Moral Luck* (Cambridge: Cambridge University Press, 1981), pp. 101–113.

13. Derek Parfit, "Reasons and Motivation," *Aristotelian Society* (1997), Supp. Vol. 71: 130.

14. E.g., see James Rachels, "Ethical Egoism," in *Reason and Responsibility,* ed. Joel Feinberg and Russ Shafer-Landau (Belmont: Thompson Wadsworth, 2008), pp. 532–540.

15. See Parfit (1984), Part I.

16. Id., p. 443.

17. Id., p. 387.

18. See Jesper Ryberg, "The Repugnant Conclusion and Worthwhile Living," in Ryberg and Tännsjö (2004), pp. 239–256.

19. See Derek Parfit, "Overpopulation and the Quality of Life," in Ryberg and Tännsjö (2004), pp. 7–22.

20. See John Stuart Mill, "On Liberty," in *John Stuart Mill on Liberty and Other Essays,* ed. John Gray (Oxford: Oxford University Press, 1998), pp. 5–130; also see chapter 6 *infra.*

21. This move may be seen as an extension of some of Joseph Raz' views. See Joseph Raz, *The Morality of Freedom* (Oxford: Oxford University Press, 1986); and chapter 5 *infra.*

22. See Clark Wolf, "O Repugnance, Where is Thy Sting," in Ryberg and Tännsjö (2004), pp. 61–80.

23. See Larry Temkin, "Intransitivity and the Mere Addition Paradox," *Philosophy and Public Affairs* 16:2 (1997); and Stuart Rachels, "A Set of Solutions to Parfit's Problems," *Nous* 35:2 (2001): 214–238.

24. See Temkin (1997), pp. 138–187, and Rachels (2001).

25. See Tim Mulgan, "Two Parfit Puzzles," in Ryberg and Taännsjö (2004), pp. 23–44.

Conclusion

Both Plato and Aristotle developed their accounts of justice based in moral frameworks. For Plato, the moral framework is metaphysically driven by his theory of universal, foundational forms. In contrast, Aristotle locates justice as a virtue in the individual, a learned disposition subject to the doctrine of the mean, with living well as the proper ends of the human enterprise.

In contemporary theories of justice, moral aspects tend to be underserved as the creation of political institutions and attendant elements dominate the discourse. With regard to moral aspects that do receive attention, many contemporary accounts of justice adopt the Kantian concept of due respect and concern for persons as a foundational element, as well as approach the justice inquiry in a deontological manner.

Spurred by the ideas of thinkers such as Thomas Hobbes and John Locke, the development of individual rights in political theory and the hypothetical social contract strongly influence contemporary analyses and theories of justice. Further, the political discussion has moved from the small closed societies of Plato and Aristotle to large, complex, and diverse societies, which require, I argue, tolerance and diversity as aspects of a liberal political framework, one that also exhibits the concepts of negative liberty and equality in the sense of due concern and respect. An important debate that has emerged in this political arena is the question of whether rights should be awarded groups.

JUSTICE AS RIGHT ACTIONS

My answer to the justice question, looking back to Plato and Aristotle, is to develop a moral framework to inform the political landscape of the times. Thus, I view the proper task of justice as the development of normative guidance in the form of action-guiding principles that may be applied in the circumstances.[1] Further, the set of principles arrived upon should, critically, be able to be universalized—by which I mean principles that are not self-defeating, that are reversible, and that may be consistently applied. Thus, I arrive at a formulation of two principles of justice, in lexical priority:

> *The Responsibility Principle*: One is responsible for one's own actions.
> *The Equality Principle*: One should act with respect and concern for persons having the same right to act and to respond to one's actions.[2]

In doing so, I maintain that justice includes responsible actions based on rational and autonomous moral agency, with the individual (not groups) as the proper bearer of rights and responsibilities. In taking an analytical approach, and arguing for the right over the good, I deepen the apparent transparency of the political tenet—*do what is right*—with a morally thick register, one that recognizes the conventions, thought, and richness of moral traditions of various cultures, by framing the concept in a deontological approach.

In viewing justice as right actions, then, I assume that a person owes a duty of justice when her or his actions may affect others. This responsibility for intentional actions is set forth in the first principle of justice as right actions, the Responsibility Principle, as limited by the second principle, the Equality Principle, which advises that we consider how others might act in response to an individual's actions. Thus, the second principle, with its reference to other persons, and consequently the external world and experience, works both as a constraint on the first principle of justice as responsible actions, as well as a repository of resources for moral decision-making, as it empirically reaches into particular communities in which individuals are situated, along with the laws and customs of such communities. It also provides the touchstone for a priority rule in situations involving conflicting values.

In examining the variability of circumstances, I mention two additional concerns. First, the circumstances or facts of a situation are often not hard and nubby items. Rather, what facts are relevant in a given situation may be open to various shades of interpretation and characterization that may be critical in determining what constitutes just actions in any given event. In addition to interpreting and selecting relevant facts, addressing the question of circumstances themselves must be understood as setting the context for the application of rules of justice.

CONTEMPORARY DEBATES

The two principles of justice as right actions presented above are intended to provide a normative model or framework for the justice inquiry, and to return contemporary debates of justice to deontological considerations.

To suggest how this might be done, I have discussed various contemporary approaches in the text and how they might benefit from explicitly recognizing moral issues. Justice is, as I have argued, inextricably linked to morality and as such justice reflects and safeguards a society's social mores. Further, given the ever-changing nature of societies, it seems prudent to insert deontological concerns back into contemporary discussions.

The various contemporary approaches I discussed here were chosen to underscore and discuss the importance in today's society of understanding justice as right actions. Thus, I treated the importance of the individual's societal responsibilities; how these may be determined, distributed, and/or assessed, an especially important theme given the complex nature of the issue of group rights today; and how principles discussed may be viewed both internationally and in future generations. I have therefore examined relational and distributional approaches to justice, value pluralism, an individual's rights and responsibilities in relationship to the polity, international justice, and justice in the future.

What follows below are brief indications of how justice as right actions can inform these various approaches, in light of the need to bring moral issues back into the conversation, especially given the complexity and diversity of today's societies and the attendant need for tolerance.

Relational Justice

Contemporary debates in justice often assume a liberal political context, in which concepts of liberty and equality, especially various concepts of political equality, come into play. Critically, since distributional views tend to ignore important societal issues such as power, they ignore too that these issues are not amenable to distribution. Of course, individuals do live in groups, and consequently, the political aspect of any formulation of justice may not be ignored. A distributional approach to the question, however, insufficiently treats important societal realities. In other words, I do not view justice, as do many contemporary theorists, as a distributional matter in Aristotelian vein, whereby the task of justice is to develop political institutions, "just institutions," to distribute or redistribute liberties and social goods of society.

Rather, focusing on the individual as responsible for her or his actions, coded as such through social or political norms, I view justice as a relational matter (see chapter 7). By contrast, in viewing justice as a distributional matter, individual responsibility is ignored. Moreover, rather than assigning justice the task of distributing social goods to those least advantaged in society or otherwise, I view the task of justice as providing normative guidance in an individual's relations to others. The key to such a relational view of justice is communication, both in a substantive sense as a rational, discursive method of resolving disparate conflicting views, but also in an instrumental sense of conveying ideas, and especially the transmission of values through time.

Value Pluralism

In the approach to justice as right actions, plural values are embraced, although I do not favor a strong value pluralist account, nor one afflicted by the problem of incommensurability. Like Immanuel Kant and John Rawls, and in contrast to both Joseph Raz and John Stuart Mill, I advocate for the right over the good. The priority of the right, which Rawls presents in his theory as neutral and anti-perfectionist, may be seen as placing limits, in the interest of fairness, on differing conceptions of the good.

In arguing for the right over the good, I acknowledge attendant to the deontological approach of justice as right actions theoretical problems; and I propose a thin underlying theory of the good, which comprises four concepts, as follows:[3]

1. rationality,
2. autonomous moral agency,
3. equal concern and respect for others, and
4. plurality of values

Thus, value pluralism may be seen to enter the account of justice as right actions by means of the second principle, the Equality Principle, which states that in societal interactions, mutual respect and concern between individuals should be normative. This weak value pluralism is further supported by the concept of tolerance and diversity, as envisioned in the political context of liberalism. In other words, a politically framed, morally thick concept—*do what is right*—approached from a deontological perspective impels my argument on justice.

The Individual and the Polity

For justice as right actions, the view of liberalism that serves as the political context for the theory includes the concepts of tolerance and diversity, but not by according power to groups in a manner that diminishes the focus on the individual as a rational and moral agent. That is, while I accept a political liberal context, I believe that the individual should be the proper bearer or rights and responsibilities in political society. In other words, the appropriate political context is a liberalism that has components of negative liberty and equality of concern and respect, further including the concepts of tolerance and diversity, with the equality component acting as both a constraint and as a repository of moral resources.

More explicitly, the component of equality as embedded in the Equality Principle is Kantian in promoting equality of concern and respect while also comprising one of the components of liberalism (along with liberty, tolerance, and diversity) that serves as the political context for the approach. It is equality as well that serves as the touchstone in the priority rule for justice in situations involving conflicting values. Thus, in justice as right actions, equality is deontological in conception and as such serves as both a political measure and an adjudicating value.

International Justice

In justice as right actions, a moral basis for international relations among nations may be found in the Responsibility Principle, which prescribes responsible actions based on rational and moral agency and which further looks to the Equality Principle and its concept of due concern and respect for providing appropriate constraints on actions, as well as a view of the external world and experience for providing resources for moral decision-making. Further, my view of personal identity as largely a social construct, as well as the importance of intentions underlying actions, may map comfortably onto nations as well as individuals, and relations between and among nations. Politically, the moral agency I attribute to nations is supported by the notion that nations and states are commonly understood to be organized for the common good of their people.

In extending justice as right actions internationally, one question posed should be whether moral agency may be properly attributable to nations as actors, followed by the question of what action-guiding principles may be appropriate for nations *inter se,* as well as between nations and individuals. The next question then arises concerning what political order may be appropriate as a framework for justice as right actions internationally, especially in respect to the situation where there is no minimal state binding nations, one which may legitimately use physical coercive power to protect rights or interests of member nations.

For answers to these questions, I focus on international relations and look to communication as the key. I argue that moral agency may indeed be properly attributable to nations, and I contest the realist view that rejects morality and instead offers self-interest as the guiding principle for nations in their relations with other nations. Further, the laws and customs of people constitute part of the empirical landscape that may be reached through the Equality Principle as applied to international matters, carrying with it, in this case, the analogous concept of due concern and respect for other nations. In providing normative guidance to nations, that is, the Equality Principle may be seen as providing constraints to the responsible actions of nations, as well as resources for moral decision-making.

Importantly, in its normative action-guiding function, justice as right actions looks to parametric universalisms, as well as morally thick concepts, included in the laws and customs of various nations and peoples, mindful that with conflicting values, the particular value that best adheres to or promotes respect and concern for others is preferred over competing values in any given circumstance. Insofar as respect and concern for others receive priority, it follows that global obligations of justice are articulated for nations *inter se,* as well as in the relations among nations, states, and individuals. Clearly, approaching international justice in this manner does not reduce the likelihood of controversial conflicts of values, but in such cases, justice as right actions also incorporates a cooperative method of reasoned discourse to arrive at just resolutions of such issues.

Perhaps most critical to the arena of international justice is the Equality Principle, eliciting respect and concern for, in this case, individual nations. That is, guidance is key in international justice, rather than the delineation of specific cases of where justice should apply. For example, in universalizing fundamental rights, as articulated in the thirty Articles of the United Nations' Universal Declaration of Human Rights, much space is taken up in trying to avoid specific aberrations of moral behavior. Rather than articulating specific instances that may over time and over cultures may or may not obtain, it may prove more useful to articulate clear, overarching principles. Thus, the four goods identified in the thin theory of the good introduced above, especially the goods of equal concern and respect for others as embedded in the plurality of values, provide guidance that not only underscore the intent of the thirty articles, but also instances not covered by them.

Since justice as right actions characterizes the concept of universal human rights as instantiating a culturally contingent debate, negotiated through the Equality Principle, it avoids both Charles Beitz' resorting to what amounts to an exception, as well as the controversial setting of minimum standards as John Rawls would require (see chapter 9). Instead, justice as right actions considers human rights as part of the empirical landscape, including the questions of the content and scope of the concept of human rights as well as challenges to their universality.

Justice in the Future

Justice as right actions rests on the notion that justice is relational rather than distributive, with a key component being communication that is, as stated above, both substantive in the sense of providing a method for clarifying and resolving disputes through rational discourse, as well as instrumental, especially with regard to the transmission of values. As with international justice, the values to be transmitted into the future are contained in the theory's underlying thin theory of the good outlined earlier, whose concepts bolster both the Responsibility and Equality Principles.

To transmit these values to future generations, the Equality Principle further provides a resource, since it makes empirical reference to the external world and experience, to the laws and customs of societies. Because justice as right actions embraces a relational view, its deontological approach avoids the utilitarian infelicities of Derek Parfit's Repugnant Conclusion and advocates for transmitting values over time in a liberal political framework of negative liberty and equality of respect and concern, together with the concepts of tolerance and diversity. The empirical reliance upon persons and their societies proposed in the Equality Principle, together with the priority rule for conflicting values provided in the theory, thus serves to provide continuing relevance for future obligations of justice.

NOTES

1. See Young Kim, *Justice as Right Actions* (Lanham: Lexington Books, 2015).
2. Id., p. 23.
3. See Kim (2015).

Works Cited

PRIMARY TEXTS

Aristotle (1986). *De Anima*. Trans. Hugh Lawson-Tancred. London: Penguin Books.

——— (1992). *Politics*. Trans. T.A. Sinclair, rev. Trevor Saunders. London: Penguin Books.

——— (2009). *The Nichomachean Ethics of Aristotle*. Trans. D. Ross, rev. Lesley Brown. Oxford: Oxford University Press.

Barry, Brian (2002). *Culture and Equality*. Cambridge: Harvard University Press.

——— (1990). *Political Argument: A Reissue with a New Introduction*. Berkeley: University of California Press.

——— (2002). "Second Thoughts: Some First Thoughts Revived." In Ed. Paul Kelly. *Multiculturalism Reconsidered*. Cambridge: Polity Press, pp. 204–238.

——— (2005). *Why Social Justice Matters*. London: Polity.

Beitz, Charles (1999). "International Liberalism and Distributive Justice: A Survey of Recent Thought." *World Politics* 51.2: 269–296.

——— (1999). *Political Theory and International Relations*, 2nd ed. Princeton: Princeton University Press.

Bentham, Jeremy (1977). "*A Comment on the Commentaries and A Fragment of Government*." In Ed. J. H. Burns and H. L. A. Hart. *The Collected Works of Jeremy Bentham*. London: University of London Press.

——— (1843). *The Works of Jeremy Bentham*, vol. 1. Edinburgh: William Tait.

Berlin, Isaiah (2013). *The Hedgehog and the Fox*. Ed. Henry Hardy. Princeton: Princeton University Press.

——— (1969). "Two Concepts of Liberty." In *Four Essays on Liberty*. Oxford: Oxford University Press, pp. 118–172.

Dworkin, Ronald (2004). "Ronald Dworkin Replies." In Ed. Justine Burley. *Dworkin and His Critics*. Oxford: Blackwell Publishing Ltd, pp. 339–350.

——— (2000). *Sovereign Virtue*. Cambridge: Harvard University Press.

Galston, William (2002). *Liberal Pluralism*. Cambridge: Cambridge University Press.

——— (2007). "Must Value Pluralism and Religious Belief Collide?" In Eds. George Crowder and Henry Hardy. *The One and the Many: Reading Isaiah Berlin.* Amherst: Prometheus Books.

——— (2005). The *Practice of Liberal Pluralism.* Cambridge: Cambridge University Press.

Gray, John (1985). *Liberalism.* Minneapolis: University of Minnesota Press.

——— (1996). *Mill on Liberty: A Defence,* 2nd ed. Oxford: Routledge.

——— (2000). *Two Faces of Liberalism.* Cambridge: Polity Press.

Habermas, Jürgen (1996). *Between Facts and Norms: Contributions to a Discourse Theory of Law and Democracy.* Trans. William Rehg. Cambridge: The MIT Press.

Hart, H. L. A. (1975). "Rawls on Liberty and Its Priority." In Ed. Norman Daniels. *Reading Rawls: Critical Studies on Rawls 'A Theory of Justice.'* Oxford: Blackwell, pp. 206–229.

Hobbes, Thomas (1998). *Leviathan.* Ed. J. C. A. Gaskin. Oxford: Oxford University Press.

Hume, David (1970). *Enquiries Concerning the Human Understanding and Concerning the Principles of Morals,* 2nd ed. (Rpt. 1777). Ed. L. A. Selby-Bigge. Oxford: Clarendon Press.

——— (2001). *A Treatise of Human Nature.* Ed. David Fate Norton and Mary J. Norton. Oxford: Oxford University Press.

Kant, Immanuel (1997). *Critique of Pure Reason.* Trans. and Eds. Paul Guyer and Allen Wood. Cambridge: Cambridge University Press.

——— (2009). *Groundwork for the Metaphysics of Morals.* Trans. H. J. Paton. New York: HarperCollins.

——— (1970). "Perpetual Peace: A Philosophical Sketch." In *Kant's Political Writings.* Ed. Hans Siegbert Reiss. Trans. Hugh Barr Nisbet. Cambridge: Cambridge University Press, pp. 93–130.

——— (1970). *Political Writings,* 2nd ed. Ed. Hans Siegbert Reiss. Trans. Hugh Barr Nisbet. Cambridge: Cambridge University Press, pp. 93–130.

Kymlicka, Will (1990). *Contemporary Political Philosophy: An Introduction.* New York: Oxford University Press.

——— (2004). "Dworkin on Freedom and Culture." In Ed. Justine Burley. *Dworkin and His Critics.* Oxford: Blackwell Publishing, pp. 113–133.

——— (1995). *Multicultural Citizenship.* Oxford: Oxford University Press.

Locke, John (1980). *Second Treatise of Government.* Ed. Crawford Brough Macpherson. Indianapolis: Hackett Publishing.

Machiavelli, Niccolò (2004). *The Prince.* Trans. W. K. Marriot. London: Penguin Books.

Mill, John Stuart (1998). "On Liberty." In Ed. John Gray. *John Stuart Mill on Liberty and Other Essays.* Oxford: Oxford University Press, pp. 5–130.

——— (2004). *Utilitarianism.* Ed. Roger Crisp. Oxford: Oxford University Press.

Nozick, Robert (1974). *Anarchy, State, and Utopia.* New York: Basic Books.

Okin, Susan (1999). *Is Multiculturalism Bad for Women?* Princeton: Princeton University Press.

Parfit, Derek (2004). "Overpopulation and the Quality of Life." In Eds. Jesper Ryberg and Torbjörn Tännsjö. *The Repugnant Conclusion*. Norwell: Kluwer Academic Press. pp. 7–22.

——— (1997). "Reasons and Motivation." *Aristotelian Society* 71.1: 99–130.

——— (1984). *Reasons and Persons*. Oxford: Clarendon Press.

Plato (1993). *Phaedo*. Trans. David Gallop. Oxford: Oxford University Press.

——— (2011). *Phaedrus*. Trans. R. Hackworth. Ed. Harvey Yuris. Cambridge: Cambridge University Press.

——— (1997). *Protagoras*. Trans. Stanley Lombardo and Karen Bell. Indianapolis: Hackett Publishing Company, Inc.

——— (1970). *The Laws*. Trans. Trevor Saunders. London: Penguin Books.

——— (2003). *The Republic*. Trans. Desmond Lee, 2nd ed. London: Penguin Books.

——— (1933). *Sophist*. Trans. Nicholas P. White. Indianapolis: Hackett Publishing Company, Inc.

——— (2002). *The Statesman*. Trans. J. B. Skemp. London: Bristol Classical Press.

——— (1992). *Theaetetus*. Ed. Bernard Williams. Trans. M. J. Levett, rev. Miles Burnyeat. Indianapolis: Hackett Publishing Company.

Rawls, John (1971). *A Theory of Justice*. Cambridge: Harvard University Press.

——— (1993). *Political Liberalism*. New York: Columbia University Press.

——— (1997). *The Law of Peoples*. Cambridge: Harvard University Press.

——— (1988). "The Priority of Right and Ideas of the Good." *Philosophy and Public Affairs* 17.4: 251–276 (reprinted in Rawls 1993, pp. 173–211).

Raz, Joseph (1999). *Engaging Reason: On the Theory of Value and Action*. Oxford: Oxford University Press.

——— (1994). *Ethics in the Public Domain*. Oxford: Clarendon Press.

——— (1986). *The Morality of Freedom*. Oxford: Oxford University Press.

——— (2003). "The Practice of Value." In Ed. Grethe B. Peterson. *Tanner Lectures on Human Values*, vol. 11. Salt Lake City: University of Utah Press, pp. 113–150.

Scanlon, T. M. (1991). "Nozick on Rights, Liberty, and Property." In Ed. Jeffrey Paul. *Reading Nozick: Essays on Anarchy, State, and Utopia*. Totowa: Rowman & Littlefield, pp. 107–129.

——— (2000). *What We Owe to Each Other*. Cambridge: Harvard University Press.

Sen, Amartya (2009). *The Idea of Justice*. Cambridge: Harvard University Press.

Walzer, Michael (1995). "Response." In Eds. David Miller and Michael Walzer. *Pluralism, Justice and Equality*, pp. 281–298.

——— (1983). *Spheres of Justice*. New York: Basic Books.

Williams, Bernard (1985). *Ethics and the Limits of Philosophy*. Cambridge: Harvard University Press.

——— (1997). "The Analogy of the City and the Soul in Plato's *Republic*." In Ed. Richard Kraut. *The Cambridge Companion to Plato*. Cambridge: Cambridge University Press.

——— (1980). "Justice as Virtue." In Ed. Amelie Oksenberg Rorty. *Essays on Aristotle's Ethics*. Oakland: University of California Press.

——— (1991). "The Minimal State." In Ed. Jeffrey Paul. *Reading Nozick: Essays on Anarchy, State, and Utopia*. Totowa: Rowman & Littlefield: pp. 27–36.

——— (1981). *Moral Luck*. Cambridge: Cambridge University Press.

Young, Iris Marion (1997). "A Multicultural Continuum: A Critique of Will Kymlicka's EthnicNation Dichotomy." *Constellation* 4.1: 48–53.

——— (2000). *Inclusion and Democracy*. Oxford: Oxford University Press.

——— (1990). *Justice and the Politics of Difference*. Oxford: Oxford University Press.

SECONDARY TEXTS

Ackrill, John Lloyd (1973). *Aristotle's Ethics*. London: Faber & Faber.

Annas, Julia (1981). *An Introduction to Plato's Republic*. Oxford: Oxford University Press.

——— (1976). "Plato's 'Republic' and Feminism." *Philosophy*: 307–321.

Anscombe, G. E. M. (1958). "Modern Moral Philosophy." *Philosophy* 33.124: 1–19.

Arneson, Richard (1995). "Against Complex Equality." In Eds. David Miller and Michael Walzer. *Pluralism, Justice and Equality*, pp. 226–252.

Arrhenius, Gustaf (2003). "The Very Repugnant Conclusion." In Eds. Krister Segerberg and Rysiek Sliwinski. *Logic, Law, Morality: Thirteen Essays in Practical Philosophy in Honor of Lennart Aqvist*. Uppsala: Uppsala University, pp. 167–180.

Barry, Rachel, Brennan, Tad and Brittain, Charles Eds. (2012). *Plato and the Divided Self*. Cambridge: Cambridge University Press.

Beetham, David (1991). *The Legitimation of Power*. Basingstoke: Palgrave.

Broadie, Sarah (1991). *Ethics with Aristotle*. Oxford: Oxford University Press.

Brown, Eric (2009). "Plato's Ethics and Politics in *The Republic*." https://plato.stanford.edu/entries/plato-ethics-politics/

Buchanan, Allen (2003). *Justice, Legitimacy, and Self-Determination*. Oxford: Oxford University Press.

——— (1999). "Recognitional Legitimacy." *Philosophy and Public Affairs* 28: 46–78.

Buchanan, Allen and Keohane, Robert (2006). "The Legitimacy of Global Governance Institutions," *Ethics and International Affairs* 20.4: 405–437.

Caney, Simon (2002). "Equal Treatment, Exceptions and Cultural Diversity." In Ed. Paul Kelly. *Multiculturalism Reconsidered*. Cambridge: Polity Press, pp. 81–101.

Capaldi, Nicholas (2004). *John Stuart Mill*. Cambridge: Cambridge University Press.

Carr, E. H. (2001). *The Twenty Years' Crisis*. Houndmills: Palgrave.

Cartledge, P. (2012). *The Greeks*. Oxford: Oxford University Press.

Cohen, G. A. (2004). "Expensive Taste Rides Again." In Ed. Justine Burley. *Dworkin and His Critics*. Oxford: Blackwell Publishing, pp. 3–29.

——— (1995). "Robert Nozick and Wilt Chamberlain: How Patterns Preserve Liberty." In Ed. G. A. Cohen. *Self-Ownership, Freedom and Equality*. Cambridge: Cambridge University Press, pp. 19–37.

——— (1995). Ed. *Self-Ownership, Freedom and Equality*. Cambridge: Cambridge University Press

Coleman, Janet (2000). *A History of Political Thought*, vol. I. Malden: Blackwell Publishing.

Cornford, Francis (1960). *Plato's Theory of Knowledge.* London: Routledge and Kegan Paul.
Crowder, George (2002). *Liberalism and Value Pluralism.* New York: Continuum.
Dancy, Jonathan Ed. (1997). *Reading Parfit.* Oxfordlackwell.
Daniels, Norman, Ed. (1975). *Reading Rawls: Critical Studies on John Rawls' 'A Theory of Justice'.* New York: Basic Books.
——— (2011). "Reflective Equilibrium," In Ed. Edward Zalta. *Stanford Encyclopedia of Philosophy,* http://plato.stanford.edu/entries/reflective-equilibrium.
Devigne, Robert (2006). *Reforming Liberalism.* New Haven: Yale University Press.
Donner, Wendy (1991). *The Liberal Self.* Ithaca: Cornell University Press.
Eisenach, Eldon (1998). *Mill and the Moral Character of Liberalism.* University Park: Pennsylvania State University Press.
Eshleman, Andrew (Summer, 2014). "Moral Responsibility." In Ed. Edward Zalta. *The Stanford Encyclopedia of Philosophy,* http//plato.standford.edu/archives/sum.2014/entries/roal-responsibility/.
Fine, Gail (1992). "Aristotle's Criticisms of Plato." In Ed. James C. Klagge, *Oxford Studies in Ancient Philosophy.* Oxford: Oxford University Press, pp. 13–41.
——— (2003). *Plato on Knowledge and Forms.* Oxford: Oxford University Press, Chapter 13.
Foot, Philippa (2001). *Natural Goodness.* Oxford: Clarendon Press.
——— (2002). *Virtues and Vices.* Oxford: Oxford University Press.
——— (2002). "Moral Relativism and Moral Objectivity." In *Moral Dilemmas and Other Topics in Moral Philosophy.* Oxford: Clarendon Press.
Freeman, Samuel (2007). *Rawls.* New York: Routledge.
Goodin, Robert and Pettit, Philip, Eds. (1993). *A Companion to Contemporary Political Philosophy.* Oxford: Blackwell Publishing.
Gowans, Chris. "Moral Relativism." *The Stanford Encyclopedia of Philosophy* (Winter 2016 Edition). Ed. Edward N. Zalta. https://plato.stanford.edu/archives/win2016/entries/moral-relativism/.
Hamburger, Joseph (1999). *John Stuart Mill and Control.* Princeton: Princeton University Press.
Hardie, W. F. R. (1980). *Aristotle's Ethical Theory,* 2nd ed. Oxford: Clarendon Press.
Hare, R. M. (1998). *Essays on Political Morality.* Oxford: Oxford University Press.
——— (1981). *Moral Thinking: Its Levels, Method, and Point.* Oxford: Oxford University Press.
Harman, Gilbert (1996). "Moral Relativism and Moral Objectivity." In Eds. Gilbert Harman and Judith L. Thompson. *Moral Relativism and Moral Objectivity.* Oxford: Blackwell Publishers.
Harsanyi, John (1976). *Essays on Ethics, Social Behavior and Scientific Explanation.* Dordrecht: D. Reidel Publishing Company.
von Hayek, Friedrich (1978). *Law, Legislation and Liberty: The Mirage of Social Justice,* vol. 2. Chicago: University of University Press.
Held, David (1995). *Democracy and the World Order.* Palo Alto: Stanford University Press.
Irwin, Terence (1988). *Classical Thought.* Oxford: Oxford University Press.

——— (2012). "Conceptions of Happiness in the *Nicomachean Ethics*." In Ed. Christopher Shields. *The Oxford Handbook of Aristotle*. Oxford: Oxford University Press.

——— (1995). *Plato's Ethics*. Oxford: Oxford University Press.

——— (1999). *Nicomachean Ethics*, 2nd ed. Indianapolis: Hackett Publishing Company.

Juvenal (2014). *Satire* 6. Ed. Lindsay Watson Patricia Watson. Cambridge: Cambridge University Press.

Kelly, Paul (2002). "Introduction: Between Culture and Equality." In Ed. Paul Kelly. *Multiculturalism Reconsidered*. Cambridge: Polity Press, pp. 1–17.

——— (2005). *Liberalism*. Cambridge: Polity Press.

Kim, Young (2015). *Justice as Right Actions*. Lanham: Lexington Books.

Kleingeld, Pauline (2012). *Kant and Cosmopolitanism: The Philosophical Ideal of World Citizenship*. New York: Cambridge University Press.

Korsgaard, Christine (1986). "Aristotle and Kant on the Source of Value." In *Ethics*. Chicago: University of Chicago Press, pp. 486–505.

——— (1996). *The Sources of Normativity*. Cambridge: Cambridge University Press.

Kraut, Richard (2013). "Aristotle on Becoming Good: Habituation, Reflection and Perception." In Ed. Christopher Shields. *The Oxford Handbook of Aristotle*. Oxford: Oxford University Press.

——— (2002). *Aristotle: Political Philosophy*. Oxford: Oxford University Press.

——— (1992). "The Defense of Justice in Plato's Republic." In Ed. Richard Kraut. *The Cambridge Companion to Plato*. Cambridge: Cambridge University Press.

Kukathas, Chandran (1992). "Are There Any Cultural Rights?" *Political Theory* 20.1: 105–139.

Kukathas, Chandran and Pettit, Philip (1990). *Rawls: "A Theory of Justice" and Its Critics*. Cambridge: Polity Press.

MacIntyre, Alasdair (2007). *After Virtue*, 3rd ed. Notre Dame: University of Notre Dame Press.

——— (1988). *Whose Justice? Whose Rationality?* Notre Dame: University of Notre Dame Press.

Mason, Elinor (2006). "Value Pluralism." In Ed. E. Zalta. *Stanford Encyclopedia of Philosophy*, http://plato.stanford.edu/valuepluralism.

Miller, Fred (1995). *Nature, Justice, and Rights in Aristotle's Politics*. Oxford: Oxford University Press.

Moore, G. E. (1993). *Principia Ethica*. Ed. Thomas Baldwin. Cambridge: Cambridge University Press.

Mulgan, Tim (2004). "Two Parfit Puzzles." In Eds. Jesper Ryberg and Torbjörn Tännsjö. *The Repugnant Conclusion*. Norwell: Kluwer Academic Publishers, pp. 23–44.

Mulhall, Stephen and Adam Swift (1996). *Liberals and Communitarians*, 2nd ed. Oxford: Blackwell.

Nagel, Thomas (1979). *Mortal Questions*. New York: Cambridge University Press.

——— (1991). "The Fragmentation of Value." In *Moral Questions*. Cambridge: Cambridge University Press, pp. 128–141.

——— (1991). "Libertarianism Without Foundations." In Ed. Jeffrey Paul. *Reading Nozick: Essays on Anarchy, State, and Utopia*. Totowa: Rowman & Littlefield, pp. 191–205.

Natali, Carlo (2009). *Aristotle's Ethics VII*. Oxford: Oxford University Press.

Nehamas, Alexander (1975). "Plato on the Imperfection of the Sensible World." *American Philosophical Quarterly*: 105–117.

Nietzsche, Friedrich (1973). *Beyond Good and Evil*. Trans. R. J. Hollingdale. Harmondsworth: Penguin Books.

Nussbaum, Martha (2001). *The Fragility of Goodness*, rev. ed. Cambridge: Cambridge University Press.

Paul, Jeffrey, Ed. (1991). *Reading Nozick: Essays on Anarchy, State, and Utopia*. Totowa: Rowman & Littlefield.

Perrson, Ingmar (2004). "The Root of the Repugnant Conclusion and its Rebuttal." In Eds. Jesper Ryberg and Torbjörn Tännsjö. *The Repugnant Conclusion*. Norwell: Kluwer Academic Publishers, pp. 187–200.

Pettit, Philip (1995). "The Contribution of Analytical Philosophy." In Eds. Robert E. Goodin and Philip Pettit. *A Companion to Contemporary Political Philosophy*. Malden: Blackwell Publishing, pp. 7–38.

——— (1997). *Republicanism: A Theory of Freedom and Government*. Oxford: Oxford University Press.

Pettit, Philip and Smith, Michael (1997). "Parfit's P." In Ed. Jonathan Dancy. *Reading Parfit*. Oxford: Blackwell.

Pogge, Thomas (2002). *World Poverty and Human Rights*. Cambridge: Cambridge University Press.

Popper, Karl (1971). *The Open Society and Its Enemies*. Princeton: Princeton University Press.

Price, A. W. (2015). *Virtue and Reason in Plato and Aristotle*. Oxford: Oxford University Press.

Pufendorf, Samuel (1991). *On the Duty of Man and Citizen According to Natural Law*. Ed. James Tully. Trans. Michael Silverthorne. Cambridge: Cambridge University Press.

Rachels, James (2008). "Ethical Egoism." In Eds. Joel Feinberg and Russ Shafer-Landau. *Reason and Responsibility: Readings in Some Basic Problems in Philosophy*. Belmont: Thompson Wadsworth, Chapter 6.

Rachels, Stuart (2001). "A Set of Solutions to Parfit's Problems." *Nous* 35.2: 214–238.

Rees, John (1985). *John Stuart Mill's On Liberty*. Oxford: Clarendon Press.

Riley, Jonathan (1998). *Mill on Liberty*. Oxford: Routledge.

Ripstein, Arthur (2007). "Liberty and Equality." In Ed. Arthur Ripstein. *Ronald Dworkin*. Cambridge: Cambridge University Press, Chapter 3.

Roemer, John (1986). "Equality of Resources Implies Equality of Welfare," *Quarterly Journal of Economics* 101: 751–784.

Rothbard, Murray (1998). *Ethics of Liberty*. New York: New York University Press.

Rousseau, Jean-Jacques (1968). *The Social Contract*. Trans. Maurice Cranton. London: Penguin Books.

Ryberg, Jesper (2004). "The Repugnant Conclusion and Worthwhile Living." In Eds. Jesper Ryberg and Torbjörn Tännsjö. *The Repugnant Conclusion*. Norwell: Kluwer Academic Press, pp. 239–256.

Ryberg, Jesper and Torbjörn Tännsjö, eds. (2004). *The Repugnant Conclusion*. Norwell: Kluwer Academic Publishers.

Sandel, Michael (1998). *Liberalism and the Limits of Justice*, 2nd ed. Cambridge: Cambridge University Press.

——— (2009). *Justice*. New York: Farrar, Straus and Giroux.

Segerberg, Krister and Rysiek Sliwinski, Eds. (2003). *Logic, Law, Morality: Thirteen Essays in Practical Philosophy in Honor of Lennart Aqvist*. Uppsala: Uppsala University.

Shachar, Ayelet (2001). *Multicultural Jurisdictions: Cultural Differences and Women's Rights*. Camhridge: Cambridge University Press.

Shafer-Landau, Russ (2003). *Moral Realism: A Defence*. Oxford: Oxford University Press.

——— (1995). "Specifying Absolute Rights." *Arizona Law Review* 37: 209–224.

Shapiro, Ian (2011). *The Real World of Democratic Theory*. Princeton: Princeton University Press.

Shields, Christopher (2014). *Aristotle*, 2nd ed. New York: Routledge.

——— Ed. (2002). *The Oxford Handbook of Aristotle*. Oxford: Oxford University Press.

Shoemaker, David (2008). "Personal Identity and Ethics." In Ed. Edward Zalta. *Stanford Encyclopedia of Philosophy*. http://plato.stanford.edu/entries/identity-ethics/.

——— (2011). "Attributability, Answerability, and Accountability: Toward a Wider Theory of Moral Responsibility." *Ethics* 121: 603–32 (Chicago: University of Chicago Press).

Sidgwick, Henry (1980). *The Methods of Ethics*, 7th ed. Indianapolis: Hackett Publishing Company.

Sinclair, R. K. (1988). *Democracy and Participation in Athens*. Cambridge: Cambridge University Press.

Smith, Angela (2012). "Attributability, Answerability, and Accountability: In Defense of a Unified Account." *Ethics* 122: 575–589 (Chicago: University of Chicago Press).

Song, Sarah (2007). *Justice, Gender, and the Politics of Multiculturalism*. Cambridge: Cambridge University Press.

Strauss, Leo (2002). *The City and Man*. Chicago: University of Chicago Press.

Strawson, P. F. (2008). "Freedom and Resentment." In *Freedom and Resentment and Other Essays*. New York: Routledge.

Talisse, Robert (2007). "Does Value Pluralism Entail Liberalism?" http://ssrn.com/abstract-1005651.

Tännsjö, Torbjörn (2004). "Why We Ought to Accept the Repugnant Conclusion." In Eds. Jesper Ryberg and Torbjörn Tännsjö. *The Repugnant Conclusion*. Norwell: Kluwer Academic Publishers, pp. 219–238.

Taylor, Charles (1989). *Sources of the Self*. Cambridge: Cambridge University Press.

Temkin, Larry (1997). "Intransitivity and the Mere Addition Paradox." In *Philosophy and Public Affairs* 16.2: 138–187.

Thucydides (2009). *History of the Peloponnesian Wars.* Trans. Martin Hammond. Oxford: Oxford University Press.

Vallentyne, Peter and Vossen, Bas van der (2014). "Libertarianism." In Ed. Edward Zalta. *Stanford Encyclopedia of Philosophy.* http://plato.stanford.edu/entries/libertarianism/.

Vlastos, Gregory (1997). "Was Plato a Feminist." In Ed. Richard Kraut. *Plato's Republic: Critical Essays.* Lanham: Rowman & Littlefield Publishers, Inc.

Waldron, Jeremy (1993). *Liberal Rights.* Cambridge: Cambridge University Press.

——— (1995). "Money and Complex Equality." In Eds. David Miller and Michael Walzer. *Pluralism, Justice and Equality.* Oxford: Oxford University Press, pp. 144–170.

Weber, Max (1994). *Political Writings.* Eds. Peter Lassman and Ronald Speirs. Cambridge: Cambridge University Press.

——— (1997). *The Theory of Social and Economic Organization.* Ed. and Trans. Alexander Henderson and Talcott Parsons. New York: Free Press, pp. 324–406.

West, David (1995). "The Contribution of Continental Philosophy." In Eds. Robert E. Goodin and Philip Pettit. *A Companion to Contemporary Philosophy.* Malden: Blackwell Publishers, pp. 39–71.

White, Nicholas (1976). *Plato on Knowledge and Reality.* Indianapolis: Hackett.

——— (1992). "Plato's Metaphysical Epistemology." In Ed. *The Cambridge Companion to Plato.* Cambridge: Cambridge University Press, Chapter 9.

Williams, Howard (2012). *Kant and the End of War: A Critique of Just War Theory.* New York: Palgrave Macmillan.

Wolf, Clark (2004). "O Repugnance, Where is Thy Sting?" In Eds. Jesper Ryberg and Torbjörn Tännsjö. *The Repugnant Conclusion.* Norwell: Kluwer Academic Publishers, pp. 61–80.

Wolff, Jonathan (1998). "Fairness, Respect, and the Egalitarian Ethos." *Philosophy and Public Affairs* 27.2: 97–122.

——— (1991). *Robert Nozick.* Stanford: Stanford University Press.

Index

About the Author

Young Kim was born in Washington, DC, grew up in Virginia, and was educated at Shimer College, Northwestern University Pritzker School of Law, and The London School of Economics and Political Science. A practicing lawyer, Mr. Kim's teaching interests include corporate and securities law, international law, and legal philosophy. He has taught at the University of Colorado Law School, on appointment as a Fulbright Senior Specialist at the University of Luxembourg, and at Northwestern University Pritzker School of Law. His research and writing interests cover intersections of law, morality, and politics, including questions of justice. His previous book in the area, *Justice as Right Actions* (2015), presents an original theory of justice.